The Writer's Toolbox

Stuart C. Brown
New Mexico State University

Robert K. Mittan
Casper College

Duane H. Roen
Arizona State University

Allyn & Bacon
Boston • London • Toronto • Sydney • Tokyo • Singapore

Vice President, Humanities: Joseph Opiela
Editorial Assistant: Kate Tolini
Editorial-Production Administrator: Rob Lawson
Editorial-Production Service: Ruttle, Shaw & Wetherill
Composition Buyer: Linda Cox
Manufacturing Buyer: Suzanne Lareau
Cover Administrator: Suzanne Harbison

A Viacom Company
Needham Heights, MA 02194
Internet: www.abacon.com
America Online: keyword: College Online

Library of Congress Cataloging-in-Publication Data

Brown, Stuart C. (Stuart Cameron), 1955–
The Writer's Toolbox / Stuart C. Brown, Robert K. Mittan, Duane H. Roen.
p. cm.
Includes bibliographical references and index.
ISBN 0-205-19563-6
1. English language—Rhetoric. 2. Interdisciplinary approach in education. 3. Academic writing. 4. Study skills. I. Mittan, Robert K. II. Roen, Duane H. III. Title.
[PE1408.B863 1997]
808'.042—dc 20 96-18561
CIP

Printed in the United States of America

10 9 8 7 6 5 4 3 2 1 01 00 99 98 97 96

For Leslie, Pat, and Maureen

Contents

PART 3 Writing Strategies for Effective Listening and Discussion

PART 4 Writing Strategies for Effective Oral Presentations

Preface for Teachers

We've written this book for two groups of upper-division college students. First, we've aimed it at students enrolled in advanced composition courses—students who have some experience writing in college but who wish to take their writing to a higher level of proficiency. Second, this book will also serve the needs of those enrolled in courses in their degree majors. Research and experience suggest that students in all disciplines must learn to use writing as a tool for both learning and communicating. We assume that some content-area teachers have the time to teach their students to use writing as a valuable tool for learning and communicating in their disciplines. But we realize that most teachers in most disciplines do not have much time to commit to writing instruction because curricula are packed already and because most work days are too short as it is.

With these constraints in mind, we've written this book so that students in any discipline can use it without the assistance of teachers. This book offers your students strategies to make them more effective learners and writers. In the pages that follow, your students will learn how to use writing as an effective tool for reading, listening, writing, speaking, and thinking. Your students will also learn strategies for using writing to communicate their ideas to you and to others in your field—in *their* field. We believe they can do all of this by themselves, without your assistance.

If you choose to guide your students to use particular parts of the book to learn or communicate particular information in your course, so much the better. Your directions to students can be as general as "Use this book. It will help you in this course and in your careers." Or you can be as specific as "Try out the strategy on this page before you come to class next Monday." We also encourage you to supplement our text with specific examples of the kinds of communication that occur in your particular discipline.

Although we've done much to make this book useful to students in college courses, we've also considered the needs of former students, people who have entered their careers. To a great extent, we've tried to address your students as already on their way to becoming experts in their chosen fields. To meet the needs of both students and professionals, we've referred to situations in both worlds. We intend this book to be useful to your students years after they've left your campus.

Finally, we hope this book offers you, whether you are a first-year instructor or a full professor, some tools to make you even more effective as a teacher and writer. We don't mean to be presumptuous, but we'd like to think that there's something new and useful for everyone who opens this book. Indeed, we've learned a great deal in putting it together.

ACKNOWLEDGMENTS

We wish to acknowledge the assistance and encouragement of many people who helped us to complete this project.

We thank our mentors, Gene Piché, Nick Karolides, Mike Graves, Les Whipp, John Hollowell, Theresa Enos, Thomas Willard, Ken and Yetta Goodman, Patricia Anders, Richard Shelton, Dwight Adams, and Don Welch, for the years of gentle guidance and friendship. Without them, we probably would not be teaching and writing.

We thank our friend, colleague, and chief supporter Charles Davis, at the University of Arizona, for his never-ending support. We admire his unwavering commitment to quality education.

We thank other colleagues at the University of Arizona, New Mexico State University, Casper College, Arizona State University, Syracuse University, and the University of Wyoming for all the knowledge they have shared with us over the past few years. Their ideas have done much to shape this book.

We thank our department chairs—Nancy Gutierrez and Reed Dasenbrock—for understanding the value of books that guide learners. We thank Beth Pearce and John Tierney for assisting with the research and the indexing for this book and Michèle Drivon and staff for efficient copyediting.

We thank our families—Leslie, Pat, Kyle, Maureen, Nick, and Hanna—for tolerating us during the months we worked evenings, weekends, and holidays at our computers. Too often they have had to do things without us. Too often they have had to wait to make phone calls because we were tying up the lines to send computer files via our modems. And too often they have heard us say, "Just as soon as I finish revising this chapter."

We thank our many students for helping us to see the need for this book. From them, we've learned much about teaching and writing and caring. We especially thank those students who granted us permission to use their writing in this book. We wish that we could have included writing from more of our students; all of it gave us insights.

We thank Joe Opiela for encouraging us to undertake this project. His gentle nudging made all the difference in the world. Finally, Stuart and Bob owe a special debt to Duane. Through his teaching, his research, and his collegiality—on this and other projects—he has truly shown us what it means to be professional.

Introduction: Strategies for Active Learning

WHY THIS BOOK

To ease your passage through this text, we think it only fair to begin by explaining some of the basic principles we've used to guide us in our development of the book. Oddly, many times in both our learning and our work environments, awareness of the "rules of the game" is assumed. When you start a new job, for example, you may have an orientation or training program, but most employers still assume a fairly lengthy "breaking in" period before they can count on your being fully productive. A number of unspoken rules that take time to learn operate in the workplace. In college or other learning environments, this happens as well. Measure your first-year college experiences against where you are now. One has only to look at grade point averages of first-year students versus GPAs of students who have progressed to upper-division status to see that almost all have undergone a change in their ability to succeed at what they are doing. Tacitly, you've learned the "rules" of going to college, whether you realize it or not.

For instance, you probably receive course syllabi in nearly every one of your college courses. Usually this sheaf of papers (or increasingly, an electronic file in a computer account) includes a list of assignments, linked to specific tasks, duties, and dates. At one point, you probably weren't quite sure how to "read" these, but as you developed experience with them, you assimilated the unspoken conventions that most instructors use in constructing syllabi. You are now able to use a syllabus to orient yourself to what the class is about and what is expected of you. Syllabi act as roadmaps to give you a sense of where you're going and what you will learn in classes.

The syllabus and opening class periods establish the "rules of the game" and familiarize you with the agenda, or the aims and objectives, of the instructor teaching the course. We therefore begin this book by introducing you to our agenda and the principles that guided our development of it. In the following sections, we show you some of the ideas that underlie the entire book you're now about to use.

Before you begin using this book, there are some features of its conception, its organization, and its writing that we think will be useful for you to know. First, when we initially considered writing this book, we weren't sure what to put in it. We knew from our own and others' experiences that to create a "writing" textbook for upper-division students studying in a wide variety of academic disciplines would be fraught with problems. If we chose to focus on specific writing assignments, whose would we use? Students in history courses seldom write lab reports, and they may not even write essays; physics students may write short essays, but more often they write research reports. Conversely, if we chose to focus on more generic "academic writing," we would probably not be going anywhere new, nor would we be addressing the needs of many students and professionals. Most students in upper-division courses have already gained experience and expertise with academic writing through first-year composition courses. Our initial problem, then, was to discover what aspects of writing experience such students—students like you—have in common, and to provide them with something they don't already have.

One thing that we've found all upper-division students have in common is their desire to succeed, to gain expertise in their chosen fields, and to become professionals. Whether you envision yourself as a manager at a Fortune 500 company, as a nuclear engineer exploring the potential uses of cold fusion, or as the director of an off-Broadway sensation, by getting where you are now you've shown a willingness to work hard to become a professional.

What you may be missing, we realized, are experience and advice. This book cannot give you the kind of real-life, on-the-job experience you're no doubt eager to acquire. But it will provide you with strategies to assist you in developing as a professional in your field. This book also will give you lots of advice. As with all experiences and all advice, some will be useful to you, and some will not be. We ask only that you make an honest effort in trying them.

Second, we decided early on to take an expanded view of "writing," one that recognizes the important role of writing as a means of discovering, thinking through, and extending information, as well as conveying it. If you expect this book to show you how to write a perfect sentence or to explain the different usages of *effect* and *affect*, you're looking in the wrong place. (We recommend one of the hundreds of style handbooks available at the library or local bookstores or increasingly built into word processing software for answers to questions such as these.) Instead, we view writing as one of the most important tools professionals use to discover and shape what they think and what they know. Too few students, we believe, are aware of the many valuable uses of writing—uses we describe in this book.

We also believe that becoming an expert in your chosen field requires more than learning how to use writing effectively, although that's a very important achievement. We've noted that many upper-division students need to strengthen their other language-using skills. For instance, how effectively would you say you read? What strategies do you use when confronted with special writing situations such as essay exams? If answering these questions makes you a little uneasy, you're not alone.

Our primary focus is on helping you develop effective thinking processes as you develop your expertise in a particular discipline. The units of this book are organized to get you to think through your development of language-using skills, especially in combination with writing. Each of the units, then, might be viewed as spokes arranged around this central hub. Writing, reading, listening, and speaking are all evidences of someone's thinking. But keep in mind that they are also tools; they not only produce thinking, they shape it as well.

This book is designed as a toolbox to assist you in accomplishing the many tasks in your classes and in your professional lives. We don't expect you to be able to use all of the tools equally effectively nor master all of them at the same time. The Contents and Index will help you decide which parts of the book will be most useful today. Tomorrow, you'll find other parts more useful because you'll be engaged in other sorts of academic or professional activities. Eventually, though, we think you'll use most or all of this book, because your courses and your professional obligations will engage you in all of these kinds of tasks.

This book is also designed to be interactive. The more you write on, in, and with this text, the more you pause and work through its ideas and answer the questions it raises, the more you will benefit from it.

And finally, a few comments about the way this book was written. As a truly collaborative effort, this book represents one of the most common, and complex, writing situations that professionals work within. Each chapter was drafted by an individual, but the final version you see here reflects our collective discovery of what we know about writing, reading, listening, speaking, and thinking. In fact, when we considered in what order to list our names on the title page—a very important and potentially divisive issue in all collaborative endeavors—we agreed to list ourselves alphabetically. Because we've worked so closely for so long, there is simply no way for us to measure or indicate who contributed what. We urge you to take advantage of every opportunity to work on such collaborative efforts. As we've discovered in writing this book, one of the best ways to become expert is to work closely with other experts.

THINKING ABOUT THINKING

As you get ready to use this book, we want you to think about your thinking. The name for this is *metacognition*. In some contexts, this is known as *critical thinking*, but we've done a little thinking on that term and decided that it seems a bit redundant. You can't *not* think critically. When you choose item A over item B at the grocery store, for example, you're making a selection based on a number of underlying factors—some conscious and some not. But you're also capable of much deeper and more effective thought. That is our aim here: to get you to think more effectively. And thinking about thinking is the first step.

Metacognition, at least for our purposes here, involves active and conscious inquiry into how and why we think and do things the way we do. Stop and ask yourself how much thinking you do in a day. Then consider how much attention you pay to how you go about this. You *know* you think all day long, but do you *understand*?

"Knowing" and "understanding" are not the same. Most of the time, people use the words *know* and *understand* interchangeably. That's unfortunate, we believe. There are differences between the concepts represented by these verbs. We'll elaborate on our understanding of the distinction by using a series of questions. To really see our point, though, you need to answer each question yourself as it comes up in the text, and before you read what follows. More importantly, you need to answer it in writing.

Here is the first question:

1. What happened in 1492?

____

____

In demonstrating the principle that *knowing* and *understanding* are quite different, we've asked this question to hundreds of students over the past few years. We always ask them to write down their response, and they nearly always look at us as if we're crazy. Now, you may have learned a little rhyme in grade school that begins

In fourteen hundred ninety-two
Columbus sailed the ocean blue

Many of us learned that little nursery rhyme and learned that Columbus's voyage took place that year. In short, we *know* it for a fact. Responding to this first question demonstrates something we've come to call WHAT-type thinking. No, not all WHAT-type thinking comes from questions that begin with the word *what*. But WHAT-type thinking generally deals with factual information. And it's generally linear. Furthermore, if asked a question that encourages WHAT-type thinking, we often recall one and only one answer that's directly related to that question. In our minds, 1492 = Columbus's voyage, even when we realize that many other things happened that year.

There's nothing inherently wrong with WHAT-type thinking; it serves us quite well. The students we've discussed this type of thinking with tell us that it's what they spend most of their time doing in courses. But how useful is this type of thinking in solving complex problems? Now, answer the second of our questions:

2. How was Columbus's voyage related to the economic situation in Europe at the time?

____

____

When we ask this question of groups of students, there's usually silence—at least at first. This type of question requires a great deal more "processing," as students develop a more complicated response to our inquiry. Questions such as this one elicit HOW-type thinking. Again, we use the word *how* as shorthand. It signifies thinking that uses much more complicated associations, connections, and awareness of relationships than does WHAT-type thinking.

Question 2, in fact, asks you to consider a particular relationship—between a factual event (Columbus's voyage) and other, larger circumstances (economic situation). You might have thought about Columbus's purposes for his voyage. Certainly exploration was one, but most obviously, he was more interested in a shorter route to Eastern spice sources, where products, if readily and cheaply available, could stimulate economic activity throughout Europe.

Because this type of question produces more complicated answers (ones that are often arguable rather than definitive), you might be wondering, "Is HOW-type thinking better than WHAT-type thinking?" This is a good question. But we suggest you go at it in a slightly different way. Ask yourself, and answer, this question:

- How are HOW- and WHAT-type thinking different?

____

____

No doubt you've realized that we just asked you to apply HOW-type thinking. HOW-type thinking is multifaceted, multidimensional. It's not linear; if you were to visualize HOW-type thinking, you'd see a number of "bubbles" of WHAT-type information clustering around the key question. So, HOW-type thinking usually includes some WHAT-type thinking. For instance, to consider question 2, you had to "know" when Columbus's voyage took place (you replayed question 1). You also had to "know" something about Europe and economics and the larger historical context of Columbus's time.

One more question:

3. Why is Columbus's voyage considered significant?

____

____

Sure, we know we've opened a huge can of worms with this. It has been a few years since the quincentenary of the voyage, but the debate over this one still rages. No doubt you can come up with a number of responses. This type of question invokes WHY-type thinking. Again, take some time now to think and respond to these follow-up questions:

- How are WHAT-, HOW-, and WHY-type thinking different?

  ____

  ____

- What processes do I use to do WHAT-type, HOW-type, and WHY-type thinking?

  ____

  ____

- When, and why, will it be valuable for me to use each type—individually and collectively?

  ____

  ____

WHY-type thinking encourages evaluation, consideration of causes and effects, and recognition of actions and results. Like HOW-type thinking, it takes time and can generate lots of output. But perhaps even more than HOW-type thinking, WHY-type thinking leads to new thinking. It is where humans invent or construct or discover new knowledge. And, we argue, WHY-type thinking characterizes not only the activity we call "understanding," but also what we call "awareness of our understanding." WHY-type thinking can give us insight into our process of creating knowledge.

Let's try one final question:

$$1 + 1 = \_\_\_\_$$

If you provide the standard response, that *one plus one equals two*, you're probably pretty safe, most of the time. But so what? In your quest to develop expertise and to share the benefits of your expertise, you need to think less conventionally. What if we complicate the notion by asserting that one plus one can equal one, as in the case of a river merging with another river? Or if we suggest another context: putting one male laboratory rat in with one female laboratory rat? The simple arithmetic construct *does* have its uses and *does* provide us with a certainty about the world we live in. But is this necessarily a place to stop thinking? Thinking critically—thinking about our thinking—involves using all of these types of thinking. We intend this textbook as a tool for doing that.

THINKING LIKE AN EXPERT

If you are reading this paragraph, despite how confused, irritated, or dazed you might be by now, you do already know and understand quite a bit about the underlying practices of communication that you, the reader, and we, the writers, are practicing. You know the letters of the Roman alphabet and how English as a language strings them together into word groups and sentence constructions and paragraph units and so forth. You also understand that a lot more is going on for this system to work and for you to get anything out of your investment of time, energy, the cost of this book, and the course you're taking. Speakers and listeners, writers and readers take part in a whole myriad of activities that surround something they have in common—what we call throughout this book a *text*.

We've written this book with the basic assumption that you know and understand more about communication than you're likely to give yourself credit for. Maybe more than other people have given you credit for. But we believe that part of becoming expert involves paying attention.

First, let us explode some myths about experts:

1. Experts don't know everything about their area of expertise, although they are expected to know a lot.
2. Experts don't understand everything about their area of expertise and sometimes understand even less than they think they do because they confuse "knowing" and "understanding," just like nonexperts.
3. Many experts aren't even sure why others see them as experts.

If you don't believe us, we suggest that you interview an expert, someone who you believe is definitely an expert on a topic. (We provide some guidelines for conducting interviews such as this later in the book). Ask her or him these three questions that underlie the myths we've noted above:

1. Do you know everything about ________________?
2. Do you understand everything about ________________?
3. Why do you believe that people like me see you as an expert on ________________?

Based on our own experiences with experts, we're pretty sure we can predict the kinds of responses you'll get, at least from *real* experts, those whose peers agree have expertise. Rather than be dismayed by their responses, we hope you'll see that they provide you the opportunity to assume not only the role of being an expert, but the excitement and challenges of contributing to the knowledge of your field.

It is never too early to begin developing a sense of yourself as a professional. Most disciplines have their own professional organizations that can assist you in this. Many have several, each with a different emphasis within the field. Consult instructors or other members of your profession about which of these organizations you may want to join. Many professional societies are eager to gain members. Some even offer reduced student membership rates, local student chapters, and job placement opportunities.

These organizations have much to offer. Most publish journals, bulletins, and newsletters that will keep you current on the latest developments and research. These are tremendous information sources that you probably already use. Adding them to your growing personal library assures that you'll have them around when you need them. Other benefits include receiving calls for papers and opportunities to publish your work. Conferences and professional gatherings are often sponsored by these organizations. Attending these—again, sometimes at a reduced rate—offers excellent opportunities to meet other professionals in your discipline, to present your own work, and to build and maintain professional relationships that are often lifelong. Becoming a member of your discipline's society demonstrates your own growing professionalism, not to mention looking good on a résumé. Don't overlook joining your profession formally. You'll be accepted as a valuable addition.

In developing your own expertise and in developing your capabilities as a critical thinker, you'll first want to do some self-appraisal. Throughout this book, we ask you to pay attention. We ask you to consider:

- What you know and what you don't know
- What you understand and what you don't understand
- What you do and what you don't do to find out

- How you do what you do
- Why

We want you to know that you already have different kinds of expertise and interests and experiences that will contribute to your further development as an expert. We also want you to recognize how these differences allow you to contribute unique and useful ideas and solutions in your area of study or professional life.

People in the United States have conflicting ideas about individuality. We stress our individuality, and yet, we usually want to see ourselves as normal. Ask yourself, however, whether you're "average." Normalcy, or "fitting the norm," is a condition of averaging. Our culture is driven by attempts to manipulate our sense of ourselves. At times, this manipulation stresses our uniqueness. At other times, we are being manipulated into seeing ourselves as part of a group. Is a best-selling novel better for being read, or at least bought, by more people? Do we like a particular music CD better because it has gone platinum? As consumers, we're constantly reminded of quantity as a measure of quality. Yet, what does this say about our individuality?

As the cognitive psychologist Howard Gardner proposes, there are multiple intelligences rarely captured by a single number or intelligence quotient (IQ). He suggests that there are linguistic intelligence, musical intelligence, logical–mathematics intelligence, spatial intelligence, bodily–kinesthetic intelligence, and personal intelligence. What we would like you to consider in your role of becoming an expert is that you recognize your own unique intelligences and their combinations. An honest self-assessment about what you know and how you know it is a first step toward distinguishing yourself from the rest of the crowd. This, and attention to the tools that we discuss in the rest of the book, will provide you the means to becoming expert.

▶ 1

Understanding Writing Processes

Overview

Getting Help From Others

Understanding Your Own Writing

Procrastination

A Look at Composing Processes

Topics for Writing

Writing is simple. Writing is easy. Writing is fun.

Of course, we're lying. It's neither simple nor easy, but it is useful. It's also very important in your life, both as a student and as a professional. Some of this, we're sure, is bad news, but anyone reading this book can learn to use writing to succeed in school or on the job. Writing well is much like doing anything well. It requires practice, some guidance, and a fair amount of awareness of what you're doing.

Throughout this book, we offer ideas for using writing as a tool for doing many things: reading, listening, speaking, thinking, learning. As you use writing to accomplish these other tasks, though, you're also practicing writing. We recommend looking for every possible opportunity to write anything. For example, each time you get a gift from a friend or relative, write a letter of thanks—even if you also offer thanks over the phone or in person. Keep a diary; it may even turn into a bestseller, as Bob Green's high school diary, *Be True to Your School*, did. It's also easy to find opportunities to make lists—something that professionals do many times a day. Like most people, you probably already make grocery lists, lists of things to do, lists of gift ideas for an upcoming holiday. These are only a few examples of everyday opportunities to write; you'll certainly find many more.

Finding such opportunities for writing may not pay large dividends immediately, but we're confident that it will eventually. When you hit the job market, for example, letter writing will become a way of life for you. You'll be writing letters to apply for jobs, to thank potential employers for interviews, to establish terms for contracts. And, according to surveys of writing in the professions, you'll become an even more prolific letter writer once you've landed a job. Research further indicates that, with each job promotion, you'll need to write more often and more effectively.

Finding opportunities to write every day will help you to become more fluent as a writer, to put words on a page with greater ease. And the easier it gets, the more likely we are to want to do it. Of course, as we get better at writing or anything else, we develop higher standards or expectations for ourselves. Those higher standards sometimes make it seem as if the task is not getting any easier, but it is. Developing writers need to think about how much easier it is today to achieve yesterday's standards. That helps to put increased achievement into perspective.

GETTING HELP FROM OTHERS

Almost anyone can help you to become a more effective writer simply by responding to your writing as an attentive reader. Writing is effective, after all, because it does something to, for, and with readers. It's only logical, then, to seek the responses of readers to see what effect you have on them.

We've found that the best method for training readers is a four-step procedure borrowed from writing expert Peter Elbow and modified by others. After you've read some of your writing to your readers (or they've read it themselves), ask them first to tell you two or three things they identified with in the writing. That is, have them tell you how their experiences relate to those described in the piece of writing. Second, ask them to tell you several features of the writing they liked. Third, have them ask questions to clarify points from your writing. Fourth, encourage them to offer suggestions for improving the writing.

It may help your readers if you go so far as to give them part of the wording for responding:

- I identify with . . .
- I like . . .
- I have these questions: . . .
- I suggest . . .

This procedure works successfully for training your readers because it accommodates both your needs and theirs. The first step in the procedure allows a reader to establish a sense of community with you. You need to feel confident that everyone in the room is committed to whatever writing project you've undertaken. The second step gives a reader a chance to communicate what the writer's strengths are in this specific work. Once these first two procedures have made both you and your readers more comfortable with the transaction, the third step—asking questions—will work to show you how better to meet readers' needs. It helps you see ways of translating "writer-based prose" (writing that meets the *writer's* needs) into "reader-based prose" (writing that also meets *readers'* needs). Answering these questions helps you, as the writer, to understand that, although readers can read your words on paper, they cannot read your mind. The fourth step, if it were not preceded by the first three, would be difficult for both you and your readers; it's not always easy to offer or to accept suggestions. But because it follows the first three steps, you and your readers trust each other's commitment enough to feel comfortable with suggestions. In fact, you may find that carefully guiding readers through the first three steps makes the fourth step unnecessary, especially if readers are encouraged to ask a sufficient number of questions at step three.

Elicit feedback often. This works especially well if you jot down your readers' responses to your writing so you can begin to see the patterns that emerge; a tape recorder can also come in handy in a conversation with your readers. Identifying patterns is a useful tool for becoming expert at writing. Expert chess players, for example, see patterns on the chessboard the instant they look at it, whereas novice chess players tend to see fewer and smaller patterns. The same is true for experts and novices looking at players on a basketball court, numbers on a balance sheet, artifacts at an archeological site. When an expert sees a pattern, he or she knows what to do with it. Novices are often those who don't—or can't—take action because they can't see any pattern.

UNDERSTANDING YOUR OWN WRITING

Just as there are many ways to practice writing and to get guidance, there are also ways to develop awareness about composing, especially your own composing. Understanding your own composing is not easy because, if you're like most people, you probably have not spent much time thinking about it. You probably also haven't spent much time thinking about how you think or how you walk or how you throw a ball or how you chew food or how you move your tongue when you pronounce words. Thinking about such activities can interfere with our performance of them. But with writing, which is mostly thinking, thinking about the act of writing—and examining how you do it—helps you understand your own cognitive processes.

In addition to getting feedback on your writing, another good tool for understanding your writing is to write about your writing habits and strategies. You might, for example, describe the chronology of how you wrote your last course paper. The following questions will help you recall what you did:

- When did you begin thinking about the paper?
- When did you begin putting words on paper?
- What did you do before you produced the first draft?
- What did you do to create a setting in which to write?
    - What writing tools did you use?
    - What did you do to make yourself comfortable as you wrote?
    - What location did you choose?
    - At what time(s) of the day did you write?
- When did you revise your paper?
- What kinds of revisions did you make?
- What kinds of editing did you do?

After you've recorded what you did as you composed your last paper, you might consider how this particular episode was typical or atypical of your usual writing habits. By doing this, you will again begin to see some emerging patterns of behavior. To reiterate, seeing patterns is an important step in changing and improving how you do something. Many athletes and performers use sophisticated video and computer equipment to capture their performance for later analysis. You too should find out what you do when you write. But knowing *what* you do when you compose is not enough. You also need to think about *how* and *why* you do what you do.

PROCRASTINATION

A word about procrastination: Don't do it. In a news item we saw a few years ago, Susan Cantrell, a reporter, noted that time management experts say that some people procrastinate because "it reduces anxiety by reducing the expected quality of the project from the best of all possible efforts to the best that can be expected given the limited time" (B1). You may respond to this with, "But, I do my best work under pressure." That's a common response, but it's more self-deception than anything—especially if you're referring to writing under pressure. You may do your best first drafts under the pressure of impending deadlines, but most evidence indicates that first drafts are pale imitations of careful, thoughtfully revised, and polished writing. Good writing requires time—time for generating ideas, time for drafting, time for revising, and time for editing and polishing. It also requires you to allow for time away from the writing after you've generated ideas, after you've written drafts, and after you've revised. This time away allows you to be a better reader of your own writing. Without time away, you can't think about it as carefully as good writers must. How much time you have to let a piece of writing "settle" is, unfortunately, rarely completely up to you—deadlines and due dates are usually set by other people.

A LOOK AT COMPOSING PROCESSES

We've mentioned the terms *generating, drafting, revising*, and *editing*. Essentially, these designate the major mental operations or cognitive processes involved in composing a serious piece of writing. Writers rarely move through these four operations in a linear, step-by-step progression; rather, most engage in these composing activities *recursively*, moving back and forth among them as the need arises. But for your purposes, it's probably helpful to focus on the four activities in the following order: generating, drafting, revising, editing. Be aware of each of these major activities in this order, and you can devote more of your cognitive resources to actually producing effective text. It's a matter of dividing and conquering, seeing writing as a manageable set of tasks, not an overwhelming array of too many things to do at once. Jugglers learn by starting with one ball, not four. By keeping your impulse to write the draft, revise, and edit on hold while you generate ideas, you can concentrate on getting the ideas out where you can see them. Then, while you actually draft the material into text, you'll need to try to ignore too much revising and editing until you have something to work into a good draft.

It's important to distinguish between generating and drafting. When you generate material, try not to worry too much about the form it will eventually take, because worrying about form is one more ball to juggle. Of course, as you generate material, you very well may discover the way you want or need to shape your piece of writing; in some cases, the shape is already specified. For example, a memo is not likely to end up as a poem. If you feel comfortable generating and drafting simultaneously, and if it works well to do so, go ahead. If you feel the need to focus your mental energies, though, generate material without worrying about how you're going to draft it.

Throughout this book, we offer strategies for using journal writing to help read, analyze, and understand material. In Part 2, we present strategies that are time tested for these purposes. However, these same strategies—dialectical entries, time lines, lists, forms, pedigree charts, and the like—all can be used to generate material for more formal writing. If you use these strategies in the journals you keep on a regular basis, you'll find that you'll also be creating a storehouse of material for the formal writing projects that you undertake.

It's also important to distinguish between revising and editing. Revising means "re-seeing" what you've drafted. When you revise, you *re*focus on the ideas that you've put into the draft. That is, you *re*consider the development of your ideas, the organization of your ideas, the support for your ideas, the logic of your ideas. In theory, revising comprises four basic operations: adding, deleting, moving, replacing. That is, when you revise, you add ideas, delete ideas, move ideas, and replace ideas. All of this sounds like a lot to juggle—and it is. That's why revising is sometimes the least favorite and least-often-completed activity. Later chapters provide some strategies to make this easier and more effective.

For now, consider the following illustration of what revising can do to turn your writer-based prose into reader-based prose. Assume that you make a grocery list before you go to the store. Your list reads: milk, coffee, bread, cereal. You, the writer of the list, have enough information to buy exactly what you wanted: 2 percent milk in half-gallon paper cartons (you always buy in paper rather than plastic for environmental reasons and because you know that light penetrates plastic to destroy vitamin D); whole Colombian coffee beans, which you'll grind at home just before you use them; Rhodes frozen whole-wheat dough, which you'll bake at home; and Post Raisin Bran.

Your list simply reminds you of what you don't want to forget. It's very likely that the cryptic list would also work for a roommate because roommates tend to know the preferences of one another. But if you were to give the list to some friend who offered to do your shopping, it wouldn't work quite so well. The list would work even less well if you were to give it to a casual acquaintance.

When we write for ourselves, revising is usually irrelevant. As our readers become less familiar, though, revising becomes the crucial way we negotiate our relationship to them, their needs, and our own communication agenda.

There are many reasons for focusing on editing last. First, editing involves what Robert Pirsig calls the "table manners" of writing. Careful editing is a courtesy to your readers. And like good table manners, careful editing will help you leave a positive impression on your guests and your readers.

A good reason for focusing on editing last comes from Ann Duin, a writing expert, who compares editing to putting a coat of paint on a house; it's that final touch that makes the house look as attractive as possible. It makes little sense to put paint on the lumber when you've put it in piles ready for construction. Just like some of the ideas you've generated (piled), some of the lumber will end up in the scrap heap; some will be hidden under sheetrock or paneling. Paint only what shows; edit only what shows.

Editing should wait until after revising. Revising is like remodeling a house; editing is like painting after remodeling. It makes little sense to paint a wall that may get ripped out during remodeling, just as it makes little sense to edit a sentence that may get ripped out during revising. Besides, you can't paint a wall you haven't yet added during remodeling. You also can't edit a sentence that you haven't yet added during revising. When everything is there and in place, then it is appropriate and necessary to make it look good. And just as careful painting protects the wood or the sheetrock from the effects of moisture, careful editing protects the credibility of the writer.

Now we need to qualify what we've just said about moving through generating, drafting, revising, and editing operations. Although it will certainly help you to understand how you write if you focus attention on each of these operations as you move through them *more or less* one at a time, don't feel chained to that sequence. Many writers find that they engage in all four operations even when they're focusing on generating or drafting or revising or editing. When you're editing, for example, you may see the need to generate more material or to move a paragraph or delete a sentence. Do it. Don't wait until you're finished editing.

Depending on your situation, your audience, and who you are, the amount of time and the order of occurrence and simultaneity of these mental operations will vary. Drafting this particular unit of this book, for example, involved three primary operations. Generating and drafting occupied us initially, although some revising and editing occurred (especially because we used word processors). Next, we focused more on peer revising, in which the person who drafted a chapter asked the other two authors questions to guide their reading of the chapter. These questions often were requests for "a second opinion." Just as often, though, they might read, "I don't know what to do here. What ideas do you guys have?"

These kinds of peer revising led to further generating and drafting, with only a little attention to editing. Finally, we moved almost entirely to revising and editing, with only minor generating and drafting. This was loosely *our* process for *our* particular collaborative situation.

The way we wrote this book illustrates how recursive writing often is. We generated material in all sorts of ways: by discussing ideas in our weekly meetings, by jotting notes to ourselves and sending e-mail to one another or calling one another whenever an idea came up, and by asking our colleagues and students what they thought.

Almost all of our revising was collaborative. That is, after one of us had drafted a chapter or a portion of a chapter, he printed it out in compressed typeface, leaving lots of white space on the right side of each page. He then gave it to the other two, who wrote comments and questions all over it. Those responses served to guide the revisions that followed, which led to further generating and drafting and revising and editing. We include one of these draft pages on page 8 to show you what it looks like.

example, involved three primary operations. Generating and drafting occupied ~~you~~ us initially, although some revising and editing occurred (especially since we used word processors). Next, we focused more on peer revising, which led to further generating and drafting with some attention to editing. And, finally, we moved almost entirely to revising and editing with only minor generating and drafting. This was loosely our process for our particular collaborative situation.

Some of us have trouble not editing!

Explain how we did this. We asked Q's of each other when we exchanged. Use this to reinforce your peer stuff above.

The way ~~that~~ we wrote this book illustrates how recursive writing often is. We generated material in all sorts of ways: by discussing ideas in our weekly meetings, by jotting notes to ourselves and to one another whenever an idea presented itself, by asking our colleagues and students what they thought. While we had originally planned to write a book with five chapters, after we began drafting material ~~for the book~~ we realized that we needed five units, not five chapters, to say what we wanted to say. We drafted the first unit of this book before we moved to other units. We then drafted and revised chapters in the second and third units of the book. At one point, one of us was drafting three chapters simultaneously, in 2 different units? That is, three chapters were on the computer screen at one time. Also, while we were drafting chapters in Unit 2 and Unit 3, we were revising and editing other chapters in those same units.

And, of course, within each, the writer was also generating, drafting, revising and editing all (more or less) simultaneously.

We should note, by the way, that almost all of our revising was collaborative. That is, after one of us had drafted a chapter or a portion of a chapter, he printed it out in compressed typeface, ~~and left~~ leaving lots of white space on the right side of each page. He then gave it to the other two, who ~~would write~~ wrote all sorts of comments and questions ~~in the very wide right margins~~ all over it. Those comments and

**We're not telling you this to impress you with our writing prowess. In fact, we consider*

FIGURE 1.1

We're not telling you this to impress you with our writing prowess. But what we would like to impress on you is this: Anyone who takes the time to examine consciously what happens when he or she writes can learn to do this. And that's really what we mean by becoming a proficient writer.

TOPICS FOR WRITING

Consider the writing you do in your leisure time. Personal letter writing is a common type of leisure-time writing among people we've surveyed. Less frequently, people also report they keep diaries or journals. Some also indicate that they write poetry or fiction in their leisure time.

Think for a moment about the topics you include in your personal letters. You probably don't write about the gross national product, the Pythagorean theorem, the structure of an atom, or the economic system of czarist Russia. Instead, you write about friends, classes and instructors, finances, frustrations, and aspirations. In short, you write about things that matter to you.

Of course, very few of your college instructors or your bosses are going to ask you to write about those topics that show up in your personal letters. Often you don't get a choice of topics. But whenever possible, try to pick topics that play to your knowledge and interests. The following examples help illustrate this point.

A few years ago in one of our courses, students were assigned to write comparison/contrast papers. One student, Lindsay, a member of the University tennis team, chose to compare and contrast the accuracy of metal and graphite rackets. Another student, Abby, chose to contrast Jean Piaget's and Lev Vygotsky's explanations of social speech in preschool children. As a psychology major, she was particularly interested in child development. Annie, majoring in music history, contrasted Mozart's and Beethoven's composing habits.

For these students it was relatively easy to find topics that drew on their interests and knowledge. In many courses, the task is a little more difficult. For example, a few years ago in a course in which students wrote about specific works of literature, Gardie, another psychology major, found a psychological approach to each work of literature. When she wrote about George Orwell's *1984*, she argued that the main character, Winston Smith, goes through specific stages as he comes to accept the totalitarian government of Oceania. Those stages parallel the ones that Elisabeth Kübler-Ross attributes to terminally ill patients. Another student showed how each of the characters in Henrik Ibsen's *Enemy of the People* fit into Lawrence Kohlberg's stages of moral development.

In some courses, the assignment can be so restrictive that it seems impossible to write from your knowledge and interests. One strategy that can help you in such situations is to keep a list of topics and subtopics that appeal to you most. If you do this from the first day of the course, most likely you'll find a way to draw on what matters most to you in the course material. Instructors *want* students to explore areas of interest—as long as the exploration falls within the context of the course. Some students, instead of following their own interests, try to write what they think the instructor wants. When they do this, they often end up writing something that satisfies neither them nor their instructors.

On the job, keeping lists of potential projects or ideas makes it easier to have choices when the need or opportunity arises. It's sometimes possible to initiate writing on topics you're interested in. In many governmental agencies and corporations, workers receive cash awards when they suggest ideas that end up saving money. Bosses don't want to sit around thinking up things for employees to do, and employees who sit around waiting for things to do will spend lots of time waiting—in the same job.

2

Purpose and Audience

Overview

A Sense of Purpose

A Sense of Audience

Audience Types
The Complexity of Audiences: A Scenario
Audience Analysis

Whenever you communicate, especially at work, you're trying to change something, if only in a small way. You attempt to change things from the way they are now to the way you want them to be. Basically, five elements contribute to the nature of any communication:

- Why (the purposes)
- You (the writer)
- Them (the audiences or readers)
- Where (context: the situation or surroundings)
- How (the medium or physical form of the communication and its structure; e.g., letter, report, speech, conversation, e-mail, video, telephone, World Wide Web Homepage)

These elements appear in all communications. A text has some purpose behind it, usually a specific one set by the writer for a reader or group of readers who have reasons for reading the text. The text also has a context, a situation that surrounds it and influences writer, reader, and their respective purposes. Additionally, a text is presented in a certain medium and has a form within that medium. The medium may be oral, written, or electronic. The form may be restricted to written texts such as memos or letters, or it may be as freewheeling as a brainstorming session with colleagues over coffee. Whatever the exact nature of a communicative act, these five elements all come into play. In your development as an expert, recognizing and using them can enhance your expertise and how you demonstrate that expertise.

It's nearly impossible to separate these elements in any but the most theoretical sense. We present them somewhat separately in the following chapters, but keep in mind that we do so only for the sake of explanation and demonstration.

The last four of these features both direct and are directed by the first: the purpose for writing. It is essential that you recognize that purposes have two parts: *your* purpose for writing and *their* purpose for reading. These continually shift and act on each other. Communication is a messy enterprise. The writer's responsibility, your responsibility, is to be alert and to accommodate these shifts. You are more likely to get what you want that way.

The following chapters will help you understand these elements so that you'll be able to design effective texts for your own contexts, your own purposes, your own audiences. By applying this understanding and these tools to your own particular discipline, you assist yourself most in becoming expert.

A SENSE OF PURPOSE

Writing is dangerous. Some countries go so far as to register typewriters, just as others register firearms. The young, revolutionary United States established, as one of its founding principles, the freedom of the press. Several of the greatest transformations in human history involved the technology of writing: the inventions of the alphabet, paper, and printing presses literally changed the world. Demonstrations by students in China in 1989 underscored the importance of text: newsletters produced by the demonstrators were so greatly sought that they were distributed by students perched in trees. The uprising in Chiapas, Mexico, came to the world's attention because of electronic mail posted to the Internet. This is said to be the Information Age. There is now an Information Superhighway to transport us around.

Probably of more concern to you, and to most of us, however, is the local or individual power and effect of our texts on specific audiences. "What does writing *do for me*?" we ask. After all, we usually have some self-interest in committing the time and energy to a task as difficult as writing. Whether we're trying to write a novel, a letter home, music lyrics, a sales contract, or a chemistry lab report, we have a purpose in mind and an audience for that purpose.

Just as an actor or comedian "plays" to an audience, a writer addresses an audience. The means for doing this and the constraints on those means are different, but the importance is the same. If a writer doesn't successfully approach the audience's needs, the writer's work and energy are wasted.

To be honest with ourselves, most of us would rather be doing something, anything, other than writing. It's a difficult task for many of us. There's rarely enough time to write as well as we should. Writing involves risk—a piece of writing makes its writer exposed, vulnerable, responsible. It can be a record that haunts. When you *commit* yourself to putting anything in writing, you're certifying with your personal assurance, with your name, that it's worth the reader's time and energy to read it. But—and a big *but*—if you have upheld your responsibility to that reader, and have a clear purpose behind your document, the payoffs can be tremendous. You get the good grade, win the contract, or achieve a promotion.

Recognizing the out-and-out mercenary aspects of many communications is the key to being a critical reader and an effective writer. As a reader, identifying what a writer wants from you allows you to decide whether to give it. As a writer, identifying what *you* want from the reader allows you to develop the necessary strategies to get what you want.

Your purpose as the writer of a document can be major or minor, depending on the situation, the task, and the audience. You may have several purposes behind what you write. Examine the list we've started below and add some of your own goals:

Writer's Goals

- I want to propose certain recommendations to decision makers.
- I want to convey to technical experts that I indeed know what I'm talking about.
- I want to convince my superiors that my work is sound and that I possess skills that merit recognition and promotion.
- I want to sell a product or an idea to a client.
-
-
-

The items on this list will, of course, change from situation to situation. Before getting too far into creating a document, however, make sure you're clear about the rewards, results, or risks involved because you wrote the document.

Generally, you should be aware that change occurs as a result of communication. Both reader and writer will be different people, perhaps only slightly, as an outcome of the effort of writing or reading a document. You might play with the idea of charting or mapping this process. Recognizing this potential to change may help guide what changes you effect and how you create them. The critical feature is to recognize your responsibility as a writer and to see the opportunities and pitfalls in all that responsibility.

A SENSE OF AUDIENCE

We all have various purposes for writing. A document can be as mundane as a grocery list or as critical as an environmental impact statement. Whatever its purpose, we create a document so that it will be read. Sometimes we are our own readers, as in the case of a grocery list or a phone message or a journal entry. At other times, we write for an audience we know on a personal level, such as friends or family. These personal audiences are not our primary concern here. Do not, however, dismiss them. These more private audiences may not seem to impinge much on your professional development, but careful attention to them can enhance your capabilities in reaching more public audiences, audiences that you affect in your professional capabilities.

Our primary attention, however, focuses on the *public* kinds of writing we do in our roles as professionals and the kinds of audiences we can expect to read that writing. The following two sections direct your attention at the different types of audiences professionals write to and tools for identifying those audiences and their needs.

Audience Types

In most efficient communication, concern for audience is central to the writer's purpose. The writer, investing time and energy, expects a return for that investment. Usually that return involves some form of payoff from the reader, whether explicit or implicit or both. Explicit returns can be anything from a good grade to an accepted business plan to high praise on a research report from a supervisor. Implicit returns can be as subtle as gaining a reader's sympathy for your point of view or as significant as winning a reader to your side of an argument. Often there are both implicit and explicit rewards from the same document. A proposal that results in a bank offering a loan to start a day care center, for example, is likely to get you not only the money but also a pat on the back from investors.

Integral to achieving your purpose is knowing who your readers are, what they need, and what you can give them. Most documents you write will encounter one or more of a number of *audience types*. We discuss here the five most common kinds of audience to expect in your role as a professional or expert in your discipline. We've arranged our presentation into an acronym that may help you remember the various types: ELECT. Note that our arrangement is merely for the sake of the acronym and is not hierarchical. At times, you may write primarily for only one kind of audience; for example, as you complete your education, your instructors are a primary audience. At times, you may need to cover the gamut. Most likely, though, your writing will be directed toward two or three of these audiences, with occasional situations that include the others.

Audience types are by no means as distinct from each other as they may seem. They're only roughly defined categories, often with a great deal of overlap. An executive audience may well include people with as much technical expertise as you have, a not uncommon situation in an engineering firm, for example, in which its managers have been drawn from its engineering staff. Or your document may encounter a mixed audience, such as the Mayor and City Council of Tucson, which, at one time, included an engineer, a professor of political science, and several other representatives of different professions.

Our acronym, ELECT, is designed to help you keep these audiences readily in mind. We've created ELECT to help you recognize that how you "choose" to approach an audience is determined greatly by who and what that audience is. ELECT represents the following audience types: Executive, Lay, Expert, Combined, Technician.

Executive

Executive audiences are best recognized as decision-makers, people who control resources such as time, money, personnel, and facilities. They may or may not have technical experience directly related to the topic. They do have expertise and training in management, accounting, social sciences, or humanities. This type of audience reads to make decisions. They appreciate less technical language and fewer definitions of special terms. Executive readers will be particularly attentive to alternatives, recommendations, results, conclusions, and professional judgments. Cost versus benefits is often of critical importance to executive readers.

Proposals and business plans are frequently directed toward this type of audience. A document written to an executive reader may be addressed to a supervisor or manager within a company, a client outside the company, or a funding source such as a bank or government office.

Lay

Lay readers or audiences are loosely defined as those who are working with a text whose topic is outside their particular field(s) of specialization or expertise. They are usually quite varied in their range of educational levels. Many lay readers are expert in some field, just not the one presented in the text. Often, lay readers read for practical application to personal interests. Text addressed to these readers requires a high degree of background information and definitions. These readers appreciate more generic terminology and more use of visual representations and graphics.

Writing for lay audiences usually means converting highly specialized information into a form and language that those outside the field can understand. An architectural plan presented to a homeowner is one example: many of the technical issues the architect needs to convey to the general contractor are not relevant to the person deciding what to build and how much to spend. For instance, references to the "HVAC systems" and "fenestration" will most likely appear as "furnace," "air conditioner," and "windows." Still, writing aimed toward a lay audience may be quite sophisticated, such as that found in such widely read magazines as *Scientific American* or *Nature*.

Expert

Expert audiences generally have at least as much professional expertise on the subject of a document as the writer. This audience is composed of people who have advanced degrees in the field plus years of experience. They know their field, and they know other experts in that field. Experts read for both *how* and *why* things work; they normally demand that *all* of the facts, calculations, and assumptions be presented. They need very little background information. They can usually handle specialized/standardized language, abbreviations, formulas, tables, and graphs. Jargon (field-specific terminology) is often not just accepted but expected by these readers—it's the language of experts speaking to one another. Of prime importance to this type of reader are the writer's methodology, inferences, and conclusions, *as long as* supporting evidence is presented to substantiate the findings. A cautious audience, these readers expect to see data. Reporting to these audiences often involves using a specific format or convention.

Texts presented to members of communities of experts must conform to stylistic features, such as APA style in a social sciences journal. The text must contribute knowledge to the field, demonstrate understanding of previous research in the field, use appropriate methodology, meet test design and analysis standards, and adhere to certain expectations of accuracy to be considered acceptable by this community of experts.

Obvious examples of expert audiences are your instructors. They report their work to peers and colleagues as highly knowledgeable in their field as themselves. An astronomer writing for a journal will address her colleagues in a much different manner than she will talk with her Astronomy 101 class. But her graduate-seminar approach may closely mirror her professional one. Different audience levels require different approaches.

Combined

The combined audience involves any combination of two or more of the other types. It's usually the most difficult, and also the most common, audience many texts are written for. The more multipurpose a document is, the more likely that it will encounter combined or multiple types of audiences. This audience type is defined by its varieties of readers and their different needs, backgrounds, interests, and purposes for reading the text. It usually requires "compartmentalizing," or segmenting information so that the various readers can choose which part(s) they need to read. Documents addressed to a widely varied audience are often written collaboratively, with different authors contributing different sections that address specific audience requirements. These sections are then assembled into a whole text.

A good example of a document addressed to a combined audience is a corporate financial report or annual statement. These usually contain a company history and a background written for the lay reader, but they also include highly technical material of interest and accessibility to executive and expert audiences—people who can look at a balance sheet and make something of it.

Technician

The technician—sometimes called the "user" audience—is one composed of those people who will *do* something specific with what the writer provides. Those who build equipment, then use and maintain it, are a common example. They often have years of experience in a special area and are sometimes therefore mistaken for expert audiences. But their primary interest is application: they want to get something done. Educational levels for technicians often range from high school and vocational training to a bachelor's degree in a technical area. Such readers usually have experience in a particular area and are extremely practical; they tend to be less interested in theory, but are familiar with it. Most have a general background knowledge in the specialized field but are not as strongly theoretical as an expert audience. They usually appreciate analogies that bring general knowledge to bear on a specific subject.

Typical examples of documents prepared for technicians are operating instructions, blueprints, schematics and diagrams, specifications, technical manuals, and instructions. These are documents that also may be directed at lay audiences. A common difficulty with such documents as computer software manuals or VCR operating instructions, for example, is a misreading of the audience level. The texts are user oriented and technical, but the primary purpose is to convey information to lay readers. Such documents often seem to assume more technical expertise than many of us have.

The key to using all of this information about audience types is to identify the principal or primary audience members and write to them, keeping in mind the needs of any important secondary audiences and your purpose for writing to them. Begin reading the various professional documents in your field to develop sensitivity to a variety of audiences and the approaches you will need to engage them. See how other professionals achieve this connection to audiences. Knowing what's expected of you by various audiences enables you to provide what they need.

Two instances of documents written for different audiences appear below. Although the topic is essentially the same, the writers of each chose very different strategies. Label each excerpt by identifying it by its principal audience type. In the margin, note the differences between the two texts.

audience type ______________________________

Dead and dying robins began to appear on the campus. Few birds were seen in their normal foraging activities or assembling in their usual roosts. Few nests were built; few young appeared. The pattern was repeated with monotonous regularity in succeeding springs. The sprayed area had become a lethal trap in which each wave of migrating robins would be eliminated in about a week. New arrivals would come in, only to add to the number of doomed birds seen on the campus in the agonized tremors that precede death (106).

audience type ______________________________

During 1963, 151 specimens (29 with tremors) or thirty-four species were found in Hanover; ten dead birds (none with tremors) were found in Norwich. In 1964, seventy-two birds (six with tremors) came from Hanover, while eight (none with tremors) came from Norwich. Most dead birds, especially small, obscure ones, such as sparrows or warblers, will not be found, so (that) these data presumably represent a minor fraction of the total dead birds (90).

The first excerpt, by Rachel Carson, an environmental activist and biologist, has a much different appeal to its readers than the second, by research biologists Wurster, Wurster, and Strickland. Although these texts are separated from their full context, it should be clear that the piece by Carson is directed at a lay audience. The second piece, much more specific and more precise in its reporting, is directed at an audience concerned with detail, verifiability, and accuracy. Carson is being no less precise in her telling, but her level of accuracy is not the same as the scientists', whose report was aimed at the readers of *Science*. Although it could be argued that Wurster, Wurster, and Strickland wrote with a lay audience in mind (their report did not appear in an ornithology journal), their approach and concerns are much more technical than Carson's. The article relies on readers having a certain amount of expertise.

The Complexity of Audiences: A Scenario

The following scenario, prepared by the librarians at the University of Arizona Science–Engineering Library, represents a common career path for an expert; in this case, an immunologist. Although we've taken a few liberties, most of what occurs to Dr. Provanovich is not that far removed from what many of you will be expected to do. Read the text and identify the various audiences and purposes Dr. P. writes for. A clue: you should find more than a dozen ways that scientists convey information.

> This is the story of Dr. Susan Provanovich (who will be known as Dr. P. throughout the story), a highly respected biochemist known for her research on the common cold virus.
>
> Dr. P. often traces the beginning of her interest in colds to her work as a research assistant to Dr. Welby. They worked together on the chemical composition of a strain of rhinoviruses and published several papers under Dr. Welby's name. Dr. P.'s dissertation developed some of the ideas first presented in the articles. These ideas were further explained in a paper she gave at the Western Regional Conference on Immunology. There, she met Dr. Night and Dr. Day (hereafter referred to as Drs. N. and D.), who were also interested in the same viruses. After the meetings, they met for happy hour and discussed mutual problems and interests. From this meeting, they decided to apply for a grant to work on a collaborative project. Their grant proposal was approved by the National Science Foundation (NSF), and even though they were working at different institutions in different parts of the country, they were able to correspond through the mail and communicate almost daily with each other using the Internet. They were also able to share laboratory results by faxing pages from their lab notebooks.
>
> The three scientists presented preliminary results of their research at the annual American Chemical Society conferences and reported their findings to NSF in their annual research reports. They were also successful in getting their research published in such esteemed journals as *Nature* and the *Journal of the American Chemical Society*. By this time, Dr. P. was becoming well known in her field. She was asked to contribute a chapter for a book on the synthesis of antiviral compounds.
>
> After years of research, Dr. P., along with her associates Dr. N. and Dr. D. and their graduate students, finally synthesized a compound effective against the common cold virus. The group immediately applied for a patent for the preparation of the compound, and held a news conference to announce their discovery. Their announcement resulted in general pandemonium and an immediate drop in orange futures. They appeared on the cover of *Time*, and *Newsweek* did a five-page article about them and their research. Dr. P. got to meet Ted Koppel, and the *National Enquirer* reported that a similar result would occur if you ate a pound of garlic every day.

Five years later, Dr. P., along with Dr. N. and Dr. D., was awarded the Nobel Prize for Chemistry. By this time, they had published their seminal work, *Synthesis and Activity of Antiviral Compounds*. Merck Pharmaceuticals had obtained the manufacturing rights and processes and was producing the compound as an over-the-counter drug. Because of her reputation, Dr. P. was asked to write a long essay on antiviral compounds for the new *Encyclopedia of Bioactive Compounds* and became the editor of the journal *Viruses and Antiviruses*.

This scenario is a fairly compressed version of one person's career and her use of communication in that career. Consider the variety of communication demands, though. And imagine the "rewards" Dr. Provanovich has garnered: professional stature, secure income, high interest (and likely, satisfaction) in her job, public recognition. Here is a professional who is reaching her audiences. We've extracted below the various "media" our immunologist uses to convey her expertise to the world. As you look through what we've identified, write in the type of audience she addressed in each instance. Remember, there may be more than one.

Professional papers and journal articles

Dissertations

Conference presentations and proceedings

Informal discussions

Grant proposals

Teleconferencing and interactive electronic mail

Faxing

Laboratory notes and research data

Research reports

Patents

News conferences and interviews

Newspaper, television, and radio coverage

Awards and prizes

Manufacturing processes and procedures

Encyclopedias and reference sources

Editorships

You should have identified, at least once, all five of the audience types we discussed earlier in this chapter.

Audience Analysis

Determining the audience or audiences you write to is highly dependent on why you are writing—your purpose. But some general techniques are available to help you identify your audience and what you need to provide that specific audience to achieve your purpose. The following questions will help you determine some of the characteristics of your audience or audiences. You need to extend and adapt our suggestions, like most of our advice, to your own particular needs and situations.

Who are they? What are they to me? This question is central to any document you design. You need to identify the predominant type of audience you are addressing and then examine that audience more closely. Determine the following:

- What are their predominant characteristics: for example, friendly to me/my ideas? known to me? voice on the phone? another writer? fiscal conservative? efficiency expert?
- Where are they in the hierarchy, and does it matter: supervisor? subordinate? peer? expert in the field? novice?

Simply thinking about your audience very consciously will provide a great deal of information. But there are other equally direct means as well:

- Ask others who know or who have written to your audience.
- Read the kinds of texts members of your audience read (and write).
- Ask them personally.

Many situations call for close contact with your audience. A great deal is usually at stake for both you and them. Try to check with the audience as directly as possible about who they are and what they expect. Both you and they are more likely to end up with satisfactory documents as a result.

What is their interest in the subject? Another effective tool for audience analysis is to examine your readers' motivations for reading your writing. We've isolated a few questions you might apply to your audience before you deliver a document to them. If you can readily and clearly answer these questions, your document should be effective.

- What is their reason for reading what I write?
- How will they use what I write?

- What is *their* goal in terms of future action?
- What action will they take?
- What do I need to do or say to influence their decisions?
- What kind of responses can I expect?
- What other possible responses might they consider?
- How informed are they?
- Are they: decision makers? advisers? implementers?

If you have difficulty answering any of the above, we advise further investigation and a certain amount of rewriting before you submit your document to your audience. Use the above questions as a checklist to make sure you have provided everything you need to provide.

What do they know about the subject? This question often requires further investigation on your part. Some of the means for finding out about your audience that we have mentioned are applicable here as well. These next questions, however, focus particularly on the professional credentials and capabilities of your readers, especially in relation to how expert they are on your topic. Consider:

- What is their degree of familiarity/background with the subject?
- What questions will they be asking about the subject?
- How much technical language will they be able to follow?

A good understanding of these aspects of your readers will enable you to tailor your document accordingly.

How do they feel about the subject? This question raises lots of risky issues. Yet, not asking this question about your readers is even riskier. Whenever writers write, they run the risk of presenting material that their readers may not feel kindly about. The "rightness" of your material may not be viewed that way by the reader. It is advantageous to have a sense of what opinions and attitudes readers have toward the topic. And readers do have attitudes. We all normally have personal feelings and emotions about topics. Anticipate preexisting attitudes that will affect your readers. Here are a number of potential attitudes we've identified, along with phrases often associated with them:

- Delight: Positively charming.
- Hostility: Not *this* again!
- Surprise: Oh good! I've been waiting for this.
- Interest: I hadn't thought about this before.
- Expectation: I was hoping something like this would come along.

- Anxiety: I was worried this might come up.
- Rapture: This takes care of all my problems.

Your readers may not have the kinds of attitudes toward your topic you would like them to have. But it's better to know in advance and take action to avoid a potential negative response just because you didn't realize that you struck a nerve.

What do I expect them to do? Last, a major concern in your audience analysis should be what you expect readers to do after they've read your document. Do you intend them to:

- Take action?
- Change their minds?
- Respond?
- Consider possibilities?
- Be informed?
- Trust you?
- Buy something?
- Accept an idea?

This question ties closely with your own sense of purpose. It's intended to match that purpose with the audience's purpose for reading your document. Consciously consider the outcome of your document.

Admittedly, all of this is a lot to keep in mind. We've left it somewhat vague, as well. Our intention—the outcome we aim for—is that you will begin applying these questions to your own particular contexts and situations. And, if you use this questioning technique (or better yet, a list of your own devising) as both a planning tool and a revision checksheet, you should be able to arrive at a fairly complete picture of your prospective reader. Remember: each situation calls for its own analysis. For every document you prepare, some form of this analysis is necessary. Even though it's unlikely that your "portrait" of the audience will be completely accurate, it is likely to provide you with some indication of how to approach a reader so that you can get what you want from that reader.

We've boiled down this material to a list of five primary areas of concern. Concentrate initially on these. As you get more sophisticated in your audience analysis, refer back to the more detailed material. Begin devising your own schemes of inquiry.

Questions for Analyzing Members of Your Audience

- Who are they? What are they to me?
- What is their interest in the subject?

- What do they know about the subject?
- How do they feel about the subject?
- What do I expect them to do?

To further reinforce what we've conveyed and to further emphasize its importance to your becoming an expert in your discipline, we offer a review quiz below. Take a few minutes and put into your own words your understanding of what you've just read about the five types of audiences. It doesn't have to be exact, but it does have to mean something *to you*. You might also note questions appropriate to an analysis of each audience type.

Five Types of Audience

E________________ Audience

Definition:

Characteristics:

L________________ Audience

Definition:

Characteristics:

E________________ Audience

Definition:

Characteristics:

C________________ Audience

Definition:

Characteristics:

T________________ Audience

Definition:

Characteristics:

Our discussion may seem peculiarly applicable to those who are already professionals in a discipline. But, even if you're still a long way from completing your schooling, these concerns apply to the writing you do for courses. You have audiences in them as much as you will anywhere else. Given any assignment—work or school—two immediate questions should immediately arise:

Who is the audience?
What is the purpose?

If the answers to these questions are not perfectly clear from the outset, use the checklists we have provided as tools to discover them.

3

Structure and Content

Overview

Planning Your Writing

Divide and Conquer

Outline Is Not a Dirty Word

The Obvious Components

Beginnings
Middles
Ends
Appendices

Collecting Material from Sources

Using Libraries and Other Repositories
Informational Interviewing

Structure is basic to almost everything. The history of science can be looked at as a history of the search for structures. As James Gleick points out, recent interest in chaos theory is a recognition that structures and systems are more complex and more integral to the nature of the world than had been previously thought.

Texts are no different. Mastery of structural understanding and technique is no less important for the writer than it is for the architect, the engineer, or the physicist. It is as organic to text as molecular structure is to chemistry. Scholars and researchers are discovering that language structures—how words and text are arranged in the process of communicating—are complicated reflections of our own cognitive processes.

Discourse, written or oral, has structure even if it is not readily apparent or if it is poorly conceived. Determining this structure is not entirely the responsibility of the audience, although the message receiver has more options for understanding and analyzing the message by being aware of its structure and intent. A sensitivity to discourse structures provides listeners and readers with a means to keep track of the points in a message and to anticipate further ones. Such awareness also enables you to determine what emphases to look for, or, in other words, what you should get out of what you're hearing or reading. Finally, awareness of structure and intent allows you to defend yourself against spurious claims and arguments.

This passage, for instance, has a definite and easily discerned structure:

> *The mechanics of a revolver are very elementary—a lever, a spring and a hammer. It takes eight to twelve pounds of pressure to pull a trigger, roughly equivalent to putting a finger in the handle of a gallon jug of milk and lifting it off the refrigerator shelf. That energy is stored in a spring as the hammer is forced back. Then the hammer reaches the cocked position and is released. The hammer strikes the shell casing, detonating a small amount of primer inside the shell, which in turn ignites the smokeless powder. The powder burns so fast that the result is an explosion. The expanding gas from this explosion forces the lead 158-grain projectile out the end of the barrel at somewhere between 750 and 900 feet per second. Spiral grooves along the inside of the barrel give the bullet the spin that keeps it going in the direction the gun is aimed. (Baker 167–68)*

In this text, we're being given an analysis of what occurs when a revolver is fired. Yet this analysis follows a certain order—this happens, then this, then this, and so on. We have a chronological sequence of events. Instructions to assemble something, to get somewhere, or to perform an action usually follow this structure.

In straightforward instances such as this example, we note the structure and then begin to anticipate what will follow even though we may have little knowledge about the process itself. When A happens, we can expect B to follow. The example begins with a list of components, a descriptive sentence. Specifications, descriptive detail such as "eight to twelve pounds," are brought to the reader's attention.

Speakers and writers do not rely on only one kind of arrangement in any extended discourse. However, most writers and speakers usually have a dominant strategy around which they arrange their material. You're familiar with all of them. Your own writing and speaking rely on them. Becoming conscious of these tools will enhance your use of them. Recognizing a particular kind of structure or discourse arrangement makes it much easier to determine the kind of notes you take in a lecture or as you read. Learning to use the different arrangement strategies in your own writing enables you to consider alternative presentation and also alternative ways of thinking through a writing task.

PLANNING YOUR WRITING

Time is a precious commodity to most professionals, something you, too, realize. As you become more expert in your discipline, the less time there is to get to everything you would like. Below, we suggest a few steps to assist you in making the most of your time whenever you approach a writing task. The sequence here is arbitrary. You, your specific project, and the context will determine the order that works best.

Organizing Your Writing Plan

1. Identify the purpose of your writing.
2. Identify the audience for your text.
3. Determine the message content.
4. Organize the content by priority.
5. Set a time schedule.
6. Devise a system for monitoring your progress.

The first two activities are essential. Most communication courses, whether focused on written or on spoken texts, could easily be summarized as courses in audience and purpose. Your responsibility as a writer is to deliver the purpose, although you may not have had much say in determining it. Class assignments do not always allow you much freedom to determine the purpose of the document you are asked to prepare. The instructor often does that. The audience is often specified as well, whether it's for an instructor or a client. However, how skillfully you satisfy the audience and purpose is determined by you. Your purpose can be as ambitious as writing an award-winning play. It can be as noble as enhancing public understanding of groundwater conservation. Or it can be as mundane as wanting a good grade in a class or wanting to impress a boss or client. Whatever it is, acknowledge this bit of self-interest and keep in mind that your writing will have your name on it.

Activities 3 and 4 directly involve arrangement. Both message content and priority depend on when you present them to the reader. We discuss this in more detail later, but keep in mind that your planning needs to take these into account from the beginning. Quick sketches, a chart of things to cover, or a planning outline may be useful at this point. Remember, though, that just because you've put your outline on paper doesn't mean it cannot be changed. Very few projects of any kind escape major modification before completion, usually because of input from your audience.

The last two activities—organizing by priority and setting a schedule—are critical as well. Time is allocated just as other resources are. Your instructor recognizes (although it may not seem like it at times) that his or her course is not the only one you're taking. Supervisors and bosses frequently have you working on more than one project. Your responsibility as an expert is to make the most productive use of the time you're allotted. Deadlines for your writing, whatever the project, are established for reasons.

The following discussion is designed to help you design your documents. In Figure 3.1 we've provided an example of a coversheet that we recommend to both students and professionals to help produce a text on time. When faced with a substantial writing task (or oral presentation, for that matter), use this as a planner. It can further be used as a document control device to help you keep track of the text, because only rarely do students or professionals have the luxury of working on one project uninterrupted from start to finish. It also can be extended into a progress chart. Finally, it can act as a checklist for completion, before the document leaves your hands and becomes public.

Put your name on the coversheet: this identifies the project to others as yours and emphasizes a sense of personal ownership and responsibility. Classify the document as part of a particular project or course. Create a working title (but do not hesitate to change this title as the document evolves). Note critical dates, whether imposed on you by others or self-imposed. Time lines are effective in planning and maintaining a sense of progress. They provide a scorecard and act as a psychological boost—there is something gratifying about checking off completed tasks, especially on large or long-term projects. Time lines also make writing a progress report, if necessary, easier.

As succinctly as possible, state the primary purpose or purposes for the document. This will help keep you focused, "on task." Do not ignore secondary purposes, such as getting a good grade or a promotion, even if they seem obvious. Specify the audience or audiences who will receive your document and note any characteristics about them that you need to keep in mind. Indicate your sources of information, whether the library or interviews or an experimental study. Jot down additional sources as well. You might need them if your primary information sources are unavailable. Last, consider possible difficulties or barriers you might encounter. Because time is an immediate limitation in most cases, the availability of specific research materials may add complications to the project. Delays in getting

Name: ______________________	Course or Project: ______________
Title: ______________________	Start Date: ____________________
Priority: ____________________	Due Date: _____________________

Primary Purpose(s):

(1)

(2)

Secondary Purpose(s):

(1)

(2)

Primary Audience(s):

(1)

(2)

Secondary Audience(s):

(1)

(2)

Primary Source(s):

(1)

(2)

Secondary Source(s):

(1)

(2)

Perceived Difficulties:

(1)

(2)

Presentation Format(s):

(1)

(2)

Attached Appendices Checklist

[ ] Proposed Table of Contents	[ ] Budget
[ ] References	[ ] Timeline
[ ] ______________	[ ] ______________

Notes:

FIGURE 3.1 Document Coversheet

equipment or information may cause problems. And so on. Try to anticipate these.

We also encourage you to create attachments or appendices to your coversheet and provide boxes to mark as an encouragement toward incorporating a working outline, time line, and so forth. Above all, adapt this to your own needs.

Below is one example of how one student used this coversheet to design a proposal for restructuring a foster parent training program. The student, a child development and family relations major, attached a detailed outline of her project that later went on to become the table of contents for the report itself. Your coversheet can also be used at later stages in your writing process—when you're revising, for instance.

Name: ____________ Course or Project: Tech. Writing

Title: Suggested Restructuring of Foster Parent Training Program

Start Date: June 19, 1989

Due Date: July 5, 1989

Primary Purpose(s): Improvement of current foster parent training program.

Primary Audience: (1) Director of Foster Parent Training Program.
(2) Employees of Foster Home

Secondary Audience: Technical writing instructor

Primary Research Sources: (1) Interview with Director.
(2) Interview with Head of foster parent recruitment.

Secondary Research Sources: (1) Books on foster care—library.
(2) Journal articles comprised of foster care, sexual abuse, child abuse—library.

Perceived Difficulties: Scheduling interviews with employees.

Presentation Format(s): APA style.

Attached Appendices Checklist: [x] Proposed Table of Contents
[x] References
[x] Graphs
[x] Worksheets

FIGURE 3.2 Working Document Coversheet

Many of us work or will work in large organizations that generate a large number of projects and enormous amounts of paper. This coversheet can be useful for you, your peers, your subordinates, and your supervisors by providing a system for internal tracking. You can state confidently, "the project is now at this stage and sitting on so-and-so's desk awaiting such-and-such." These coversheets also can be designed to yield progress or status reports.

Organization of resources, especially time management, is critical in most professional situations. But the organization of information within a communication is also key. It's especially essential in written communication. Readers rarely have the writer on hand to answer questions or provide explanations. Your own readers had better not need you to be around to explain your texts. We know of an instance in which an architect in southern Arizona was working with a client in northern Arizona. The client received the architect's proposal for a multi-million-dollar shopping center design and was so confused by it that he flew his private plane 400 miles to find out what the plan was all about. Needless to say, he was not happy with the architect. You probably don't go to such lengths to get further clarification when you read; don't expect others to.

Also, effective organization is efficient, and the more efficient your communication is, the happier the readers are: you save them time and effort. Readers of most professional documents (and remember that your work submitted to instructors is a demonstration of how professional you are) rarely read the way most of us were originally taught to read.

Most experts read texts in their disciplines just as most writers write them—in sections. That doesn't mean starting with word one in paragraph one on page one. Those readers who encounter many documents during the course of their day have neither the time nor the need to read everything you have provided. Your document, whether a report on single-side drive wheelchairs for your mechanical engineering design class or a three-million-dollar grant proposal to fund tissue culture research, competes with other documents written by other writers who want just as much as you do from the reader.

Although the percentages vary from study to study, professionals report that, typically, they first read the summary or abstract of a document. This enables them to determine whether it's important for them to read or even if it is *worth* reading. Those who decide to read on usually either go to the introduction or turn immediately to the conclusions or recommendations. Some few of your remaining readers will bother with the body and the appendices. Let's say that you start with one hundred readers: perhaps ten of them will ever get through the entire document. That doesn't mean you can skimp on these less frequently read sections—readers are too individual to count on their not reading everything.

As a means of helping your readers and as a means of helping you write your document, we provide these suggestions for you to apply to your own writing:

- *Arrange your material into units of information.* Think about your readers and your purpose; use these as criteria to build your units. For example, executives normally want costs segregated, then benefits, and so on.
- *Establish a hierarchy among these clusters of important information.* We often think in hierarchies: use this to your advantage to arrange your units in an appropriate sequence. Commonly, the most important information is placed early in a report, then the next most important.
- *Adjust your hierarchy to a reader-centered sequence.* Consider your readers in the act of reading: what are they doing when? This is audience awareness. Try to think like your reader and put your groups in a sequence appropriate to that reader.
- *Think visually.* Use pictures, graphs, charts, maps, drawings, tables; also keep in mind that a page of text has a visual impact. Use appropriate paragraphing, bulleting, indenting, listing, enumerating.
- *Adopt and adapt patterns used successfully by other writers.* Find models; see what patterns you can modify to your own needs.

The following discussion extends and elaborates these ideas. Try to relate each of the items on this list to one of the following sections.

DIVIDE AND CONQUER

Preparing most documents, whether a proposal to do something, a research report on what you've done, or a demonstration of how much you know, is an imposing task. Larger projects, such as this book, are even more imposing. First, we wanted to produce a book to help students use writing in their respective disciplines. Second, because the project involved three authors, which you may have thought meant the task was easier by two-thirds, the task became more difficult. Each of us has his own unique areas of expertise to apply. As a result, we broke the text into "chunks." We then divided up these chunks among us as our background and expertise and interest dictated. The Contents, for example, indicates how the task of writing a book was segmented into chunks and then organized, both for your sake as a reader and for our sake as writers.

Writing projects usually are more manageable if they're divided into components or segments in this way. Many of us will put off a project until the last minute and then crank it through the word processor or typewriter the night before. It nearly always shows. But what happens when a project won't fit into the night before? A process used by most professionals in designing most things, whether a prototype or a written document, is to break the task into parts and then assemble the parts into a whole. Variously called *segmenting* or *componentizing* or *partitioning*, this is an invaluable means of accomplishing a task without being overwhelmed by just how large a task it really is.

Think, for instance, of building a house: a lot of steps (no pun intended) go into it. The house is not done all at once; you set a foundation, raise the walls, add a roof, put in the plumbing and electrical systems, add the finish work and fixtures, paint, landscape, move in the furniture, buy a dog. Some of these occur at the same time. Some steps have to wait for others to be done. Some situations call for one step to be done before others are done, whereas other situations change the order or sequence of events.

Writing demands this kind of flexibility. A writer's best tools are those adaptable to a variety of situations. A writer's process of using those tools needs flexibility as well. Beginning to write a document on its first page is only one way of developing a document—in many respects, the weakest way of beginning. Just as a set of blueprints is composed of a number of individually complete documents (the electrical plans, the site plans, the plumbing plans, etc.), a document of any size has various components integral to the whole. An architect or an engineer will create whole sets of blueprints or design schematics piece by piece, and not necessarily beginning with page one. A great deal has to be worked out before those opening units can be created.

You can approach your writing this same way. Break the task into parts. Complete pieces in the most efficient way. Some parts are easier to do than others. Certain areas will need more time or more research or more input from other people. The idea is to set a schedule and work at finishing sections one at a time. Then assemble at the end. Another metaphor for the process might be cooking. Recipes call for gathering the materials, determining quantities, and then, in a sequence of events, assembling them. Not until everything has been done do you have edible food.

We've suggested the bare essentials in applying segmenting to your writing tasks. But only you can make it work. First, take a minute and sketch below a common task or procedure in your own discipline that illustrates this assembly approach.

____

____

____

____

____

Just as you're able to break out the elements of this process, you should be able to break out the components of a document in your discipline.

This is also a way to keep track of all of the elements that need to go into your document. Using segments is a means to *map* your communication. This is an organizational tool that makes your task easier, as well as the readers'. Mapping is, as its name suggests, a visual trail for both the reader and writer to follow. Look at this chapter, for example. We've attempted to set up a logical, progressive flow from point to point and to provide an easily discernible visual flow with our format of chapter title, major head, minor head. The chapter can be easily outlined using these segments.

Here are several suggestions to enhance your use of mapping:

- *Use headings often.* Think of them as signposts for the readers and for you; these act as *sub*titles to your major title.
- *Phrase each heading to tell what specifically follows.* Be direct and specific: use a question, the main point, a key word or phrase.
- *Use parallel structure wherever possible for heading titles.* Each heading has its own function: to announce its topic. However, each heading is also a segment of the whole and establishes an outline or scheme for the reader to follow. This is a crucial concept—it requires consistency whether in the form of maintaining the same class of objects (e.g., apples, pears, and peaches) or the same grammatical form (e.g., verb, then object).
- *Regard these headings as visual aids.* Make sure the layout corresponds to your hierarchy of importance.

Be generous with paper when mapping out a text. Write a single subheading at the top of each sheet of paper. Use this sheet only for material that belongs to that unit of text. Using individual sheets of paper helps you to shuffle them about for better fit in the final assembly. Notecards work too, the bigger the better. Using a word processor makes this task easy as well: set up your subheadings and then simply "spread" them as you add material to a unit and move them about as the need arises. Some word processing systems have built-in outlining systems for doing this.

An effective illustration of this process is a textbook—this one, for example. Look at the table of contents. You can see the various *layers* that went into its composition: overall is the title of the book, then you see chapters, then within chapters are hierarchical levels of headings. Those distinct units were written and rewritten and then brought together to form the chapters, which were brought together to form the larger units, then the book as a whole. You can visualize this process as a series of nested boxes, one inside the other. Apply this to your own writing tasks—you'll be surprised how quickly you'll be able to build an impressive document, and how much more manageable the task is.

OUTLINE IS NOT A DIRTY WORD

The use of outlines is closely aligned with segmenting or creating text components. We've detailed instances of these in later chapters on reading and notetaking, but we want to remind you that they will work for your writing as well. Take a creative attitude toward them: develop a system that works for you, not one that is rule bound, in which Roman numeral *I* means you have to have Roman numeral *II* and so forth. The outlining rules many of us were taught in our early education have some use, but consider them breakable. Cognitively, some of these rules make sense, though. Developing a sense of parallelism may be one of the principal motivations behind the suggested arrangement patterns. Because making outlines has so many negative connotations, we prefer to call them *schematics* or *sketches* or *text blueprints.*

Below is a schematic developed by a molecular biology student. The purpose of his proposal was to solicit assistance from a pharmacy professor he worked for in applying for a large grant to study tissue co-culturing. He

```
  I. Transmittal letter
 II. Table of Contents
III. List of Figures and Illustrations
 IV. Audience Requirements
     A. Proposal targeted towards a formal grant
        application
        1. Chosen: National Institute of Health Foundation
        2. Determine audience requirements
           a. Acquired previous grant application as model
           b. Focus audience as proposal to my supervisor
  V. Specific Aims of the Proposal
     A. Intent: establish a suitable method of co-culturing
        vascular smooth muscle with sympathetic ganglion
        cells.
        1. Develop a primary cell culture
           a. Use previous techniques to culture ganglion
              cells
           b. Develop new method of culturing smooth muscle
              cells
        2. Record synaptic transmission from both types of
           cells
        3. Determine the characteristics of each
```

FIGURE 3.3 Sample Schematic *(Continued)*

FIGURE 3.3 *Continued*

```
   VI. Significance
       A. Background of the two types of cells
          (Developmental)
          1. Sympathetic neurons
          2. Vascular smooth muscle
       B. Description of the two types of cells
          (Morphology)
          1. Sympathetic neurons
          2. Vascular smooth muscle
       C. Innervation of the two types of cells
          (Functional)
          1. Sympathetic neurons
          2. Vascular smooth muscle
  VII. Methods
       A. Supplies needed for culturing cells.
       B. Primary cell culture of guinea pig inferior
          mesenteric ganglion cells.
          1. Animals
          2. Dissection
          3. Dissociation and Plating
       C. Primary cell culture of guinea pig inferior
          mesenteric vascular and superior mesenteric
          vascular cells.
          1. Animals
          2. Dissection
          3. Dissociation and Plating
       D. General culture methodology
          1. Proposed method one
          2. Proposed method two
 VIII. Discussion
       A. Relating to established methods
          1. Discuss the advantages and disadvantages
             a. Method one
             b. Method two
          2. Limitations in the project
   IX. Conclusion
       A. Summarize the benefits
          1. The applications of this type of project
          2. The types of knowledge to be obtained
    X. References
       A. List of all the resources used for this project.
```

broke out in great detail the various segments needed to explain his proposal and to convince his reader of both the value of his project and his knowledge on the topic.

Although his proposal was far from complete when the student submitted this outline, it does provide an idea of the *what*, *why*, and *how* of his project. It is of even more value to him in that it enables him to keep track of his progress, extend certain areas, add depth to others, and delete several components.

Using the "Divide and Conquer" strategy in conjunction with a schematic or blueprint is a way to determine the order or arrangement of your text. It makes your final assembly much easier. It has the added advantages of working as a check sheet and being easily converted to a table of contents (often all you need to do is add page numbers). If you look at our Table of Contents to this book, you'll see the final version of our outline of its components; we drastically altered sequences, made additions and deletions, and rewrote subtitles and headings so much that our initial outline is barely recognizable as this book, but that is always a writer's prerogative. Just like an iceberg, the text you see is rarely all there is to it.

THE OBVIOUS COMPONENTS

Communications have three parts: a beginning, a middle, and an end. However, these three parts often have their own components or segments. On the surface, these components are familiar, readily understood concepts. You've known them since your first encounters with text.

Yet, what distinguishes a beginning from a middle from an end? Mere location or placement on the page? If so, where does a beginning end? What about its middle? Where does one end? With what does one begin? Many writers seem not to recognize that the apparentness of beginning, middle, and end in their own writing is not so obvious to the reader. Each of these three concepts is actually a lot more complex than it seems.

Purpose, audience, and context, of course, determine the particular approaches a writer will take in establishing the "how" and "what" of each component. Each of these segments has its own integral purposes and principles: together they operate on your readers in meaningful patterns, and they dictate meaningful patterns to you as you write. How your patterns and the readers' patterns match probably is as much a study for chaos theory as anything, but your principal concern should be to get your purposes satisfied. Effective and intentional (that is, conscious) use of these obvious components makes your task and your readers' task easier, and more likely to be successful.

Beginnings

Oddly enough, many professional writers in many writing situations do not get to the beginning, or introduction, until the project is largely completed. How it appears is not necessarily how it came about. For instance, in writing this book, we *thought* about the introduction, but it wasn't until we had completed a great deal of the book as a whole that we got around to *writing* it. Later, when we revised this book in some very drastic ways, we threw away the first introduction and started over on a brand-new one. And *that* one also was not finished until the rest of the book was finally revised.

As a writer, you perform at least three distinct functions in the beginning:

- You use it to persuade the readers to read attentively.
- You shape their responses to what they are about to read.
- You offer a preview of coming attractions.

For the reader, a strong beginning accomplishes a number of things as well:

- It tells the reader what the text is about.
- It tells how it is organized.
- It generalizes about its contents.
- It keeps the reader reading.
- It tells the reader what parts of the text need to be read.

The guidelines we provide here will not work in all instances. Essays and most literary forms rarely abide by them. Think, for example, of mystery novels in which you find out "whodunit" early in the book. The writer uses other strategies to keep the reader reading, such as the suspense of the detective proving who did it. Most of your readers, however, are not reading for enjoyment. They're reading for utility, for application, for pragmatic reasons. The strategies you use need to be more direct, less mysterious.

Remember that in any kind of communication, exceptions abound. Good writers continually "break the rules." Most readers in professional and classroom situations are after what you have to say first and are only secondarily interested in how you say it. The catch is that how you say it helps readers get to what you have to say. Keep in mind that your text is competing with other texts and distractions for the reader's time and attention. Get the important material to that reader as quickly as possible. The following suggestions will help you do that.

At the beginning, tell what your document is about. Announcing this first helps readers understand *and* remember what you've written. And it helps readers find particular, relevant information and helps them decide if they should read the text and how.

At the beginning, tell how your text is organized. This forecasting of your structure enables the reader to look for key points. It also provides for effective repetition and emphasis without seeming to be redundant.

At the beginning, generalize about the contents of your document. Readers generalize about particulars as they read: help them out in a way that meets your purposes. By introducing the overall topic and its points, you can help readers anticipate and extend the evidence and support you bring in later. Introducing readers to a general commentary also enables them to activate background knowledge and to locate your text in relation to other information they might have.

Put the most important information first. This increases the probability that your readers will read the important information, and it increases the likelihood that they will remember it. It also makes this information easy to find if readers need to come back for it at a later time.

Forecast and answer your readers' most important questions as they arise. As we read actively, we raise questions, concerns, issues with the text and its writer. Use this to your advantage. Readers most often ask three types of questions:

1. "Can you explain?" (The readers cannot understand some word, concept, or statement because the material is unfamiliar.)
2. "Can you tell me more?" (The readers understand but want more information.)
3. "How can you say that?" (The readers question the validity of a point or statement.)

Provide transitions. Think of transitional devices as part of the "glue" that holds the text together. However, transitional devices work only if the underlying ideas are connected. View your text as a flow of ideas, and ensure that your readers do also. Transitions can be as simple as repeating key words and phrases. Consciously directing readers' attention (e.g., "Now let us turn our attention to . . .") creates a transition. Enumerating the text is another means of providing a signal to the reader that a new, but connected, point is being made. Subheadings and chapter divisions can work as transitional devices. The English language has a large number of techniques for moving the audience from point to point. Become more conscious of these in your reading—you'll find that you develop a larger and more diverse repertoire for your writing that way.

The following example is from the molecular biology student whose document blueprint we included earlier. Recall that the writer is seeking support and assistance from a professor to write a proposal for funding to investigate a new technique in cell culturing. Note the various introductory features as they appear.

> *The intent of this proposal is to establish a suitable method of co-culturing vascular smooth muscle together with sympathetic ganglion cells isolated from the guinea pig. The overall goal is to understand the previous methods used in culturing other types of cells and to use this information in developing a suitable alternative. To accomplish these aims, I will*
>
> 1. *Develop an understanding of the developmental background of the sympathetic neuron and the vascular smooth muscle cell.*
> 2. *Review the literature on the morphology of each of the cells.*
> 3. *Determine the functional significance of the innervation process between the sympathetic neuron and the vascular smooth muscle cell.*
> 4. *Provide a list of the materials needed for the proposal.*
> 5. *List the methods involved in the preparation of each of the cells.*
> 6. *Discuss an alternative in the methodology used to successfully culture both of these cells together.*
> 7. *Provide an appropriate discussion relating this proposal to established methods and indicate limitations that might occur.*
> 8. *Summarize the benefits of this type of research project.*

We are immediately made aware of the purpose behind this document and the goals of the project. Furthermore, we're given a specific list of what is contained in the following twenty or so pages of the text and the order in which they will appear. Direct and detailed, this opening strategy introduces the topic very briefly, states the purpose of the document, and then forecasts its contents.

One way to make sure you have enough of these elements is to follow the process we suggest below. Once again, however, we want to remind you that for this tool to be successful you need to consciously adapt these steps to your own processes and needs. And *practice.*

1. *Imagine your readers and their possible responses.* Keep in mind their roles, jobs, specialties, goals, personalities, and attitudes.
2. *Tell your readers how your communication is relevant to them.* Be able to answer these questions:
   - What is the problem?
   - What has (or has not) been done?
   - How will this help?
3. *Tell how your communication is organized.*
4. *Tell the scope of your communication.* State what it contains and what it doesn't contain.

5. *Tell your main points.* Get the most important information to the reader quickly.
6. *Provide any necessary background information.* Beginning, or "opening" a document, whenever purpose and audience allow, should be:

   - Engaging
   - Positive
   - Cooperative
   - Short and concise
   - From the reader's point of view

The beginning of a document must persuade readers to read attentively and must convince them that the document is worth their while. Teachers are perhaps the only audience you can count on to read something that they may not want to read: if they assigned a paper, then they are obliged to attempt to read it. Yet, why is it that some students get good grades on their papers and others do not? The teacher, like any reader, wants to be engaged by the writer. Put yourself in the instructor's place: would you want to read what you turn in? And then multiply that answer by the number of students in your class. Outside of a class, your writing will not get the same treatment. The professional world does not share the academic world's sense of obligation. Readers simply will *not* read a poorly designed document. And all of your hard work will do no one any good if your documents are not read. Identify for yourself the elements that appear in the opening reproduced below. It's excerpted from a request directed at a university president to include student representatives on a task force concerned with child care facilities on campus.

> A need and a desire for some sort of campus child care programming has been expressed by various members of the faculty, staff, and students. To make significant advances in this area and to avoid the exclusion of any campus constituency, these groups must work in concert, not as separate groups with parochial goals. Through this proposal, we intend to demonstrate the need to include student representation on the University Committee to Review Child Care Assistance. This goal will be achieved by demonstrating the importance of child care as a national, state, and campus issue. This proposal will also discuss the existing University Committee to Review Child Care Assistance and examine the manner in which students can work with the committee to achieve overall campus goals.

Written by a political science student and a child development student working as a team, this document establishes a clear topic and purpose. The writers then indicate what they cover in the rest of the document so that readers know what is conveyed and when to look for it.

The opening of any document gives readers an immediate sense of whether the document is worth their while. It also implicitly shapes readers' responses. The opening of your text tells readers if they should read it, if it's likely to be worth reading, and if you're the person who should have written it.

You have undoubtedly written successful papers to get where you are now. Think a bit about opening strategies you have used in an attempt to engage your reader. Or think about effective openings you have seen others use. Scan through a book or journal that you *enjoy* reading and identify effective openings.

We find that many students and many professionals spend the least amount of attention, effort, and imagination on their openings. They just start. And the cost is tremendous. Openings often seem as if the writer is bored with what he or she is reporting, is not very knowledgeable, has not put in any time or thought to the matter, or worse. Readers notice.

In the following paragraphs, we discuss some of an almost endless array of opening strategies. Let your purpose and audience guide your own development of a repertoire of possibilities. But use these to begin developing your sense of what it takes to "hook" the reader.

Definition Opening

This is a classic. You probably began using a version of this one in elementary school: "*American Heritage Dictionary* says that a 'definition' means 'The act of stating a precise meaning or significance, as of a word, phrase, or term' (346)." This approach rarely does much for a reader, however. The reader can too easily look up the word; an expert reader is likely to be insulted. In many disciplines, however, terms and concepts are not known to the reader, nor are they defined in any but the most specialized dictionaries. At times you'll want to use a term in a novel or unique way. In these cases, it's wise to clue readers in or to engage their interest by beginning with a definition. Loren Eiseley, the naturalist and essayist, begins a chapter with this opening:

> It is a remarkable fact that much of what man has achieved through the use of his intellect, nature had invented before him. *Pilobus*, another fungus which prepares, sights, and fires its spore capsule, constitutes a curious anticipation of human rocketry. (75)

Neurologist Oliver Sacks starts a chapter by defining "a phantom, in the sense that neurologists use, is a persistent image or memory of part of the body, usually a limb, for months or years after a loss" (66).

Anecdotal Opening

Historian Jacques Sadoul opens his study of alchemy this way:

> During the severe winter of 1956 I was caught in a snow-storm which obliged me to take shelter in a bookshop in the rue Saint-Jacques in

> Paris. It was a shop specialising in occult works on magic, astrology, clairvoyance and alchemy. (15)

Russian psychologist A. R. Luria opens the second chapter of his study of a man with photographic memory like this:

> The actual beginning of this account dates back to the 1920's, when I had only recently begun to do work in psychology. It was then that a man came to my laboratory who asked me to test his memory. (7)

This approach often intrigues readers to read further, provided they are interested in the person telling the anecdote or the anecdote is interesting in itself. Do not neglect humorous opportunities here. Most of us like to be amused and are willing to keep reading for the promise of more. Darrell Huff begins his classic text *How to Lie with Statistics* with a mildly humorous and telling anecdote:

> "There's a mighty lot of crime around here," said my father-in-law a little while after he moved from Iowa to California. And so there was—in the newspaper he read. It is one that overlooks no crime in its own area and has been known to give more attention to an Iowa murder than was given by the principal daily in the region in which it took place. (7)

Question Opening

This is another old standby, especially if used rhetorically (that is, a question with only one answer or one that expects no answer). Because it's so common, and often badly handled, this opening strategy could lead readers to mistrust you immediately. Done well, or inventively, however, it can suffice. In this example, naturalist Joseph Wood Krutch uses this strategy in the Prologue to *The Great Chain of Life*:

> Whenever men stop *doing things* long enough to *think about them*, they always ask themselves the question: "What am I?" And since that is the hardest of all questions to answer they usually settle for what looks easier—"If I don't know what I am, then can I tell what I am like?" (xx)

Historical Opening

Historical accounts are often quite engaging, providing both focus and background information while generating interest. In a discussion on the physics and chemistry of matter, Stephen Toulmin and June Goodfield begin a chapter with historical information:

> In 600 BC, when Thales of Miletos was in his twenties, the traditional mythologies had not yet been seriously questioned. Two hundred years later the intellectual environment was very different. (73)

Scenario Opening

Bronislaw Malinowski opens a unit of his classic anthropological study *Argonauts of the Western Pacific* with this intriguing scene:

> Imagine yourself suddenly set down surrounded by all your gear, alone on a tropical beach close to a native village, while the launch or dinghy which has brought you sails away out of sight. Since you take up your abode in the compound of some neighboring white man, trader or missionary, you have nothing to do but to start at once on your ethnographic work. Imagine further that you are a beginner, without previous experience, with nothing to guide you and no one to help you. (4)

Malinowski draws us into the experience by enabling us to place ourselves there with him.

Other approaches are equally useful. Lewis Thomas, a medical doctor and popular author, begins an essay with a twist on our perceptions: "Warts are wonderful structures" (76). He starts another as a letter addressed to medical doctors (12). He raises our concerns with this opening: "The Meningococcus, viewed from a distance, seems to have the characteristics of an implacable, dangerous enemy of the whole human race" (93). He attacks as an adversary: "The influence of the modern medical school on liberal-arts education in this country over the last decade has been baleful and malign, nothing less" (137). And these are only a random sample of *one* writer's strategies, in only *one* of his books.

These illustrations demonstrate but a few of the many variations that writers have adopted to entice and ensnare readers. Be inventive. Note also that none of these examples is very discrete—several of them could just as easily illustrate a number of opening strategies. The classification of a strategy as one kind or another is not important. Work at finding just the right opening, even if it means attempting several and throwing away the less successful. Keep a file folder or a record in your journal of examples of effective opening strategies, especially those that occur in the writings in your discipline. Think of these strategies as "opening hooks," lures that you use to fish for reader interest and attention. Change them depending on who your readers are and what they will be interested in. Give too little attention to your opening, or use too little bait, and you'll likely go hungry.

Middles

The middle of a document is usually the largest part of it. And surprisingly, the middle or body is usually the easiest to write. It's also the part that is read least in the professional world. Some research suggests that as few as 10 percent of a report's readers will read its middle sections. A business plan presented to a bank to secure a loan, for example, usually has a large middle that demonstrates all of the research and detail necessary to convince the reader that it's a good idea to lend *x* number of dollars to a company. Often it's not read. Many scientific publications and reports have large chunks of text that detail the experiment and its results; but most of their readers concentrate on the conclusions drawn from the research. Readers of feasibility studies may read only the recommendations. Those deciding to fund a proposal may read only the rationale and the budget.

As the writer, however, you cannot count on readers *not* reading the whole text. Smaller documents are likely to be read in their entirety. And when writing for a course, you must assume that your entire text will be read by your instructors. Your responsibility is to provide the most effective, most complete, most efficient text you're capable of—one that demonstrates, throughout, your competency and professionalism.

Audience and purpose guide your selection of what is; but to satisfy that audience and purpose, certain organizational concepts have "evolved." Most of us remember having to write a comparison/contrast paper sometime in our schooling. What generally escapes us when we're taught this is that these discourse strategies invariably involve using more than one arrangement—just as most carpenters use more than one tool, most anglers have more than one lure, and most artists use more than one brush or knife. It's not uncommon to find several types of arrangement used simultaneously. For instance, an architectural proposal for a parking lot might have both a problem/solution (not enough parking/propose a parking structure) and a spatial emphasis (given *x* number of cars using the lot and only so much space available, the solution is . . .). However, writers and speakers usually select a dominant arrangement around which to structure the discourse and then bring in other kinds to help convey their message. Spotting the strategies is helpful to listeners and readers in ordering and remembering what they hear or see. Having strategies available and then using them helps writers get things done.

We've categorized some of the more common types of arrangement below, but remember that they are in no way discrete. They rarely occur by themselves. These and other arrangements create a sense of structure for the reader and the writer.

Chronological

This arrangement is sequence oriented, usually based on time. First A happened, then B. Various kinds of instructions, recipes, directions, narratives, experiments, and lab reports are often structured according to what happens first, then next, and so forth.

Cause/Effect

Item B resulted from Item A. Or A causes B. "Because" is a strong signifier of this type of arrangement. This arrangement often causes problems for writers because, as ecologists say, "You can't do just one thing." A single cause rarely results in a single event. Still, cause/effect analysis is often seen in news reports, history, and other genres in which the analyst is attempting to explain why something happened.

Comparison/Contrast

Item A is like Item B or is not like Item B. Similarities and differences among items from the same class or category are emphasized in this kind of arrangement. Note that contrast assumes some similarities, just as comparison assumes some differences. Two principal types are used: *chunk* or *block*—Item A is presented fully, then Item B; *sequence* or *integral*—Items A and B are discussed side by side, point by point. *Consumer Reports* is an excellent source for models of this pattern.

Problem/Solution

A fairly obvious and much-used arrangement, it implies "We have a problem, and this is our solution." In many respects, almost any writing task you approach is one involving problem/solution. Note that identifying a problem is usually only part of the process; most times, you need to be able to provide some idea of a solution as well.

Topical

This arrangement is based on subdivisions of a topic, usually either presented *numerically* or *alphabetically*: "I will discuss three points. First, . . ." To avoid a hierarchy of importance suggested by numbering the points, writers sometimes designate their subpoints alphabetically or with bullets.

Order of Importance

Often used with a numeric system of arrangement, writers order their supports in a hierarchy and present them in either ascending (*climactic*) or descending (*anticlimactic*) order of importance. Intensifiers such as "first and foremost" or "last and most important" are giveaways of this strategy.

Spatial

This approach uses the location of what is being discussed as its key emphasis. Much architectural and engineering design focuses on where something is located. For instance, in a parking lot proposal, emphasis might be on locating it where it would serve the greatest number of people in adjacent or nearby buildings.

Another way to view these arrangement patterns (also commonly called "modes of discourse") is to examine not just what they are, but also what they do and how they work.

To look at these strategies in more detail, we'll set up a scenario and use aspects of it to provide an example. We'll use a fictional university that has a perceived parking problem. Our task is to solve, or at least abate, the parking problem. Plus, we would like to be able to park when we come to school. Immediately, we can see that we have many alternatives, whatever our expertise. These alternatives may draw on our backgrounds in ecology, psychology, and sociology (getting people to walk, bike, take a bus, carpool) or our expertise in architecture and engineering (designing parking structures, using space more effectively, enhancing traffic flow). We have at hand our entire repertoire of writing and thinking strategies to solve the problem.

One possible strategy is *classification*, creating hierarchies. We classify or segregate material into groupings based on our purpose. Either formal (groupings based on some objective, observable characteristics) or informal (groupings based on more subjective, intuited characteristics) classification is a tool that can:

- Arrange material in a way useful to readers
- Create groups (and subgroups) that are inclusive
- Separate mutually exclusive items into unique categories

Some guidelines for using classification are to:

1. *Choose principles of classification suited to your readers and purposes.* Identify logical characteristics that group important items.
2. *Use only one principle of classification at a time.* Provide one slot for each of your items at each level of your hierarchy.
3. *Use parallel groups at the same level.* Make your groupings of equal rank.
4. *Avoid overlap among groups.*

In our parking proposal, we could use classification to convince our readers of the problem or of the usefulness of our solution. For instance, in identifying the problem, we could categorize or classify the various people who encounter this problem (students, faculty, staff, people living in the neighborhoods bordering the campus, etc.). We could identify sets of problems these people encounter (environmental—air pollution, dwindling natural resources, traffic noise; emotional—frustration, anger, fear; physical—long walks to class, danger crossing streets, confrontations with other "competitors" for parking spaces, etc.). The idea is to set up categories and demonstrate or establish criteria for membership in that set. Venn diagrams are often useful visual tools for such an effort.

Partitioning, another strategy, is a means of organizing a description. To use it, think of an object or concept as a collection of parts. The two most commonly used principles are *location* and *function*.

When using partitioning, be sure to:

1. Choose a principle for partitioning suited to your readers and purpose.
2. Use only one principle at a time.
3. Arrange the parts of your discussion in a logical sequence.

Our parking solution would likely involve elements of partition. We might propose a multifaceted attack on the parking problem by proposing alternative transportation instead of, or in addition to, more parking facilities. Partitioning would enable us to break the problem/solution into more manageable parts and to come at the issues from several directions.

Segmentation is a way of describing a process or the relationship of events over time. It's often used when we want to describe:

- How something is done
- How something works
- How something happened

In using this strategy, keep in mind the following:

1. Choose a principle suited for your task.
2. Arrange your groups in an understandable sequence.
3. Make your groupings of manageable size.
4. Make the relationships among the steps or groupings clear.

Tied to our example, segmentation might occur if we proposed a long-term approach. First, we'll provide single-level lots as we implement a campaign to get more people to take the bus or ride bicycles to school and as we wait for multilevel parking structures to be built. Our proposal would describe the process of taking care of parking problems over time.

Another conceivable strategy is *comparison*, which is ideal for helping readers make decisions or helping readers understand something by means of analogy (using the familiar to explain the unfamiliar). Two patterns of comparison are common:

Alternating Pattern

Statement of criteria
Overview of two alternatives
  Evaluation of Alternative
    Criterion 1
      Alternative A
      Alternative B

Divided Pattern

Statement of criteria
Description of two alternatives
  Alternative A
    Overview
      Criterion 1
      Criterion 2

Criterion 2
Alternative A
Alternative B
Criterion 3
Alternative A
Alternative B

Criterion 3
Alternative B
Overview
Criterion 1
Criterion 2
Criterion 3
Comparison of Alternatives

When using comparison, remember to:

1. Choose points of comparison consistent with your purposes and readers.
2. Arrange the comparisons hierarchically.
3. Arrange your groups in a logical sequence.

Considering that parking itself is an expensive proposition, most readers will want to know if we have examined a number of possible alternatives. They will also want to see the criteria we used to make the comparisons before they will accept or reject our recommendations.

The following are more global strategies or approaches to a writing situation. The first here is almost impossible to avoid. It comes into play during nearly every communicative act. Simply considering audience and purpose necessitates a certain concern for *persuasion*. But, intentional persuasion occurs (or does not occur) when you want your readers to take a certain course of action. When you want readers to accept a certain interpretation, you use a higher degree of persuasion. Readers are (or should be) skeptical—they will not accept things simply because you say they should. Your responsibility, however, is to convince them that you are knowledgeable enough and prepared enough to be worth listening to or reading.

To be more persuasive:

1. *Begin your persuasion by stating your claim.* You want your readers to accept your position consciously, so let them know what it is. The exception to this occurs when you know they will react negatively: in this case, start with your evidence and build toward your claim.
2. *Present evidence that your readers agree is sufficient and credible.* Your argument rests on your facts, observations, authority, and other evidence. They will question whether you present enough and whether what you present is reliable.
3. *Explicitly justify your line of reasoning.* Readers examine the logical soundness of your statements and its applicability to this situation. This is a predominant characteristic of an argument, not an opinion. Many people tend to confuse these two terms. Although the natures of both argument and opinion are complex, it's very difficult to refute an opinion—they usually just *are,* and they are often unexamined by their holders. Arguments, however, usually have strong reasons to support the position

taken by the advocate. It may not be the position you would take, which puts you in the position of providing suitable counter-evidence or support for your side.

Here is a suggested organizational pattern for more persuasive arguments:

1. Statement of claim
2. Evidence supporting claim
3. Justification for the line of reasoning used
4. Statement of anticipated objections
5. Refutation of objections
6. Restatement of claim

In our parking proposal, we might begin by pointing out certain facts of life at our university. For example, twenty thousand people arrive in automobiles at campus daily to park in ten thousand slots; Campus Police issue five thousand parking violation tickets and tow away three hundred cars weekly. So many vehicle-related incidents a month involve loss of life, limb, and property. And the president of our university was late for a meeting because someone had illegally parked in her slot. We could go on and develop this more, but you can see the kinds of appeals we would make to our readers to demonstrate the problem, and then our solution.

Another approach, *cause and effect*, demonstrates consequences. Its aim is usually either *descriptive* (in which the writer wants readers to understand the cause of some action or event), or *persuasive* (in which the writer wants readers to believe that some event or action was the result of specific causes). Certain guidelines are useful to consider:

1. Begin by identifying the cause or effect you are describing.
2. Explain the links in the chain of cause and effect. Emphasize how each link or step leads to the next or is caused by the preceding.
3. In dealing with several causes or effects, categorize them. The hierarchy helps readers understand relationships in a complex chain of events.

Persuading by using *cause and effect* involves these steps:

1. State your claim at the beginning. Your claim will be that some particular effect was created by some particular cause, or that some specific cause will lead to a specific effect.
2. Present your evidence and lines of reasoning. Use undisputed evidence as much as possible.
3. Anticipate and respond to objections.

The parking lot example could use this approach and predict dire consequences unless a solution is implemented. Reduced enrollment, faculty attrition, and poor community relations all might be factors brought up in an argument. We would want to avoid being too adamant about our claims to avoid charges of faulty reasoning, but conditional phrases using words such as "might" or "could" are often effective ways of demonstrating potential or probable instances of cause and effect.

The next approach, *problem and solution*, also falls into *descriptive* and *persuasive* categories. Writers use a descriptive approach to explain things that have happened, or how things were solved. Use a persuasive approach when you want readers to agree that the particular actions you recommend will solve the problem:

1. Begin by identifying the problem that was solved. Remember to make the problem significant to the readers.
2. Explain the links between the problem and the solution. You want the readers to recognize how the solution overcame the problem.
3. Group complex actions into categories. Build hierarchies of importance for readers.

To persuade with a *problem and solution* approach:

1. Describe the problem in a way that makes it significant to the readers. Your aim is to persuade readers to take action, your recommended action.
2. Present your evidence and lines of reasoning. Use sufficient and credible evidence.
3. Anticipate and respond to objections.

Consider now for yourself how you might use this particular approach on our parking problem. Just to provide an opportunity for you to participate in this scenario, think about how to approach the parking problem from an environmental perspective.

Let us reiterate: NONE of these strategies can work independently of other strategies. Nor have we presented more than a bare sketch of the potential these have. You must recognize that writers use a number of these strategies simultaneously. Experts have learned to use them all, depending on need. Writers continuously experiment with them as well. Spend time trying each of these yourself. Notice what other writers do.

The middle of a text may not be read as often in a quantitative sense as other parts of the text are, but qualitatively, the middle is at least as important as what comes before and after. Only if you can establish the validity of the beginning and end can you achieve your purposes. That is what happens in the middles of your texts.

Ends

An ending accomplishes three essential purposes:

- Provides your readers with a sense of completion or closure
- Emphasizes key material
- Directs readers' attention to future action or study

Our parking proposal, for example, might end with a restatement of the severity of the problem, a reminder to the reader of the consequences, our recommendations, and a request for the reader to establish a committee to investigate further. We would want to convey that, up to this point, the issue has been discussed thoroughly and fairly, and that it's now up to the reader to initiate response.

And, like most of what we discuss in this book, there is no right way of providing the ending. Considering context, audience, and purpose will distinguish the more effective from the less effective.

However, we can offer some advice. Ends of documents are commonly (and unnecessarily) signaled to the reader by "In conclusion." Perhaps one reason writers use this signal is to remind *themselves* that they're trying to conclude. Another reason, perhaps, is a lack of other ending strategies. Here, then, are some others to consider when you're concluding:

- *After you've made your last point, STOP.*
- *Allude to your main point again.* You place emphasis on it this way.
- *Summarize key points.* This is not always necessary, especially on short documents.
- *Focus on a key feeling.* This is your last chance to shape your readers' attitudes.
- *Tell your readers how to get assistance or more information.*
- *Tell your readers what to do next.* Actually suggest what action they should take—don't leave it up to them.
- *Identify any further study or work that is needed.* Most work is accomplished in stages. Suggest or recommend future action such as research, follow-up study, continuation of funding, and so forth.
- *Refer to earlier goals or points that you have made.* Outline the next stage or stages.
- *Follow the social conventions that apply to your situation.*

Philip Rhinelander, a philosopher, closes his essay, "Stereotypes—Their Use and Misuse," with the following:

> But I have said enough to suggest that the first task of rational inquiry is either to avoid such terms altogether, or to make sure that

> they be clarified. This requires looking behind the labels and the stereotypes to the issues. The main difficulty is that the more complex our problems become, the more pressure there seems to be to find simplistic solutions. Let us do our best to avoid yielding to that pressure. (150)

Even out of the context of the whole essay, we can see a number of the above features. Note everything occurring in this brief passage. Identify its elements of closure.

As a restatement of the above, closings should:

- Be positive
- Appear confident and successful
- Reemphasize key material
- Be written from the reader's point of view
- Be specific in requesting an action or suggesting an attitude
- Sound final (as though you are closing)

The end of a piece of your writing is usually the last impression the reader carries. It's sometimes the first thing a reader reads—or the *only* thing. Many readers, especially those who have solicited a document from you, want only to know the solution to a problem or your recommendations.

Appendices

Appendices are handy tools, but there is no easy formula for deciding what to put in them, especially if your document is for multiple purposes or multiple audiences. Appendage is probably the best way of thinking of them—as an added attraction or supplement to what you have to say. Material in appendices is usually not critical to your audience and purpose, but it can be a nice bonus for the reader, depending on interest and need. Some readers will need or want the material you include in an appendix; others will not. The guiding rule is that if it's necessary to satisfying your purposes and the purposes of *most* of your readers, it had better be a part of the main text. If it's necessary or desirable to *some* of your readers, then relegate it to an appendix.

In many instances—technical reports, for example—the appendices are larger and more numerous than the text itself. Surveys and questionnaires used to gather data, the data themselves, specifications for materials and equipment, certain kinds of costs, maps and charts, resources used or available, additional visual displays secondary to the ones in the text, personnel biographies or resumes, and other information of this sort can be included here. Note that you need to title an appendix with a more descriptive name than *Appendix A*. Use a title that describes the contents of the appendix just as you would any other subunit. Also, list your appendices as *Appendix A: [descriptive title], Appendix B: [descriptive title]*, and so forth in the Table of Contents.

COLLECTING MATERIAL FROM SOURCES

Finding information, the contents of your documents and presentations, is a nearly endless task. You can't know too much. Limited time, money, and access often constrain how much you are able to gather. And in your role as an expert, you will continually face these constraints. The more you learn, the more you realize how much you don't know, or need to know, or want to know. What you and others in your profession don't know is what keeps your discipline dynamic. What you don't know can also be exciting: as professionals and experts, we're all detectives in many ways, investigators in our own little areas of expertise.

In the following section, we present a very brief overview of information sources. We have limited our discussion of these sources because a comprehensive discussion is beyond the scope of this textbook. Furthermore, because these sources—and their general availability—change literally every day, it's impossible to know what you have access to. In the final section of this chapter, however, we provide extensive suggestions for conducting informational interviews. We have found that talking to people—especially experts—is a valuable research tool, especially if you know how to do it well.

Using Libraries and Other Repositories

For experts, questions necessarily lead to finding answers and problems lead to proposing solutions. Interviewing for information, which we will discuss in the next section, is a valuable and necessary tool, but it does not replace the library or the new information technologies. You are probably already highly proficient in using libraries or you wouldn't be where you are in your field of study. We merely want to remind you that an array of information is available, information that increases at a staggering daily rate, information that you need to seek out. We've highlighted some of the key resources. If you're unfamiliar with them, take some time to get acquainted with their use.

An obvious place to start a search for information is in the *card catalog*, or, as these are phased out, *online library catalogs* (or *public access catalogs*). These will get you to books and periodicals that establish a foundation for your project. *Bibliographies* and *periodical indices* are undoubtedly familiar as well, especially the general ones such as the *Reader's Guide* and *electronic databases* such as Infotrac. You may also be aware of the *specialized indices* and *abstract collections* that compile the reports on research in your particular discipline, both in conventional print volumes and in *CD-ROM* versions. Increasingly, this literature is referenced and available through *online search services*, as well. If you are not familiar with how to gain access to this material, find out from your instructors what they use or consult a reference librarian. Many disciplines also have their own special *encyclopedias, dictionaries*, and *handbooks* that are invaluable professional tools and can direct you to other information sources. *Directories* and *compendiums* of all kinds are published in almost every discipline. Browse the central reference collection of your library to see what resources are available. Many libraries now have these materials and others on computers, or they are linked to computers that contain them.

Don't ignore the *government documents collections*, either. The extent of these holdings varies greatly from library to library, but indices are usually available even if the documents themselves are not. Libraries share with one another through *interlibrary loan* agreements. Just because your library doesn't have a book or document doesn't mean it can't be obtained. The U.S. Government, by the way, is the largest publisher in the world. Your tax dollars are at work in these documents, so make use of them; the government is also making an effort to digitize (put into electronically accessible form) almost everything it publishes. Again, don't be afraid to ask for assistance. *Reference librarians*, highly skilled professionals themselves, are eager to help you gain expertise in using the resources they maintain.

You should develop basic research strategies for yourself. The new technologies have made this easier and much more efficient. Technology continues to radically alter our access to information. Enormous *computer databases, microfiche*, and *microfilm collections*—now routinely available on CD-ROM and through the *Internet* and *World Wide Web*, have rapidly enlarged our search capabilities to the point that we worry about being smothered in information. In developing a project or paper topic, your first step might be to browse these electronic databases to see what has already been done. This, in turn, will help you refine your idea and lead you to key information sources.

Access to electronic sources of information is now available at most colleges, universities, workplaces, and, increasingly, at your local public library. You may already be "online" from your home with your own personal computer and modem link through one of the *commercial online service providers*, such as CompuServe, Prodigy, or America Online. All of this access puts at your disposal an unfathomable amount of information. It also enables you to travel the world, at least virtually. With *World Wide Web browsers* and *gopher search services*, you can visit nearly every major library in the United States, most major corporations, and many professional organizations. You can also gain entry to discussions among experts—and not-so-experts—in many fields by *"lurking"* (listening in) on specialized *electronic bulletin boards* or *newsgroups* established on a particular topic. In many cases, you can seek information directly from the experts themselves through these forums. But keep in mind that this quick and expedient access has some drawbacks. As with all information sources, be sure that you are receiving accurate information from knowledgeable people. A recent query to one such discussion resulted in three responses, all of which were different, and only one of which was correct.

Not surprisingly, reference librarians are often the best place to seek help on gaining access to these new information technologies. It is their business to know where and how to find out. Your instructors and classmates are also good sources for where to go and how to get there, especially because both the access to and the nature of the new information tools are changing so rapidly. Our best advice is this: Seek out every tool and information source you can find, and become familiar with all of them.

Informational Interviewing

The information sources that we see neglected at every grade level, from kindergarten to graduate school, are people. The overly familiar "if you don't know, look it up" usually sends writers and speakers to the library. Yet, some of the primary sources of information are the experts and authorities all around us. They are sometimes responsible for what's in the library: they may have written it, or they may have suggested that the library acquire it. And most professionals rarely rely on extensive library searches. The time involved and the datedness of even the most current material decrease the value of library information in many fields. So, we urge you to do what these professionals do: go directly to "the horse's mouth," so to speak.

Although this technique is called many things, the most descriptive is "informational interviewing." It involves using primary and secondary research materials that you acquire firsthand by talking with your sources. Admittedly, this is an intimidating strategy. But after requiring hundreds of students to use "live" research materials in addition to conventional library sources, we are happy to report that all of the students have returned safely. Some even enjoyed it. A few developed job offers, internships, friendships, and dinner invitations.

Tremendous resources are available through informational interviewing, with equally tremendous payoffs for the enterprising researcher. You add verve, authority, originality, and contemporaneity to a document or a presentation when you include living and breathing sources. Reflect on how much the various media use (and abuse at times) on-the-street or at-the-scene interviews. Unfortunately, most of us are ingrained with the idea that research begins and ends at the library or in the lab. We ignore a facility that we have used and practiced and refined since before we were able to walk: the ability to talk and to listen. Inquiring minds want to know. Some of them interview experts.

We suggest you add to your research repertoire this simple strategy: reach out and *ask* someone. Often this is a complete stranger, someone with extensive expertise and authority, a professional in your area of inquiry. This strategy does cause some anxiety. However, this anxiety won't be fatal unless you let it paralyze you. Surprisingly, most experts and professionals you would want to approach will be receptive. Perhaps this is not so surprising: after all, they *are* people, and most people like to talk, especially about their expertise. You are recognizing their expertise—a compliment. Furthermore, you are giving them an opportunity to discuss areas of their lives that are important to them. And all it takes is a bit of nerve on your part.

The Plan for an Interview

Your first hurdle to tapping these sources of information is self-imposed: "Why would they talk to me?" Overcoming this obstacle begins with finding an interview subject and preparing for the interview to avoid wasting this person's time.

To do that, consider two elements of communication situations we discuss throughout this book: audience and purpose. Clearly identify your purpose for seeking out and talking with authorities. Determine how these information sources will assist you in achieving your purpose and in conveying to your audience what you have to say. We suggest that you start with some informal writing and brainstorming, answering the following questions:

1. What is my purpose for the interview?
2. Who is my audience for the text I'm producing?
3. What kind of information do I need?
4. Who can give me this information?

The first three of these questions we discuss many other places in this book. The last question is our focus here. Who you interview depends, of course, on your audience, purpose, and the information needed. Look around you. The university or college you attend is full of experts: professors, researchers, administrators, and fellow students. If you work, even part-time, your place of employment may be full of excellent resources as well. The town or city where you live is also a resource for experts and authorities. Government—federal, state, and local—is replete with experts, many of whom are paid with your tax dollars to be information sources. Industry and business are created and maintained by experts. Be imaginative: browse through the yellow pages, inquire at professional organizations, and look in research and trade journals.

So, the first step is to establish who you want to talk to in a general sense. Decide what type of person in what kind of position who does what kind of work related to what topic(s). These, then, become your guidelines for selecting potential interviewees. With this information in hand, you're ready to build a list of possibilities. Sources are only as limited as your imagination and time constraints in finding them. Talk with faculty members, friends, family, librarians, and classmates. Ask them to recommend people who fit your criteria for an interview source.

Approach this search just as you would a search through the library: keep records. Notecards are invaluable records of potential contacts, just as they are for sources found in the library. And don't stop with only one or two names. Experts are busy; you may have to try several before finding one who can squeeze you in.

Next, outline very specifically the information you want. Structure and organize it in some way using the strategies we discuss in Part 3. You may even want to begin drafting specific questions you want to ask. At the very least, determine what you *most* need to find out during the interview.

The following outline was developed by a student in response to an assignment to talk with a professional. The student was asked to interview someone in a position that the student would like to be in five years after graduating. The purpose of the interview was to gather and report on the kinds of communication the professional engages in as part of his or her job. This student's outline is very detailed. Looking at it, you may be able to envision the exact questions the student posed for the interviewee.

```
 I. Interviewee requirements
    A. non-academic
    B. 5 or more years of experience
    C. willingness to share time and writing samples
    D. non-relative
II. Personal background and perceptions on writing
    A. academic degree(s): what, where, when
    B. specific writing courses: what, when, where,
       description, comments
    C. courses with writing requirements: what, when,
       where, description, comments
    D. on-the-job training in writing: description,
       requirements
    E. style manual(s): in-house, recommended, personal
    F. comments on the pleasure(s) and pain(s) of
       writing
    G. perceptions of own strengths and weaknesses in
       writing
    H. perceptions of own writing style(s)
```

```
III. Profile of current writing
     A. subject matter
     B. types of writing: letters, memos, reports, etc.
     C. audience(s)
     D. purpose(s) of writing: affirm, argue, calculate,
        challenge, classify, compare, conclude, corroborate,
        deduce, demand, demonstrate, describe, design,
        dispute, evaluate, examine, explain, instruct,
        infer, investigate, question, recommend,
        re-establish, revalue, review, survey,
        synthesize, test, theorize
     E. % of total work time spent on writing tasks
     F. % spent on each type
     G. system of writing: pre-writing activity,
        individual vs cooperative authorship, editing,
        publishing
     H. tools of writing: dictation equipment, computers,
        typewriters
     I. relative importance to the person's job
 IV. Related activities
     A. other communication skills: speaking, reading,
        listening, dictating, collaborating
     B. relative importance to the person's job
     C. % of total work time spent on each
     D. specifics about the most important
  V. Request for writing samples
     A. note audience and purpose of each document
     B. have each document initialed
     C. obtain signed release
 VI. Importance of good writing
     A. to the interviewee
     B. to superiors, associates, subordinates
     C. to the company or business in general
     D. to the interviewee's profession
     E. to the interviewee's audience
VII. Advice for students entering the profession.
```

FIGURE 3.4 Sample Outline

Although this outline is tailored to a specific interview, it shows the kind of detailed planning necessary for successful informational interviews. Your own purpose and context will be different. But taking the time to prepare a detailed questionnaire or checklist assures that you "cover the bases," present yourself as efficient and knowledgeable, and get what you need from the interview. Once you've established your purpose and identified what type of person you are looking for, you're ready for the next phase: contacting potential sources. Pick up the phone and call. It's a pretty safe and efficient way to make a first contact.

The Etiquette of Interviewing

Like many social encounters, a certain etiquette or code of conduct is expected, if not required, by the parties involved in interviews. As the interviewer, you have additional responsibility as the one who initiated the process: you are the one in control. You—not the interviewee—are responsible for conducting a professional and productive interview.

Whether your initial contact is with the potential interviewee directly or with a receptionist or secretary, these guidelines represent a suitable approach. Prepare and practice, if necessary.

- Explain, briefly, who you are, what you are doing, why this person seems an appropriate source, and what you will do with the information you receive.
- Ask if this person can supply the information you need; if not, ask for suggested alternatives and thank the person for the help.

When you find the person you want to interview:

- Set up a time and place where the interviewee can give you uninterrupted time and attention.
- Suggest how much time you think you need, then negotiate.
- Express your thanks, in advance, and reconfirm the time and place for the interview.

When making initial contacts, keep in mind that secretaries and receptionists often can help you identify exactly who you want to talk to or they can recommend alternatives. Also remember that they often control who gets in to see the boss, for how much time, and which boss they get in to see. Expressing gratitude to them—professionals in their own right—is both polite and a wise investment.

The Interview

It's essential to your interviewing success that you remember that the professionals you seek out are very busy doing what they do. The time that they have taken from their schedules to talk with you is a gift, one of the most precious gifts to ask of a professional. Following these suggestions will help you indicate your gratitude to your interview source.

1. Dress neatly and arrive on time.
2. Begin by thanking your respondent, in advance, for giving valuable time.
3. Restate the purpose of your interview.
4. Tell your respondent why you believe he or she can be helpful.
5. Discuss your plans for using the information.
6. Ask if the respondent objects to being quoted or taped.
7. Avoid small talk.
8. Be clear, direct, and orderly with your questions.
9. Be assertive but courteous. Don't be afraid to ask pointed questions, but remember that the respondent is the giver and you are the receiver.
10. Let your respondent do most of the talking. Keep your opinions to yourself.
11. Guide the interview carefully. Keep the conversation central to your purpose.
12. Be a good listener.
13. Be prepared to explore new areas of questioning. Sometimes answers will uncover new directions for inquiry.
14. Keep notetaking to a minimum. Note key words and phrases to later refresh your memory.
15. Ask for clarification or further explanation of a response when necessary.
16. After all of your questions have been answered, ask for any additional comments that might be helpful.
17. Thank your respondent for the time and assistance and leave promptly.

After the Interview

Get a summary of your interview down on paper as soon as you can, even if you've taped it. Get it while everything is still fresh in your mind. Don't wait until evening or the next day. Schedule your interview so that you have thirty minutes or so afterward to write. Be as detailed as possible. Many of the strategies we discuss in Part 3 can be used to record interview notes.

One final gesture further demonstrates your professionalism: write a thank-you note. Do so immediately after the interview while it's still fresh in everyone's mind. If possible, you might include the document that resulted from your interview. A thank-you doesn't have to be long, doesn't take much of your time, and doesn't cost much. And writing it may be to your personal advantage at some future point, especially if you are entering the same profession as your interviewee. It's a smaller world than we sometimes recognize. And even if you don't receive any sort of payoff, you will still know that you have been courteous.

▶ 4

Global Revision

Overview

Revise: To see again.

Sounds pretty simple, doesn't it? Just look at that writing one more time. Well, "just looking at" a piece of writing and truly revising it are very different activities. When effective writers truly revise—see again—they do so from diverse perspectives, and with a variety of purposes in mind.

Before you read on, take a moment to carefully consider your current thinking and understanding about revision by responding to these questions:

- When I revise a piece of writing, what is my purpose? What do I intend to achieve by revising?

  ___

  ___

- What activities or strategies do I associate with "revision"?

  ___

  ___

- How are "revising," "editing," and "proofreading" related?

  ___

  ___

If you found it difficult to respond to these questions, you're not alone. Because writing is a complex and arduous process, and because human nature urges us to write at the last possible moment, many writers skip or abbreviate revision. Then, too, you may not know why or how to revise effectively. So, you might view revision as editing, which may consist of running the spellchecker just before hitting "Print."

At the beginning of this chapter, we discuss the purposes for revising, drawing attention in particular to the key distinction of "global" versus "local" revising. We also explain how changing your perspective—from that of writer to that of your reader—helps you revise. Then, in the rest of this chapter, we offer some very specific strategies that writers use to accomplish their re-seeing of a text in terms of its audience and in terms of its overall structure and content.

We suggest such a variety of strategies because no strategy works every single time for every single writer working on every single text. And, as with all our advice, merely reading about these strategies is not enough. Becoming expert means gaining experiences using a variety of tools in many contexts and for many purposes.

WRITING FOR THE WRITER VERSUS REVISING FOR THE READER

One reason writers revise their texts is to make sure that the writing will actually *work* for a reader. When writers generate or draft material, they often do so with only themselves as an audience. They may jot down lists of words, draw some funny-looking diagrams, or even dictate some random thoughts into a tape recorder. But they don't intend that material to be read or heard by someone else.

Material such as this is what some writing experts refer to as "writer-based prose," text whose only intended audience is the writer. This self-as-audience writing serves some very important purposes: it helps us see and think through our thinking, "dump out our brains," and rehearse our understandings before a fairly safe audience. But writer-based prose is most definitely different from "reader-based prose," writing that is intended for—and carefully shaped toward—a specific, identifiable audience *other than the writer*. Reader-based text includes and makes explicit as much as writer-based text leaves out: the details that support and explain the list of key words; the lengthy descriptions showing where those funny-looking diagrams came from, how they work, and what they represent; the kinds of cues that guide readers from the beginning to the end of our otherwise random thoughts.

So one key activity that writers undertake when they revise is to shift their writer-based prose to reader-based prose. To do that successfully, the writer must effectively change his or her perspective. Having generated and drafted the text as the writer, he or she now must become the reader.

Now, most of us have experienced something like the following scenario, which pretty closely parallels what needs to happen during revising for a reader. You jot down some little bit of information—say, a couple of words from a phone message, thinking you'll flesh them out a bit more when you write up the "real" message to give your roommate or colleague in the next office. But then, something interrupts; you get called away and don't get back to that little note until the next day. At that time, you look at the note; you scratch your head; it resembles your handwriting; you vaguely recall being present when *someone* made those marks. But you have no clue what they mean.

Our scenario may be overdramatic, but it's pretty much the perspective that effective writers try to take when they approach a reader-based revision of their texts. They try to approximate that kind of distance—from the writer writing to the reader reading.

GLOBAL REVISION VERSUS LOCAL REVISION

Most experienced writers also approach revision of their texts at different levels. They re-see their texts both globally and locally. Global revision is something like looking down at your home from a helicopter hovering at about one thousand feet: you can see the house, notice how it's situated on your street, and maybe even see patterns of traffic coming and going to it. This kind of fly-over is useful for getting a sense of your house in the larger context, the community. But you certainly can't see into the rooms.

Local revision, however, is analogous to a very careful house inspection—the kind you might make before buying a house. You might start outside, on the sidewalk; you'd pay close attention to the steps, the entry door, where the light switches are located—and if they work. You might even get down and look at the carpet to check for stains. And you'd continue like this through every single room. And the basement. And the attic.

Some writing experts refer to global revision as "text- and paragraph-level revising" and local revision as "sentence- and word-level revising." We prefer the words *global* and *local*, however, because, for us, these labels reinforce the way the two levels constantly interact. Experienced writers know that they can't really revise their texts at only one level, and often not even at one level at one time. For instance, if we decide to change the word *experienced* in the preceding sentence to the word *expert*, we've made a very local revision. However, in its meaning, that sentence connects to the idea of "experienced writers" that we used to start off this subsection of the chapter. Would we, then, change the word we used there? Would we next find ourselves using the search-and-replace function of our word processor to hunt down every occurrence of the phrase? And, having done so, wouldn't we have changed the whole meaning—that is, wouldn't we have made a global revision? These are the kinds of decisions that writers make when they revise.

One final distinction needs to be made. Although you've probably heard the terms used interchangeably, *revising*, *editing*, and *proofreading* are not the same activities. As we've already shown, *revising* means to re-see a text's meaning and its shape. *Editing* often refers to what we're calling local revision: alterations at the word, sentence, and paragraph levels, which may subtly alter the text's meaning but may not affect its overall shape. Finally, *proofreading*'s function is only to bring the text—in its final, revised, and edited form—into agreement with standard conventions of spelling, punctuation, usage, and document formatting. As we sometimes say, proofreading a text that really needs revising is like putting mascara on a pig: it annoys the pig, and it gets you nowhere.

STRATEGIES FOR READER-BASED REVISION

Analyze Your Audience, Again

In Chapter 2, we discuss the value of analyzing your audience as you begin a writing project. One way to put yourself into your readers' shoes when you revise is to repeat that process. Here, again, in a slightly different shape, are some questions to help you think about your readers and their attitudes toward your text. Answer each of these questions as fully and completely as possible.

Questions for Analyzing Your Audience

- Who are my primary readers? That is, who is this writing directly aimed at? Name them, either singly or collectively, but as specifically as possible.
- Who are my secondary readers? That is, who might ultimately see this writing, perhaps because a primary reader has passed this text on to someone else?
- What do my readers know about my topic already? What do they need or want to know that they do not already?
- What are my readers' attitudes toward the topic? For instance, are they already disposed to see it my way, are they tired of hearing about it, are they uncomfortable reading about it?
- What one thing about my readers must change as a result of this writing for me to consider it successful? For instance, will they know something new, will they vote a certain way, will they call me and thank me, will they rise up in riot?

Analyze Your Purpose, Again

Many writers find that what they thought they were going to do for their readers when they started writing a text is not what they end up doing. In effect, the text decides what it wants to do; it takes on a life of its own. But presenting such a two-minded text to readers will almost surely confuse them because it pulls in two directions. So, critically reanalyzing your purpose, especially from your readers' perspective, is another good way to begin a reader-based revision. Answer each of these questions, as fully and completely as possible, to assess the *current* purpose for a piece of writing.

Questions for Analyzing Your Purpose

- What one thing must happen as a result of this writing for *readers* to consider it successful?
- What other results would readers find nice to achieve as well, but are not necessary for the success of this writing?
- What are the primary or essential points that readers need to see covered to achieve these results?
- What supporting material—details, facts, background information, evidence, visual aids—will help me present these primary points to my readers?

- How will achieving this purpose change my readers' attitudes and opinions about
    - The subject?
    - Themselves?
    - Me?

Write a Letter to Your Audience

Write a letter to your audience in which you explain what you are trying to accomplish in the piece of writing and how you are going about doing it. As you write, try to imagine your audience as a single person to whom you are speaking directly. You may find it necessary or useful to write a series of notes, memos, or e-mail messages to several individuals who may represent the range of your audience. These might include anyone from a very close confidant to a very distant enemy (of your ideas, not of you, we hope).

To be most effective in helping you get a sense of your readers, these should be very informal, friendly letters. But you also may want to think, for a moment, under what conditions you would *not* write a friendly, informal letter to your audience.

Get Feedback from a Trial Reader

Ideally, to find out how your readers will eventually react to your finished text, you should run it by them beforehand and ask them. That's the ideal; it's not always possible. But with some careful preparation, you can "construct" a trial reader who can give you some good feedback to guide your revising. (We also discuss this practice, and offer some slightly different strategies for using it, in Chapters 1 and 7.)

A couple of suggestions, though. First, both the quality and the quantity of the feedback you get are directly related to the "set-up" you provide. If you hand your roommate or colleague a text and say, "Read this and tell me what you think," you're likely to get something about as useful as "Seems okay to me" in return. (We know this from experience. We are frequently asked in just this way to provide feedback on our students' and colleagues' writing. We're seldom able to say anything intelligent to them unless we first find out more about their writing context.)

Second, many very experienced writers use this strategy on *every single piece* they write. That way, they get better and better at asking good questions—and at listening critically to their readers' feedback. These writers also seek multiple sets of feedback from different readers. They know better than to expect one trial reader to magically have all of the answers. They also know that, with practice, their trial readers get even better at being trial readers.

Writer: ______________________________

Project: ____________________________________ Due Date: ________________

Reviewed by: ________________________________ Date: ____________________

This writing is: ______ an early, sketchy draft
______ a working version
______ a finished version

The *AUDIENCE*(s) for this document is/are:

primary:

secondary:

The *PURPOSE*(s) for this document is/are:

Please respond to these specific questions about the document:

1.

2.

3.

Reviewer's comments and suggestions:

FIGURE 4.1 Document Review

So, use this strategy consistently and frequently to get the very best results from it.

The following are some general suggestions for setting up and getting useful feedback from trial readers. We also provide an example of a document coversheet that you can use to supply all of the necessary information to your trial readers (Figure 4.1, above).

Suggestions for Getting Useful Feedback

- Set up the writing situation for the reader *before* you turn over your writing. Explain who your audience is, what your purpose is, and where you think you are in the overall process of writing the piece (e.g., still just getting started, about half done, ready to proofread).

- Establish the *one or two specific questions* you would like the reader to respond to about your writing. If you have lots of questions, spread them out among several different trial readers.
- When constructing your questions, try to avoid "Yes/No" questions: they almost always get "Yes" answers, and they never get a full enough answer to be much help. Instead of "Is the sequence of ideas logical?" ask, "Where do you have trouble following the sequence of the ideas?" or "How would you explain the sequence of ideas?" In responding to questions like these, trial readers are encouraged to point to a specific place—or to explain that they have no such trouble anywhere.
- Give the reader space to write comments—both on your text and separately. We've found that offering a half-page space for comments (as on the document coversheet) tends to encourage readers to write *longer* comments than suggesting that they turn the coversheet over and use the back. We suspect that, because they don't think that they *have* to fill up a page, they frequently write more than a page. Curious, but true.
- Allow for plenty of time to discuss your writing after the reader has considered it. Take careful notes—or even tape record these oral comments. Often, the really substantive and helpful feedback comes when your trial readers explain the *reasons behind* their answers to your questions.
- Offer to return the favor for the person who reads your writing. Being a trial reader for someone else is extremely good practice for putting yourself into your own readers' perspectives. And this is a great way to develop good habits for working on collaborative teams.

Write an Informative or Evaluative Abstract

Using the guidelines for Informative and Evaluative Abstracts in Part 2, write a summary of the information in your text. It might help to imagine that you work for a very busy executive who just does not have time to read everything being published. Instead, she relies on you to keep her up to date, to summarize materials neutrally, and perhaps to offer some succinct commentary on their usefulness. Now, having put yourself in that position, write an abstract of the text you've been working on.

This strategy helps you take on a reader's perspective because it encourages you to see your text not as "all those words I've worked so hard to get down on the page," but rather as "when it's all boiled down, this is what readers will take away from it."

Analyze a Model—Good or Bad

One of the surest ways to get an idea of what is expected of you by your readers is to look at other documents that have been successful. Bad examples are often useful as well; they show you what you don't want to do. Model your own text on what seems to work well. Start where other writers have finished and then try to improve on it. Many faculty keep files of previous student papers, especially very good ones, and are willing to let you look at them. On the job, don't overlook the obvious resources: the filing cabinets. They often contain several years' worth of examples, both good and bad, of nearly every kind of document you'll be asked to create. And a friendly file clerk may be able to direct you straight to a good one.

But we don't recommend that you merely find a text similar to the one you're working on and copy it. Instead, you must look carefully and critically at *how* the other text does what it does, *why* it works—or doesn't work—effectively, and how similar your writing situation is to the one that generated the other document. In short, take it apart. Being a critical reader of a model text helps you take on the critical perspective necessary to revise your own text for your readers.

Develop Visual Aids for Your Reader

As important as it is to consider your text for what your readers "hear" when they read it, you should also give some attention to the visual elements of your text. Developing visual aids is a useful reader-based revising strategy. Not only can these elements add dimension and reader accessibility to your text, but creating and then explaining them often helps writers think through what they're trying to say.

What do visual aids do for readers? Many readers first scan an entire text, stopping briefly to examine visual information as they go, to "look at the pictures." This helps them develop an overview or framework on which to "hang" the ideas in your text. Readers also use visual aids as "rest stops" during their reading: they pause to consider—and consume—the text they've just read while they take in the visuals. Finally, some extremely busy readers may rely on a good reading of *just* the visual elements of your text to give them a summary of key information. If you don't believe that visual elements are an important reader item, consider how much money publications like *USA Today* now spend on them every single day.

Visual aids can be any of a number of different kinds. You're already familiar with the most obvious ones, having seen them in textbooks, mass media magazines, newspapers, on television, and on computer screens. You may have experience reading and drawing graphs. But graphs are much more various and complex than the line graphs we're usually taught in high school. Bar graphs, picture graphs, and pie graphs all have uses as well. Additionally, photographs, line drawings and sketches, artist renderings, blueprints and schematics, maps of all colors and sorts, and tables all have tremendous potential to assist both you and your reader. Small pictures or icons can help you and your readers identify key points.

New technologies like digital scanners, color laser copiers, and multimedia computer applications make it possible—even easy—to include many of these in your texts. But before you load up a document with exploding pie charts just because you love creating them, here are some considerations from the reader's perspective.

Suggestions for Creating and Incorporating Visual Aids

- *Determine where visual aids are needed.* Ask yourself, "Where would a drawing or other visual representation of my information be
  - Fast
  - Clear
  - Easy

  for my reader to understand?"
- *Identify the best type of visual aid to use.* A chart is not a chart is not a chart. Look around you at the various visual aids that you encounter as a reader. Which ones work for you and which do not? Which can "say" what you need to convey, and which cannot?
- *Consider what types of visual aids your readers will expect.* Just as each field has its own common text types and formats, so do they also have certain preferences for visual aids. Become familiar with the ones your readers are likely to know—and be able to read, quickly.
- *Ask a trial reader to suggest both which type of visual aid to include and where.* Sometimes the most valuable feedback you can hear is, "Draw me a picture of *this* idea."

This very brief discussion of visual aids for readers is designed more to jog your memory about potential ways for you to "illustrate" your texts than to provide detailed instruction on how to do so. It should also encourage you to be on the lookout for the kinds of visuals you find effective as a reader. Recognize how you use visuals as a reader and then, as you revise, bring that recognition to bear on the documents you create.

STRATEGIES FOR GLOBAL REVISION

Annotate or Gloss Your Text

In Chapter 9 we describe annotating, our name for "writing and drawing in the margins," as a strategy for more effective reading. In fact, it's also one of the more effective ways we know for writers to "re-see" their own texts. There are many variations that you can try, depending upon the aspects of your text that you want to focus on in your revision. Here are the steps that writers most often use when annotating or glossing their own texts while revising.

Suggestions for Annotating Your Text

1. Mark the text off into "chunks," subunits that seem to be complete. Do not be fooled into believing that each paragraph is a chunk! Sometimes, a chunk is only a sentence. Sometimes it's a series of paragraphs.
2. Here are a number of different ways you can proceed:
   - In one margin, identify the key topic that you find presented in each chunk of text. You might ask yourself, "What is this chunk *about*?"
   - In the other margin, identify the functions that the chunk serves—or could serve—in a finished text (e.g., opening material, presentation of alternative viewpoint, thesis or focusing statement). You might ask yourself, "What does this chunk *do* for this text?"
   - Other elements you could annotate include stylistic features (e.g., passive and active constructions), sentence structures (e.g., compound, complex, and simple sentence variation), and paragraph structure (e.g., topic statement, illustration, explanation, transition).
3. Once you've annotated all of the chunks of the text, consider the annotations *separate from* the text itself. It's a bit like removing the skin and flesh to work with a skeleton. Some writers who annotate on the margins of their texts fold back their pages after annotating so that they can just focus on the narrow strip of notes. Others use a stack of 3 × 5 cards, copying a single annotation onto each card and stacking them up in the order in which they occur on the text.
4. Now that you have this "skeletal" view of your text, you may want to use another global revising strategy to consider ways to change and reshape it. Returning to our discussion of the obvious components of a text in Chapter 3 may be useful at this point.

Use Cut and Paste

There is a good reason why your word processing program has little scissors and paste bucket icons at the top of your screen: writers have been using cut and paste as a revising technique forever. On the computer screen, cut and paste can be a handy way to rearrange some sentences in a paragraph, or maybe to move a whole paragraph somewhere else. But most experienced writers—and computer users—recognize a serious limitation to this as a *global revising* tool: you can only see one screenful of text at a time. To get the very *most* out of cut and paste, we suggest that you print out the text—at least double-spaced. Then, get out the scissors and paste, or tape.

Use Your Word Processor's Outline Feature

Most word processing software includes an outline feature that you can use to get a "skeletal" view of your text—and cut and paste efficiently. If your text includes headings and subheadings already, you can probably use this feature by merely switching from "text" or "normal" view to "outline" view of your document. You can then choose which levels of your document to display in the outline. For instance, you might show two levels: the headings and the subheadings. The text paragraphs that follow each subheading will then disappear from the screen, although they're still "attached" to their subheadings. When you rearrange or change the elements of the outline, these text paragraphs move—or are deleted—along with the headings to which they're attached.

Even if your finished text will not include headings (for instance, if it's a short text), you can still use this valuable feature. First, annotate your text by identifying the topic of each "chunk" of one or more paragraphs. Then, insert these annotations as temporary headings. You can use the outline feature to revise; later, remove the headings. Or, you might decide to leave them in after all, as valuable cues to your readers.

Consider Your Document's Format

Your document's overall appearance and the way its headings, text, and visual aids are arranged on the page are referred to as "document formatting." Sometimes, writers have freedom to choose how they present their documents. At other times, document format may be stipulated, either by a stylesheet followed by a particular discipline, which we discuss in the next chapter, or by a company's guidelines for documents produced by its workers. When you revise globally, you need to take time to consider these aspects of your text. Here are some suggestions for doing that.

Suggestions for Document Formatting

- *Find out which elements of document formatting, if any, are stipulated.* Then, follow the guidelines *to the letter.* Although they may be unclear to you, there are reasons for these stipulations—if only to make all documents look alike.
- *If you have some freedom to develop your document's format, consider some models for ideas.*
- *Ask yourself, "How conventional or unconventional do I want to get?"* If you put page numbers in the bottom right corner of each page instead of in the top right, will this make your document "distinctive" or merely "annoying" to readers?
- *Consider how page layout is related to your document's content.* If, for instance, your text includes many visual aids and you want to present them next to the accompanying text, you might consider whether a "landscape" layout (with pages turned sideways) rather than the standard "portrait" layout would work better for your readers.
- *Consider different typefaces, within reason.* Most page designers agree that using more than two different typefaces creates a "busy" looking text.

And there are definite differences in the readability among typefaces. The standard among printers is to use a sans serif typeface for titles and headings and a serif typeface for text. (This book uses Optima for headings and Palatino for text, for instance.)

- *Print out sample sections of your text showing different formats or typefaces to check them.* As good as computer screens are getting, there's no substitute for a printout to judge the visual effect of a text.

▶ 5

Local Revision

Overview

Hemingway: I rewrote the ending to *Farewell to Arms*, the last page of it, 39 times before I was satisfied.

Interviewer: Was there some technical problem there? What was it that had you stumped?

Hemingway: Getting the words right.

Yes, even experienced writers—*very* experienced writers—have to do lots of editing. Although we would argue that in "getting the words right" Hemingway was probably engaging in *both* global and local revising, he clearly worried over the words. But thirty-nine times? What could he possibly have been doing on each of those passes over the text?

In this chapter, we describe how some experienced writers go about the often daunting task of getting the words, the sentences, the paragraphs right. But we do not try to tell you everything about editing, or about the qualities of effective writing. Instead, in our discussions of style handbooks and stylesheets, we point you toward the many other very good resources that you can, and should, use on your own. We finish by drawing your attention to the moment that all writers work toward: the presentation of their text.

STRATEGIES FOR LOCAL REVISION

Use Your Word Processor's Tools

Most word processing software now contains many features that can help you begin editing a text. You probably know about spellcheckers. And you may have used a built-in thesaurus to find an alternative word for one that you find yourself overusing. But you should also check whether your software has a built-in grammar or style checker, as well.

This feature can help you identify sentence-level problems, sometimes offering a suggested revision. Of course, as with spellcheckers, you must make the final decision whether to accept the revision or reject it. Style checkers can also give you comments on the "readability" of your text; that is, they can calculate the average length of your sentences and the general vocabulary level of your text. This can help you decide, for instance, that you want to combine some of your short sentences into more complex constructions.

One other useful editing feature of most word processing software is the "Find" or "Search" or "Replace" function. It may take a little thought for you to see how you can use it, but it's very powerful. One valuable use for the Find function is to check on homonyms, those words such as *to*, *too*, and *two*, which sound the same but are spelled differently. Spellcheckers don't catch these (although some grammar checks will) because they recognize each spelling as a word. If you have trouble with a specific set of homonyms, you can use the Find function to go through a document and stop on each occurrence of one of the forms; then you can decide whether you have the right form.

Another use for the Find function is to locate your "favorites," those words or phrases that you've fallen in love with and use at every possible chance. We found ourselves starting far too many sentences with "For instance" throughout this book. When one of our trial readers pointed it out, we used the Replace function of our word processor to change every occurrence to *FOR INSTANCE* just before printing out a copy for our final editing. It was easy to see the phrase on the page and decide which ones to change or to shift to another position in the sentence. Then we reversed the Replace process to put the remaining ones back to "For instance."

Use Both Sets of Ears

We all have two sets of ears: one on the outside of our heads, one on the inside. The outside pair—the ones we decorate with jewelry or cover with our hair—is very experienced at listening to text. (We discuss their usefulness, and their limitations, in Part 3 on listening.) The set of ears inside our heads is generally not as experienced at listening to text. Unfortunately, too many writers try to rely only on their less-experienced ears when editing their writing and completely pass up a very obvious and useful tool right there on the outsides of their heads.

After you've globally revised a text to your current satisfaction, read it aloud. Under ideal conditions you might read it aloud to an audience who can respond to it in the ways we've suggested in the previous chapter. But under less-than-ideal conditions, you can simply read it aloud to yourself—with pencil in hand. When you hear something that goes "clunk," make a mark in the margin. The key is to listen and mark only during this first pass; you can concentrate on fixing the problems in a later pass.

You might be surprised how effective this procedure can be. Reading aloud, you'll hear how your text sounds. Some words, phrases, and sentences will cause you to falter or even stumble because they are just plain hard to read in their current form. When you've finished reading, go back through and investigate those marks you've made in the margin: try to recast the phrasing, move the pieces around, or just state the meaning a different way.

Many writers have found that three or four oral readings can do wonders for the flow of a paper. One of our colleagues even tape records her reading so that she can "hear" the paper much the way a larger audience does. A variation on this strategy is to have someone else read your writing to you. That will allow you to hear the prose in another voice. And when the reader stumbles or falters, you know that you need to edit.

One final variation: try this strategy in different locations. The same text read in different kinds of rooms will sound very different—and show different problems. Try one reading in a very small, cozy place. Bathrooms work well: they're usually small, lined with soft towels, and private. Next, choose a very large, open space. A large classroom works well. They often are (unfortunately) very stark rooms that resound with echo. It's amazing what you'll hear when your text bounces back at you! Finally, try a moderately sized room with carpeting—such as a living room or a small meeting room. Read your text while sitting down at a table. In this way, you'll encounter the text as some of your readers are likely to "hear" it with the ears inside their heads.

USING REVISION TOOLS: STYLE HANDBOOKS AND STYLE SHEETS

When you hear someone use the word *style*, you probably connect it with fashion, flair, elegance, a certain way of dressing or acting. When you think of style in terms of writing, you might think of it as a combination of unique characteristics, a fingerprint that clearly identifies the writing with a specific, usually well-known, writer. Given those two predominant views, you might then say that "style is what my writing doesn't have."

But that's not true. Each writer's writing, just like each person, does develop unique characteristics that identify it. Second, most writing styles—like most people—don't stand out that much. Most people and most readers prefer it that way because a flashy writing style attracts attention to itself and away from the content of the message. One important part of developing expertise in your field is developing your own style as well as adapting it to meet the needs and conventions of your profession.

If you use the writing strategies we discuss throughout this book and if you do lots of writing, you will develop a personal style. If you also pause from time to time to examine closely your own and other people's writing, you can fine-tune your style even more. You can also consult some resources that will help you both to develop and polish your style and to conform to the expectations of readers in your specific discipline.

There are two very different kinds of resources that help you do each of these tasks. Both have probably been suggested—or required—as textbooks for one or more of your college courses. You might even own them right now. But, based on our experience with students and professionals in a variety of disciplines, you are confused about the differences between these two types of resources; therefore, you don't use either one as much as you could—as much as you should. We intend to clear up that confusion.

The first type of resource, which we call the *style handbook*, is a general reference book that explains and usually demonstrates the finer points of Standard Edited English. We briefly describe their uses—and abuses—and offer a list of style handbooks you might consult. The second type of resource, which we refer to as the *style sheet*, is a highly specialized set of rules for preparing documents. Each style sheet provides authors and publishers in a specific field—sometimes in several fields—an established set of conventions for such matters as page format and layout, standards and methods for proper citation of source material, accepted abbreviations, and manuscript preparation instructions. We discuss when, why, and how to use a style sheet.

Facts and Fallacies about Style Handbooks

Style handbooks are among the most widely misused (not to mention disused and underused) reference books. And there are hundreds of them, with various purposes and degrees of usefulness. Here are some insights about handbooks that will help you sort out those most useful to you for your specific needs.

Using a style handbook will make me a better writer. Fallacy. Writing, plus rewriting, reading, throwing away, writing some more, revising, asking readers to comment on your writing—in short, a lot of practice—will make you a better writer.

But style handbooks can help you *polish* and *fine-tune* your writing by answering such questions as when it's appropriate to use *imply* and when you really mean *infer*, whether the question mark belongs inside or outside double quotation marks, or how to create a parallel construction. Not even expert writers know the answers to every question all of the time. One thing that makes them experts is that they recognize their limitations and they know what resources can help overcome them. They use handbooks.

The most effective way to use a style handbook, *any* style handbook, is to use it when you need it. Handbooks are not meant to be read from cover to cover and then put on a shelf. In fact, we can't think of a less interesting read than a handbook. But you do need to have a working knowledge of your handbook so you can recognize when it would be useful to you. And you also need to give any handbook you're considering a really thorough going-over to make sure it contains what you need.

All handbooks are alike. Nothing could be further from the truth. There are many out there. Some are intended for specialized audiences. Some are very comprehensive in their scope, covering everything from usage and punctuation to how to avoid wordiness and what salutation to use on a letter to the Prime Minister of Great Britain.

You may find that you will want to have two or three different handbooks, each one for different types of questions. You might want a general handbook for usage and punctuation questions and a more specialized handbook for your profession.

I have a dictionary, somewhere, and that's all I need. First, what you need most is to find your dictionary and put it close at hand. No writer writes well without using one. Period. Second, in a pinch, a good college dictionary, especially one that includes a separate style handbook, can serve you quite well. But be sure it's a *current* dictionary; language does change, rapidly. A dictionary is only one of the resource tools that experts use. When they need advice on capitalization, or when they want to find a synonymous term, their dictionary may do the job. However, they know that what dictionaries are really meant for is defining and spelling words, not finding out what words are capitalized. And a thesaurus or dictionary of synonyms will provide a wider range of word choices.

I don't have to get it exactly right; besides, someone else will fix it. Anyone who believes those two excuses also believes in Santa Claus, the Tooth Fairy, *and* the Great Pumpkin.

Attempting to quash the first of these two fallacies has ruined the reputation of many an English teacher. Seen as harridans of correctitude who swoop down on students' papers to pick at comma splices and dangling participles, they have been unjustly accused as "the only ones who worry about such things." Not true. Anyone interested in communicating effectively and efficiently worries about getting things exactly right.

My word processing program has a grammar and style checker. Useful as these software bells and whistles are, they don't substitute for a style handbook. All they do is compare your text with a set—and a relatively limited set—of circumstances that they're "trained" to watch out for. *You*, the writer, must still make decisions about your text, often based on only a little description that pops up on your screen. A style handbook—or two, or three—can show you examples and help you fully understand the potential problem that the grammar checker is red flagging. Spelling checkers also need to be backed up with a dictionary. They can only mark words that aren't in their electronic dictionary and suggest alternative ones that are in it. *You* have to make the choices.

What's the best style handbook to buy? One way to find out is to ask instructors or colleagues which handbooks they use. Get a number of suggestions; then, look over each one carefully and decide which one will work best for you. Another way to find a good handbook is to browse the shelves, usually labeled *Reference*, at your local bookstore. Last time we checked, one bookstore we know had more than 20 feet of shelf space devoted to this type of resource book. The following *very* short list of style handbooks includes both general and specialized handbooks you might want to consider.

Some Style Handbooks to Consider

Bellquist, John Eric. *A Guide to Grammar and Usage for Psychology and Related Fields.* Mahwah, NJ: Erlbaum, 1993.

Brand, Norman, and John O. White. *Legal Writing: The Strategy for Persuasion*. 2nd ed. New York: St. Martin's, 1988.

Brusaw, Charles T., Gerald J. Alred, and Walter E. Oliu. *The Business Writer's Handbook.* 4th ed. New York: St. Martin's, 1993.

———. *The Handbook of Technical Writing*. 4th ed. New York: St. Martin's, 1994.

Day, Robert A. *How to Write and Publish a Scientific Paper*. 4th ed. Phoenix: Oryx P, 1994.

Follett, Wilson. *Modern American Usage*. Ed. Jacques Barzun. New York: Avenel, 1980.

Fowler, Henry W. *A Dictionary of Modern English Usage*. Ed. Ernest Gowers. 2nd ed. New York: Oxford UP, 1965.

Gastel, Barbara. *Presenting Science to the Public*. Philadelphia: ISI, 1983.

Michaelson, Huber B. *How to Write and Publish Engineering Papers and Reports*. 3rd ed. Phoenix: Oryx P, 1990.

Sides, Charles H. *How to Write and Present Technical Information*. 2nd ed. Phoenix: Oryx P, 1991.

Strunk, William, and E. B. White. *The Elements of Style*. 3rd ed. New York: Macmillan, 1979.

Williams, Joseph M. *Style: Ten Lessons in Clarity and Grace*. 4th ed. Chicago: U of Chicago P, 1990.

Woolever, Kristin R., and Helen M. Loeb. *Writing for the Computer Industry*. Englewood Cliffs, NJ: Prentice, 1994.

There are also many discipline-specific style handbooks. Ask your instructors or other professionals in your field to suggest which of these you should consider.

What Is a Style Sheet and Why Do I Need to Use One?

A style sheet, sometimes called a style manual, is a set of guidelines followed by a group of writers and publishers. Although some style sheets—especially in newly revised editions—contain material found in many style handbooks, their primary concern is to present systematic methods for arranging material, citing sources, and formatting the final version of a document. Most style sheets help users by providing lots of examples.

There are several very good reasons for using a style sheet. But the most important is the one many student writers misunderstand. Style sheets are like traffic laws: they are meant to be followed *exactly* and *by everyone*. If you follow the guidelines of the style sheet to the letter, you'll be in step with all of the other writers in your field. Similarly, following traffic laws to the letter helps everyone get around safely. If you don't follow the style sheet, there are penalties, albeit not usually as severe as those for breaking traffic laws. You may, for instance, get your document handed back to you, along with a terse comment (a kind of warning ticket): "Follow style sheet." Even if it doesn't get bounced back to you, your writing is sure to be taken less seriously by your readers if you're sloppy about the way you conform to the standards of your discipline. Finally, in the most extreme case, your lack of careful documentation and citation of secondary sources leaves you open for a charge of plagiarism. And that can be a whole lot worse than a parking ticket.

So, follow style sheets exactly. If that means using a ruler to measure your margins, or the amount each paragraph is indented, do it. If it means squinting at your computer screen, counting the number of spaces after the period following the title of a book in your Works Cited list, do it. And if it means hauling out your copy of the style sheet every five minutes to look up something, do that, too. Good drivers and expert writers follow the rules.

An equally important reason for following a style sheet, and one that even many seasoned style sheet users overlook, is that it reflects—often in very subtle ways—the way members of a discipline think. Consider, for example, the parenthetical documentation systems of two commonly used style sheets, often called the *MLA Handbook* and the *APA Manual*. (We don't know why their titles get abbreviated this way; but this is how we hear regular users refer to them every day.) The following two paragraphs, containing the same information, illustrate the differences between these two style sheets, and the way their users view their work.

MLA Handbook

Style sheets have an obvious influence on the way a written text appears. As John B. Howell points out, style manuals began, some 300 years ago, as guidelines for printers, who are ultimately responsible for the way a printed text looks. One of the earliest existing style sheets, Charles H. Timperley's *The Printer's Manual*, was actually a combination technical guide on printing and style handbook. Later style sheets, including the popular *Chicago Manual of Style*, eventually became less directed toward printers and more intended for writers. (ix-xi)

APA Manual

Style sheets have an obvious influence on the way a written text appears. According to Howell (1983), style manuals began, some 300 years ago, as guidelines for printers, who are ultimately responsible for the way a printed text looks. One of the earliest existing style sheets, Charles H. Timperley's *The Printer's Manual*, was actually a combination technical guide on printing and style handbook. Later style sheets, including the popular *Chicago Manual of Style*, eventually became less directed toward printers and more intended for writers. (ix-xi)

The differences are subtle, but telling. Notice, for instance, that in the first version the book cited is identified by the author's full name within the text and in the second version by the author's last name and a year. Does this indicate that writers in the social sciences, who often use the *APA Manual*, are cold and impersonal, and their colleagues in the humanities, who often follow the *MLA Handbook*, are friendly? Not really. Instead, we think it's more a matter of the way they perceive information. In both versions, mentioning the author's name serves the same function: it directs readers to a list at the end of the document that provides full bibliographic information on the text cited. But in the first version, the author's name slides rather unnoticeably into the sentence as if to say to readers, "You all know John B. Howell's work on this subject." By including the year in the text, however, the reference in the second version says to readers, "I'm referring here specifically to Howell's 1983 work." In the social sciences, where the value of information often depends on its timeliness, placing the year in the text allows readers to judge the currency of a reference without having to look at the References list at the end of a document. Conversely, the value of information in the humanities is often based on who said it, not necessarily when. Merely stating a name in the text—especially if it's a name associated with well-known and highly respected work—can cause readers to recall a whole body of ideas, either by one author or by several authors whose work is related.

These subtle distinctions also carry over in the formats for Works Cited and References lists. Here is the same bibliographic information prepared according to each style sheet.

Works Cited

Howell, John B. *Style Manuals of the English-Speaking World*. Phoenix: Oryx, 1983.

References

Howell, J. B. (1983). *Style manuals of the English-speaking world*. Phoenix: Oryx Press.

Once again, notice the placement of the information. In the second example, the year of publication and the author's name—with first and middle names abbreviated to initials—are placed close together on the page. The first example, however, gives the complete author's name and follows it with the title of the document cited. Each of these patterns reflects the way readers in different disciplines tend to remember important sources of information: in some cases they associate it with an author and year; in other cases, it's more common to link an author and a title. But both of these formats serve an important purpose that you may not have thought about. They allow readers to scan very quickly down the left column of the References or Works Cited pages to note what sources are cited in the text itself, a technique that many experienced readers use to judge whether to read an article. If they don't see certain citations that they know are important references for the topic discussed in the article, they may pass over it completely, or at least set it aside as less crucial.

We hope our discussion has convinced you that there really are reasons—beyond being told to do so—for becoming familiar with and using the style sheet followed by members of your discipline. Becoming expert includes understanding these rules and the ways of thinking that guide members of your profession. Consult with your instructor, your colleagues, or a reference librarian to find out which style sheet is appropriate for your field. Then purchase a copy. And follow it.

DOCUMENT PRESENTATION: ITS REFLECTION ON YOU

Details do make a difference. Although correct spelling and perfect margins are not usually critical to what your document "means," this level of detail is not unimportant. Notice for instance what happens when you encounter a typographical error in somehting you read; it jars your attention away from what's being said and puts at least some of your concentration toward looking for other mistakes. These mechanical features also cast doubt on your credibility. Reading "recieve" creates a suspicion on the reader's part that either you don't know how to spell it or you are not very careful. You can't win. Typos and small glitches in grammar, spelling, and punctuation—even a deviation from usual format—can suggest that you are either ignorant or sloppy, or both. These are not perceptions you want to provide for readers. Instead, let them decide these matters based on *what* you're saying rather than *how it's presented.*

But presentation is more than just bringing the spelling and punctuation into line with convention. A document, whether it's a paper turned in to an instructor, a proposal to a client, or a report to a superior, presents who and what you are. It invariably has your name on it, which means that you're certifying what's in it. Innumerable students have looked at us in amazement because of the low grades we've given for torn, dirty papers with barely legible work on them. Our reply: "If it can't be read—and read quickly—it can't do anybody any good."

Every audience you encounter will have different pet peeves and different requirements for what is excellent, acceptable, marginal, and unacceptable presentation. If you're not supplied any specific guidelines, the following suggestions could make a difference. Some of these are painfully obvious, and just as painfully (for reader and writer) ignored. Keep in mind that you present yourself with every document you submit.

Suggestions for Presenting Text

- *Present typed or machine-printed work.* As a student, outside of exam situations, everything you turn in should be typed or machine printed, clearly and neatly and as free of error as you can make it. Errors you detect in your final product should be neatly corrected by hand, if not retyped or reprinted. Increased use of word processors and the ease of producing nearly error-free text has made many readers *even less* tolerant. As a professional, your employers expect you to have this facility; so if you've been putting off joining the computer generation, now is the time.
- *Use good paper and a clear typeface.* Near letter-quality computer printer typefaces are accepted—perhaps not even detected—by most people now. On major presentations, we urge you to get laser-printed copy if you can. Don't be stingy on the paper quality either. Use a 20-pound paper or photocopy the original onto it. Make sure the photocopies are as clear as—or clearer than—the originals.
- *Fashion documents into a package.* Large projects should be bound—cheaply enough done at most photocopy shops. Smaller ones can be stapled or paperclipped together and submitted in a folder or large envelope, depending, of course, on what is specified. It is usually a small investment, and it adds to the sense of professionalism you convey. We suggest not using those clear plastic covers with the plastic slip-on binders. The binders fall off most of the time; besides, readers have to take them off to read what's inside them. Make sure your pages are numbered and identified in some way as yours, by using either your last name or an abbreviation of your paper's title as a "running head." Using a title page may or may not be called for; find out if one is expected. A "courtesy page," a blank sheet of paper at the end of a document, may also be expected.

We may be overstating the obvious, but once again, if it doesn't look professional, your work isn't going to be treated professionally.

▶ 6

Special Writing Situations

Overview

In this chapter, we address two special writing situations: creating a portfolio and writing under tight time constraints. These writing circumstances lie at opposite ends of a continuum. Preparing a portfolio is usually a long-term project for which you plan, try out ideas, revise, and ask test readers to give feedback. Writing under pressure, however, usually happens in such tight time constraints that it discourages planning, revising, and getting feedback.

Although quite different from each other, both of these writing situations require flexibility. You will need to adapt your current writing strategies to them—and perhaps adopt new ones that you haven't used before. Finally, by looking critically at how and when you make these adaptations, you will develop your ability to meet any writing situation you may encounter—in school or on the job.

PREPARING A PORTFOLIO

What Is a Portfolio and Why Might I Need One?

Whether in the workplace or in school, you are often required to demonstrate what you can do—and in many situations, why *you* should be doing it and not somebody else. All of us continually are asked, fairly or not, to justify ourselves to employers, colleagues, and teachers. These people looking over our shoulders (figuratively, if not literally) rarely take us on our word that "Yes, I'm doing a good job at what I'm supposed to be doing." Rather, they want proof.

One of the more effective demonstrations of your capabilities is a handy tool called a *portfolio*. Although your résumé or transcript or grade in a course describes what you have done, these "identifiers" don't provide a very complete description of what you have done, nor what you are capable of doing. Recognizing this, educators and prospective employers increasingly are asking for more evidence. Schools, elementary through college, are now adopting a portfolio approach to assess the job they are doing while simultaneously evaluating how well their students have done. Employers are looking for evidence that you can do what you say you can. The best way to get this information is to ask you to provide as complete a demonstration as possible. The portfolio is one such instrument.

Basically, a portfolio is a collection of various kinds of your work done over time that you can present to others. Two different orientations to portfolios currently exist. The portfolio can be a demonstration of *progress* or a demonstration of your *best work*.

Progress portfolios are being used to assess program or institutional success in education. You may not be that concerned about the institutional goals behind subjecting you to this kind of assessment. But you do need to be concerned about how this kind of portfolio indicates your improvement in a class over the course of a semester, or how it determines if you are sufficiently prepared by all of your courses to graduate. You may already have experienced progress portfolios in first-year college composition; many schools are moving toward using portfolios as graduation exit measures. This type of student assessment extends to a variety of disciplines as more and more faculty become trained to use it. We know of one introductory astronomy class that uses them. And we have many other colleagues who are considering adopting them.

The other kind of portfolio, one comprising your best work, is more common as a professional tool for displaying your expertise and capabilities. This is not new for many professionals. Architects, advertisers, visual artists, graphic designers, and technical communicators have relied on them for years to sell their capabilities. Because they may not have as many external constraints, there is more creative room in constructing this kind of portfolio. The trade-off is less assistance in determining what to include than when asked to compile a progress portfolio. In keeping with our theme throughout this book of developing expertise, we'll focus your attention on the best work portfolio, although most of the suggestions and considerations we provide apply to both types.

Strategies for Preparing a Portfolio

A portfolio that demonstrates your best work is a sales tool, one that represents your professional capabilities and disciplinary expertise. In effect, then, you must consider how you want yourself to be seen. We suggest that you consider three phases of activity in developing your portfolio: anticipation, execution, and presentation.

During the anticipation phase, you should first ask, "What am I selling?" Obviously, you are selling yourself and your abilities. But you need to consider which abilities and to whom you are selling. You need to ask, "In my field, what is the market looking for?" In the spaces below, jot down several capabilities that someone in your field should have mastered. Be as specific as possible.

____

____

____

____

____

____

____

____

A mechanical engineering student or a recent graduate in that field, for example, would include demonstrations of his or her abilities to produce proposals, routine correspondence such as letters and memos, progress reports, a patent application, computer-aided drawings (CAD), and perhaps a design project done collaboratively, either for a course or on the job. Other disciplines will expect different types of textual demonstrations. Once you begin to determine what is expected of you, you can begin to construct a portfolio that will demonstrate to particular audiences your specific abilities to meet their expectations. But because the portfolio you construct represents your abilities, you'll want to make sure that those abilities are the ones most desired in your field.

Next comes the really hard part. We provide a series of questions designed to help you do some self-appraisal. As you respond to these questions, be fair and be honest:

Questions for Self-Appraisal

- In my work to date, what materials best represent my capabilities?

____
____
____
____

- What strengths do I observe in my work?

____
____
____
____

- What weaknesses do I observe in my work?

____
____
____
____

- Of my work, what types are most successful?

____
____
____
____

- Where is my work least successful?

____
____
____
____

- What do I learn about myself from the portfolio?

____
____
____
____

- Based on my assessment of my portfolio, what learning goals shall I set for myself?

  ____

  ____

  ____

  ____

- Given my responses to all of these questions, what do I want this portfolio to accomplish?

  ____

  ____

  ____

  ____

This self-analysis should set the stage for the next phase of considerations in which you look at the audiences and purposes for your portfolio.

As we emphasize throughout this book, you need to critically and explicitly examine who you are presenting yourself to and for what purposes. The following guide contains prompts to remind you that your portfolio will be used by particular readers for specific purposes:

Self-Assessment Guide for Portfolio Construction

Audience Considerations

- Who is the audience?
- What do I know about them?
- What do they want to know/see about me?
- How will they evaluate what they see?
- In what context will my portfolio be viewed?
- What familiarity will they have with the material I include?

Purpose Considerations

- What kind of response do I want?
- What do I want the audience to think about me?
- What effect do I want to achieve with my audience?

Perception

- How do I come across?
- How accurately does my portfolio reflect who I am and what I can do well?
- What kind of person am I presenting?

At the execution phase, ask yourself, "What do I include in my portfolio?" Of course, your options will be determined by what is asked of you as well as by what you intend your portfolio to accomplish. But don't leave out something that might leave a distinctive impression on your readers simply because you didn't remember it. Keep in mind all of the different kinds of texts that you've produced in your work to date. Deciding what to include and what not to include can be a perplexing task. This is just a beginning list of materials to consider including:

Possible Texts to Include in a Portfolio

- Articles (written for technical audiences)
- Articles (written for popular audiences)
- Lab reports
- Creative writing (screenplays, stories, poems, essays)
- Design work (pamphlets, brochures, invitations, blueprints, drawings, technical illustrations)
- Research materials (annotated bibliographies, reports, fact sheets)
- Public relations documents (newsletters, news releases)
- Meeting notes or minutes
- Trip reports
- Interviews
- Formal letters
- Lab notebooks
- Proposals
- Progress reports
- Agendas
- Résumé
- Speeches
- World Wide Web homepages (and other electronic forms of text)
- Oral presentation materials (transparencies, slides, handouts, audiotapes, or videotapes)

We know that you will need to extend and customize this list for your own profession, needs, and background. Take time now to add to this list in the space below by noting the kinds of texts common to your discipline. Be specific. Use this opportunity to note particularly effective materials you've developed.

____

____

____

____

As you think more and more about constructing your portfolio, you'll begin to recognize what should be included and what should not. And you'll find that you need to adapt your portfolio for different audiences and different purposes. So get into the habit now of *saving* everything.

The presentation phase involves preparing your portfolio. We assume that you have prepared or will prepare a professional résumé. The same care and attention to detail that go into that document need to go into the presentation of your portfolio. Here are several details that you might want to keep in mind:

Suggestions for Presenting Your Portfolio

- Develop a motif or theme that can assist in unifying your work and its presentation.
- Reflect your personality and its distinctiveness throughout the portfolio.
- Use quality materials such as clear photocopies, good paper, and professional binding.
- Strive for consistency in the layout (typefaces used, borders, heading styles and sizes) as well as in the materials themselves.
- Make the portfolio easy to handle.

Like your résumé, your portfolio is a direct extension of who you are and what you are capable of doing. If it appears professional and expertly produced, you'll be treated as a professional. If it is sloppy and poorly executed, you can easily imagine how others will respond to you.

Portfolio Review Guidelines

As with any important document, you should enlist several others to help you review and assess your portfolio. You've become "too close" to it over the time you've taken to assemble it and are less likely to see the shortcomings that might hinder your best presentation. Besides, the more trial readers you consult, the greater likelihood that you've addressed different audience expectations.

Figure 6.1 is a suggested checklist you can use to evaluate your own portfolio or those of others. And do look at others, especially with a careful eye toward identifying what works and what doesn't. This coversheet—or one of your own design—also enables you to solicit specific feedback from other students, from faculty, and from professionals for revising your portfolio. Attach a copy of it each time you ask for a review. Treat the scale here as if a "5" means fantastic (no possible change could make it better) and "1" means seriously reconsider including (not without some work, anyway).

This checklist is only a crude measure of the effectiveness of your portfolio, but it should give you some idea of its overall impact and it should

Portfolio Review Coversheet

Portfolio Author: ______________________________ Date: ____________________

Portfolio Purpose(s) ____

Portfolio Audience(s) ____

(Scale: 5 = excellent; 1 = needs substantial improvement)

Approach to Audience

5 4 3 2 1 The introduction clearly establishes the purpose of the portfolio.
5 4 3 2 1 The material is interesting.
5 4 3 2 1 The material is believable.
5 4 3 2 1 The order or arrangement of material is appropriate.
5 4 3 2 1 The material is relevant to the audience and its needs.
5 4 3 2 1 Each document shows sufficient detail to demonstrate expertise.
5 4 3 2 1 The materials are coherent.
5 4 3 2 1 The material achieves the purpose of the portfolio.
5 4 3 2 1 Each unit contains distinctive material.

Notes:

Visual Presentation

5 4 3 2 1 The structure is evident and useful.
5 4 3 2 1 Demonstration of visual techniques, including graphics, is apparent.
5 4 3 2 1 The "package" is visually pleasing and professional.
5 4 3 2 1 The material is easily accessible to the reader.
5 4 3 2 1 The table of contents is clear, logical, and accurate.
5 4 3 2 1 The work is accurate and free of errors.

Notes:

Reflections on Me

5 4 3 2 1 The individual units show me as an effective and professional communicator.
5 4 3 2 1 The range of my capabilities is apparent.
5 4 3 2 1 The portfolio demonstrates my flexibility and adaptability to a variety of tasks.
5 4 3 2 1 My ability to work collaboratively is evident.
5 4 3 2 1 My ability to work independently is evident.

Notes:

Total of individual scores: _____/100 total possible points
Summary evaluation and recommendations for the portfolio:

FIGURE 6.1

point you to particular areas that need work. As with any checklist and guidelines, you'll need to adapt this to your own circumstances.

Finally, remember that your portfolio is probably obsolete as soon as it's finished, so keep *revising*. Ask your colleagues and teachers to assist you in preparing and reviewing your portfolio. Think of the portfolio as a neat, professional record of your accomplishments, one that you can carry with you as a personal history, as a tool for self-reflection, and as an advertisement of who you are and what you can do well.

WRITING UNDER PRESSURE

Because we too are under pressure (our publisher wants this book done NOW!), this discussion will be brief and practical. That's not to say that this topic is unimportant to us. Nor is writing under pressure unimportant to you, either in school or on the job. In fact, both our own experiences and those of our students tell us that there is never enough time to write something as well as we could, or want to, write it. Events happen too quickly. People need things done immediately.

Next time you take a plane trip, observe what goes on in the first-class section. Get beyond your envy of the bigger seats, the nicer meals, the free drinks. Most likely, most of those passengers are using the larger seats so that they can work more easily. Dictation equipment, laptop computers, fax machines, and cellular phones are technologies developed to speed the communication process and to get the most out of employees wherever they are. Nowadays, many documents are drafted on the airplane ride to the meeting where they're presented.

The writing and thinking processes that we present throughout this book, and that most of us would *prefer* to use, go out the window because some audience or some purpose is snatching at our documents as fast as we can get them off the printer. Federal Express and other next-day mail services, not to mention fax machine and modem manufacturers, make a lot of money as a result of the constant time pressures most of us face as professionals. The kinds of tests you're subjected to as a student, especially those that involve writing under time pressure, will help you prepare for some of the professional demands made on your writing.

In schools, one popular forum for you to demonstrate your learning, thinking, and writing capabilities is the essay test. You're no doubt familiar with them. Most likely you'll become more and more familiar with them before you finish your degree. Increasingly, colleges and universities across the United States are implementing exit exams that you must pass before graduating, exams that involve an assessment of your writing. Other approaches include sophomore- or junior-level essay exams to diagnose your capabilities for the writing expected of you in your upper-level course work.

Writing-intensive or writing-emphasis courses are also increasingly common to our educational system. In fact, you may well be using this book in conjunction with such a course. These courses often require essay or in-class writing situations, whether the traditional "here is a question and write your brains out until time is called" or more creative approaches involving case studies and elaborate scenarios in which you present solutions or analyses within a very tight time frame.

If you are planning to continue on to professional or graduate school, you face even more writing under pressure once you get there. And getting there usually involves a writing trial-by-fire. Almost all of the professional school exams such as the Law School Admissions Test (LSAT) and the Medical College Admissions Test (MCAT) now have essay components that weigh heavily.

Thus, writing under pressure—writing without the benefit of extensive time for adequate reflection and revision—is inevitably encountered by professionals and students alike. The following suggestions will help you produce better documents under limited time constraints. We focus on how to prepare for and take essay exams because they are a relatively universal experience—and frequently frustrate students. But professionals and experts in all disciplines apply these same strategies almost daily as they draft, revise, polish, and print out documents just in time to rush them to their readers.

Anticipation: Strategies for Preparing

Central to adequately preparing for an essay exam is recognizing that your response, your answer to the test situation, must be *constructed*. Many situations, a statistics test, for instance, require you to recognize a problem and its immediate answer: you apply a particular formula to the situation and then solve that formula to derive the expected answer. Usually, there is only one correct response. But in situations involving writing, the *nature* of your response, or how you present your answer, is as important as what the answer is. And in writing situations, there is usually a range of possible responses. Or there is no "correct" answer at all, but rather one that you present as feasible or probable. The central concern of a reader (the evaluator) in this case is to determine if you demonstrate proficiency, knowledge, and expertise. Your job, then, is to construct, control, and present your expertise knowledgeably and proficiently.

Although the individual nature of these exam situations depends, like every other communication situation, on your audience and purpose, it's useful to conceive of them, like a play, in terms of three acts:

1. Construct your response.
2. Organize your response.
3. Write your response.

Of course, the reader also expects all of the features of well-crafted prose—clarity, conciseness, freedom from error—features you do not have much time for in these situations. So, we add a short epilogue:

4. Revise and edit your response.

Preparation is the key to making the most of your time in an exam situation. You usually have forewarning. You may not know specifically what you will be expected to respond to but you should have a general idea of the topics to be covered. Many instructors announce in advance the number of questions, the time available to you, and even the specific topics that will be covered on the exam. In some cases, you can review exams given at other times to get a clearer sense of the exam. A sample test, when available, provides an idea of the structure of the exam and often identifies main issues or focuses on a topic.

Another way to prepare is to review your class notes and texts to determine the main points covered in the course. Using the strategies we discuss in Part 2 for generating reading notes really pays off when tests come up. Once you've identified potential topics, focus on particular areas.

Creating your own essay-type questions is useful. Look at previous exams, from any course, and model your questions on those written by instructors. This forces you both to analyze the way questions are constructed—a key to constructing your own responses, which we discuss a little later—and to synthesize the material. One instructor we know often asks his students to each submit three possible questions from which he builds the final exam in his course. Having written exams ourselves, we can assure you it's one of the most challenging writing assignments that an instructor could give.

Keep in mind, however, that anticipating potential questions is not necessarily predicting the future. "Your" question may not actually appear on the exam, although there's always the chance, especially if you really have been paying attention. But writing possible questions helps you discover what you know well and also what you're weak on. You can then use your time filling in the gaps of your understanding with more study, further research, or questions to the instructor during class or office hours. Forming a study group to create and share possible questions is also effective.

Once you or your group has created a set of questions, respond to them. Set up the time constraints you expect and take your own exam, imitating the conditions you expect in the actual exam as nearly as possible. Then, exchange your responses, or put yourself in your instructor's position, and judge your efforts. This is an effective way of analyzing your audience, another important aspect of preparing. If your efforts fall short of what you think your audience expects, you still have time to do more reading, writing, and thinking. If, however, you have difficulty deciding what is expected, you need to investigate your audience further.

Most instructors are quite clear about what they are looking for in responses on their tests. If you are unsure, *ask*. Find out the instructor's goals or purposes for the test. Exams, especially essay exams, are not usually intended to discover how little you know but rather to demonstrate how much you know and how well. Asking an instructor the specific goals for a test increases your chances of meeting them.

Also find out whether notes, the textbook, or other resources will be allowed. If so, much of your preparation time can be spent organizing these materials for easy use during the exam. For instance, you might annotate your notes and textbook and create an index, as we describe in Part 2. If you sort, arrange, and paperclip or mark with Post-It notes your materials according to specific topics, you will save valuable time otherwise used shuffling through for just the right page of notes during the exam. On the job, this is called filing, and it's a highly valued skill that you need to develop. Finally, consider whether you need to take a dictionary. Used too much, it may slow you down unnecessarily. Conversely, if you can wait to use it until you've finished writing and are revising and editing, it may be invaluable. A misspelled word, crossed out once and corrected neatly, indicates your preparation and attention to detail, not your ignorance.

Execution: Strategies for Writing

Here we'll start with the obvious: Be on time (or a little early) and bring with you exactly—and only—what you need.

Not quite so obvious, perhaps, is what to do once you have the exam in your hands. We offer the following strategy, which we have seen work successfully for dozens of students. You will need to modify it to your individual situation; but if you keep these steps in mind, you will be far ahead of those who don't. Here are the six steps:

1. Scan the exam.
2. Budget your time.
3. Reread, analyze, and choose.
4. Plan your response.
5. Write your response.
6. Revise, edit, and proofread.

Your first instinct on being handed an exam is probably to hunch over it, begin at the top, and work your way to the end—all the while disregarding the clock ticking off the minutes. A better strategy is to scan the whole thing quickly first to get an idea of what you're facing. And we mean *very* quickly.

Look over the directions for key phrases such as "Choose one of the following" or "Answer each in a short essay." Note key topic words in the question(s) as well, words that trigger memories of discussions, notes you've written, or stacks of material you have ready to use. This brief overview lets you know where you need to concentrate your efforts. It also alerts you to possible black holes in your preparation or your memory that you either want to avoid, if possible, or devote extra time to filling in.

Once you have a sense of the number, the type, and the topics of the questions, pause to make a time budget. When we suggest this to students in our classes, they usually look aghast and say, "But I don't have enough time to worry about the time!" And we say, "You don't have enough time *not* to worry about it." The seconds it takes to establish a time budget result in a better piece of writing. Write down your time budget—inside the front cover of your exam book, perhaps—and indicate the actual clock times to be finished with each phase. For instance, given one question to respond to in a two-hour exam, your budget might look like this:

Planning	½ hour	10:30
Writing	1 hour	11:30
Revising	½ hour	12:00

If you must answer several questions, or if your exam is divided into several parts, consider how much each piece of writing is worth. Instructors often list the point value of each item so you can do this. Some even suggest the amount of time you should spend on each item. Use this information to budget your time. Then, stick to it faithfully. Like money, time gets spent faster without a budget.

Now you're ready to return to the exam for a much closer reading. Take each question apart by asking yourself:

- What *task* does this question ask me to perform?
- What is the specific *topic* it focuses on?
- What *hints* does it give me about my response?

The following prompt, for example, can be quickly analyzed this way: "Define the term *Xeriscape* in relation to southwestern urban planning."

- What *task* does this question ask me to perform? Define.
- What is the specific *topic* it focuses on? *Xeriscape*
- What *hints* does it give me about my response? Relate to southwestern urban planning.

Granted, not every exam question works that well. We know; we've written a few clunkers. But these three elements—task, topic, hints—are used by many question writers. Besides *define*, some other common task words to watch for include *explain*, *compare*, and *describe*—essentially all of those words that describe language activities.

This is also the time to make choices, if you have the opportunity. If you spot a topic word that you are less prepared to write about, immediately eliminate that question and never look at it again. If you must face it, schedule it in the middle of your time budget, after you've handled an easier question or two but before you feel the crush of the clock.

Rereading, analyzing, and making choices should take no more than a few minutes. Planning your response, the next step, will take longer, depending, of course, on the number of responses you must write. Again, most students balk at the notion of spending valuable writing time planning. But once again, we assure you, it's time well spent.

To plan your response, use any of the usual writing strategies that help you get started writing. Outlining is effective, and fast, for many writers. But you also may find that quickly reviewing your notes or a specific passage in your textbook, if they are available to you, will suggest the approach you want to take. And we've seen some interesting pictures sketched inside the covers of exam books that helped writers "see" what they wanted to say.

One caution: Don't spend too much time fussing over introductions. We've seen some beautifully crafted beginnings, like half-built bridges, that went nowhere. In fact, we suggest that, when you begin writing, you leave the first page blank for an introduction yet to be written. After all, that *is* the way most texts are produced: middle, end, beginning. And it's much more effective to dazzle your reader with the "meat" of your response. Finally, if you run out of time or can't come up with something more delightful, your introduction can be a rephrasing of the question or of your conclusion. Given the speed with which most exams must be read, bland introductions are quickly forgotten.

Here are a few more suggestions to keep in mind while writing your response:

- Write in the clearest, most direct language possible.
- Choose simplicity and repetition over elegance and diversity.
- Use technical language if it is efficient and appropriate to your audience.
- Let purpose and audience guide you.
- Repair weak sentences during revision and editing, not during writing.
- End conclusively, not abruptly.

Effective writing, whether composed over ten years or in ten minutes, requires revision, editing, and proofreading. Taking the time to read through your writing to spot and fix those weak sentences and fill in punctuation marks thought but not written will definitely add to the quality of your writing. Readers notice these touches, sometimes unconsciously, as their eyes glide over the page.

But sometimes there just isn't enough time to do as much of this as you'd like. There are some shortcuts. As you write, mark in the margin a sentence or word that needs fixing, or leave a blank space if you can't think of the word you want. Then, if you don't have much revising time, you can scan through and at least fix these few items you know about. In some instances, you may discover when revising a whole paragraph that you need to reorganize: you have all the pieces, but they're jumbled. Don't waste your time recopying; simply number the elements in the correct order and add a note to your reader: "Read as numbered." This works equally well for parts within a sentence and even large chunks of your text. And it's usually much easier to follow than arrows.

Finally—and it's embarrassing to have to bring this up—write legibly. Most readers' response to illegible writing is to assume it's concealing ignorance, not wisdom. Regardless of what you've heard about doctors, illegible writing is not professional.

Desperation: Strategies of Last Resort

Sometimes—rarely, we hope—you need strategies of last resort. You haven't the faintest idea how to respond to a question, or you're sure you've never even heard of the topic before. Write something, anything. Writing, as we point out throughout this book, is the best way to think. You may find out that you did pick up a little bit, perhaps accidentally, from sitting in class. Or, you may find another angle on the topic, one that you can write from.

If nothing else, you can use the time to write out your excuse, and your apology, and your personal guarantee that such a mishap will never occur again. Even if you don't show it to your instructor, spending the exam time writing it will certainly improve your oral delivery of it. And improve your character.

Our best advice for such instances is, quite obviously, don't get yourself into them. Using the strategies we've outlined here and those discussed throughout this book, you should be fully prepared to meet any writing situation, no matter how short the time. If you are to become an expert,

[*Publisher's note: Due to time constraints, this sentence was not finished.*]

7

Collaboration

Overview

Rewards, Risks, and Objections

Getting Started

Generating Material

Collecting Material

Revising

By now you've probably heard this word in one or more of its forms: *collaboration*. Some students we know tend to ignore it as "just another big word that teachers use." (In all fairness, some faculty see it much the same way.) To other students, it translates as "oh, boy, another group project." We'll let you decide whether that's said with relish or sarcasm. But, if pressed, exactly how do you define *collaboration*? Take a moment to write down what it means to you. Jot down some experiences you've had working collaboratively, as well as any problems you've encountered with it.

____

____

____

____

____

____

Both figuratively and literally, what's at the center of col*labor*ation is *labor*; what's at the beginning is the idea of "with." So in very simple terms, *collaboration* means "working with" or "working together." But communication, in all its many shapes, is also integral to collaboration. Perhaps that's because communication is almost never *not* collaborative. Even talking to oneself, and its parallel, thinking aloud, are conversations with an "other." Some theorists have convincingly argued that individual human activity, especially language use, must be social before it can be individual. That is, before we humans can do things solo, we first need to do them with other humans.

One of our purposes in writing this textbook is to encourage you to pay attention to how you do what you do—especially how you communicate. It's hard to imagine people working together, collaborating, without communicating. So, we believe that observing and understanding collaboration, especially paying attention to how it works—and doesn't work—when you are involved in it, can give you insights into how you communicate individually. Furthermore, because we also believe that, regardless of your area of interest or profession, you can expect to find yourself working on teams at least some of the time, knowing some specific strategies for effective collaboration is also central to becoming more expert in your field. That's what we provide in this chapter.

Although we focus on collaborative *writing* in this chapter, our discussion applies equally to all the communication activities we discuss throughout this book—often carried out by teams you may not yet see as teams. As a reader of this textbook, for instance, you are engaged in a collaboration with us, its writers, this very moment. (We discuss this further in Part 2.) You collaboratively listen with your classmates to the text that evolves during any given class period, something we discuss in Part 3. And you've no doubt worked with others to plan and give a team oral presentation, a topic we delve into in Part 4. By thinking about all of this and connecting it with all of your other thoughts and experiences, you are further developing your own expertise.

REWARDS, RISKS, AND OBJECTIONS

Collaboration, like all communicative activities, is not simple. It has both rewards and risks. We speak from obvious experience: this textbook is a joint effort. But so is much of our other professional activity. We serve on committees, organize and deliver panel presentations at professional conferences, design and develop course curricula with other faculty, and even team teach some of those courses.

We don't see our situation as particularly unusual, either. Many professionals collaborate as a matter of course. IBM has entire teams of people known as "information developers" who work with a product from idea conception to point of sale. Scientists routinely work on teams. So do marketing researchers, agricultural economists, physicians, musicians, and automotive technicians.

What we and most other professionals find rewarding about collaboration is the "cross-fertilization" of ideas, the energizing discussion among people with common interests and goals, the shared sense of accomplishment when those goals are reached. If you've been involved in any kind of team sports, you probably recognize these rewards as similar to that experience.

But collaboration carries risks, too. There's an old adage that says, "You can pick your friends, but you can't pick your relatives." Often that's the case with collaborators, too. Whether you find yourself assigned to a team project with classmates or toiling with your fellow cubicle dwellers on the job, it's a reasonable bet that about half the time you'll be working with someone you don't know and wouldn't necessarily *choose* as a collaborator. By the same token, choosing your close friends as collaborators is risky, too. Friendships, and marriages, have ended when those involved thought it would be great to work as members of a team.

Another risk is credit. In most cases, the credit for the team's accomplishment is evenly distributed; each individual member's contribution gets absorbed into the whole. For some people, giving up individual recognition is difficult; sharing it with others, even harder. And, it's true, there's almost always the nagging question, "How would this have turned out if I'd done it all by myself?"

Finally, we feel compelled to address a couple of objections to the whole notion of collaboration that we often hear raised: that it's wrong and that it doesn't work. The first objection usually takes the form of "collaboration is just a fancy word for cheating, getting someone else to do *your* work." We agree that there are times when it's valuable, appropriate, or just plain convenient for people to work alone, although we're hard pressed to imagine exactly where the rest of the world goes while that's happening. However, we argue that in a *true* collaborative effort, no "one" does anyone else's work; indeed, for collaboration to be effective, all participants have to commit all of their energy to it. When that happens, they all get out of the activity more than they possibly could have put into it alone.

Does collaboration ever fail? Absolutely, and abysmally. When it does, we argue again that some measure of explanation can be traced to the fact that it wasn't a *true* collaborative effort. And a second explanation is usually that the participants had little or no training in *how* to collaborate effectively. Here's just one example of how collaboration can be disastrous if not handled well. Because it's about an attempt to write collaboratively, we think it's worthwhile to present it in some detail, as a kind of cautionary preface to our discussion.

In *Collaboration and Conflict*, Geoffrey Cross tells a story about Auldouest Insurance Corporation (a pseudonym), whose employees spent seventy-seven days writing the executive letter for the company's 1986 annual report. There were eight links in the communication chain for composing the executive letter, ranging from the writer at the bottom to the CEO at the top. Not once during the process did all participants meet together. Instead, various members of the chain passed information to others through others. As a result, as in any situation like the children's game called "Telephone," information was added, deleted, or altered as it got passed up and down the chain—much as the character Tim Taylor on the television situation comedy *Home Improvement* mangles information as he passes it from his neighbor, Wilson, to members of his family. The situation at Auldouest would be equally comic if the stakes were not so high.

Another related problem with the executive letter was that people who had information crucial to the letter's success often delegated drafting and revising tasks to people (the writer, for instance) who did not have that information—or even reasonable access to it. A third problem was that the president, the senior vice president, and the primary writer each envisioned different audiences for the letter. This problem was magnified by the lack of direct communication among all members of the team—if the word *team* applies in this case. A fourth problem was that various people in the chain held differing purposes for the letter. Again, because different members of the communication chain emphasized different purposes but did not communicate those emphases directly to other members, more conflict ensued. As a result of all of these factors, the writer worked on thirteen drafts of the letter from late October to late November. In early December, that letter was discarded, replaced by one composed by the writer's supervisor. The writer simultaneously constructed another new version of the letter. Later that month, the senior vice president composed yet another version, which was approved on December 29.

Yes, when it's approached in this way, "collaboration" will fail, miserably. And, yes, we believe that "collaborating" like this is very wrong.

GETTING STARTED

Whether you have a choice of your collaborators or are thrown together for some other reason, we suggest that you consider communication as the key factor to effective teamwork. First, last, and always: communication. Even a group of people who don't know or like each other very much, but who can communicate with one another, can form an effective team and accomplish much. And we want to stress here, again, that communication includes *listening* as well as speaking, *reading* as well as writing. You probably already know that a group composed entirely of very good talkers may not be as productive as one containing some good talkers, some keen listeners, and somebody who's watching the clock.

Although we doubt that there's ever such a thing as a "perfectly balanced" group of collaborators, we urge you to identify—and capitalize on—the complementary strengths in your team. And we do mean *your* team. It's vital that all members of collaborative groups have some sense of ownership in both the team and its work. But there's one myth about collaboration that we need to explode: teamwork is almost never *equally* distributed. No matter how you go about the task, and we discuss a variety of ways below, there will always be the appearance—and, usually, the reality—that some members of a group "do more" than others. Though we have no proof, we suspect this tendency has more to do with human perception than with actual division of labor. That's why it's so vital to ensure that every member be invested in the *team's* work, not in his or her own contribution.

So far, we've described some ideal characteristics of collaborators: a group of effective communicators with complementary strengths and a shared investment in the team's efforts. But how can you assure that your team will have those characteristics? There are no guarantees. However, employing the following strategies during the early stages of any collaboration will encourage them to develop.

Get to know your collaborators as *collaborators.* It's no secret that people love to gather around food. An informal first meeting, to which each member contributes something to eat, will help break down some barriers between people. But an even more effective first meeting is one at which the team members *collaborate to prepare the food.* It's a great way to see how each person works—and you get to eat at the end! Mix up a batch of chocolate chip cookies; make a huge salad; carve a watermelon and fill it with fruit. You'll be amazed at how much you learn about each other and about working together.

If you're collaborating electronically, perhaps even transcontinentally, such get-togethers are a bit harder to accomplish. Instead of food, try creating verse. Start with a couple of lines—the sillier the better, usually—and ask each person to take a turn adding on. Stuck for a starter? Use Dr. Seuss as a model. It's also wise to set up a distribution system so that every member of the team gets a copy of everyone else's messages. As the verse bounces around, everyone will pretty quickly get a sense of the different "voices," and the people behind them, in the group.

Clear the air, early and often. Many difficulties in collaboration can be traced to something *un*said. So encourage each member of the group to say exactly what he or she thinks—and feels. This is far easier to recommend than to do. It takes time (after all, it's really important to listen carefully to each and every member), and it requires trust. If nothing else, start each meeting of your team by having members tell what they like about how the project is going and what they are not happy with. And listen actively.

Check on each member's perception of the goal. We're frequently amazed (although we shouldn't be) to observe well-meaning faculty committees that launch into discussions of change without first finding out what result each member is aiming for. Too often these efforts end up like a Laurel and Hardy shtick: instead of moving the piano, they get exhausted from simultaneously trying to push it toward each other. We point out the importance of clarifying your purpose for a writing project in Chapter 2, but those ideas apply equally to any kind of team effort. Although it may seem that you're spending an awful lot of time talking about what you're doing—and not *doing* it, it is important to constantly ask, "What do we think we're doing?"

A parallel, and equally important, question is, "How did we decide to do this?" So, *plan the work and frequently discuss the plan.* Some team members shut down not because the group is working toward a goal they don't share, but rather because they believe the team's not getting to that goal by the "right" route. Or because they don't know what the route is.

Also, *get a commitment from each member.* Notice that we did not say *agreement;* total agreement is unrealistic, and it's less important than a commitment. But if each team member commits to something—whether to work toward the same goal, to complete a particular task, or just to show up every single time there's a meeting—other things are more likely to happen. For instance, the member who commits to showing up is pretty unlikely, after showing up, to just sit and watch everybody else contribute.

These last three activities—clarifying the goal and the plan, and getting commitments—work particularly well when all collaborators can see them unfold. For that reason, we recommend that groups work out their goals, plans, and commitments on a chalkboard or white board, or even on large sheets of newsprint. In electronic collaborations, you may want to post the goal, plan, and commitments at some mutually accessible site *and* send them out to each member regularly for clarification. As frequently as every two or three days is not too often to go back to these issues.

Finally, it may be useful to *identify individual members' roles on the team.* For instance, one team member might act as the spokesperson for the group. Another might take on the role of progress monitor, and yet another might act as "cheerleader" or "encourager" for the team. Note that these team roles differ from specific tasks that members might be working on for the project. But members' work in these roles contributes to the effective function of the team.

GENERATING MATERIAL

At first, it might seem a lot easier to generate material for writing projects when you're working as part of a team. After all, isn't it true that "two (or more) heads are better than one"? And don't "many hands make light work"? Well, those old adages notwithstanding, it's been our experience that generating ideas and material collaboratively is neither easier nor harder than working alone. But it's definitely different. Although we recommend using the same *types* of strategies and the same approach we've suggested already in Chapters 2 and 3, there are some special considerations to keep in mind when you're generating material for a collaborative project.

Try several different strategies. Some people prefer very structured strategies, and others go about generating ideas and material in more freewheeling ways. By consciously choosing a variety of methods, your team can count on getting input from all members. Here, briefly, are some different approaches to try:

- *Brainstorming*: In "true" brainstorming, no idea is discarded, discounted, or discussed until every possible idea, from every participant, has been turned up. No matter how silly or outrageous ("let's attach the wings of the Space Shuttle with bubble gum," for instance), put them all up for everyone to see. This is probably the most freewheeling approach.
- *Talk/pause/write*: Slightly more structured than brainstorming, this strategy can help bridge the gap between the "think by talking" members and those who need quiet time to reflect and write. Set a time limit—and maybe an alarm clock—for some open discussion or brainstorming; 15 minutes is a good minimum. When the time's up, take an equal period for silence *and* writing. It's tough, but enforce the silence. How you proceed from here will depend on the group. One way is to have everyone read out loud what they've written, using the same guidelines as for brainstorming: no discussion until everything has been heard.
- *Drafting specific sections*: Sometimes there's an immediate and obvious consensus about who can or should draft specific sections of a text. Get a commitment from each member, especially about when the draft will be done, and let each work, alone or otherwise. But remember that no one likes to be stuck with "leftovers." If some pieces are left unclaimed, work on those as a group rather than "assign" them.
- *Chaining*: Sometimes it takes a chain reaction to get things going. Get someone to draft a first sentence or paragraph; then, hand it off to another member of the group. Keep passing it around until there's plenty to work with. And remember that the links of a chain are not always different: some members may want to contribute an alternate version of an already existing piece.
- *Outline*: We describe a variety of outlining strategies throughout this book. Check the index for some ideas.

Agree on "acceptable" formats. Some people work best with pen or pencil and paper; others can't think without a keyboard. Then, too, there are all the different software applications—and the different computer "platforms" and operating systems. Before generating too much material in a wide range of formats, it's a good idea to settle on a couple that everyone can use. This may be even more critical when collaborating electronically. Just because you can *see* or *read* someone else's information doesn't necessarily mean that you can integrate, display, or print it with yours.

Start putting things together from the beginning. This may seem obvious, but it's not that easy to do. One of the best ways to encourage team members to see the *team's* efforts as important is to constantly look at the *team's* production. Even if it's messy and disconnected, store all the generated material together, in one file—paper, electronic, or both.

Make everyone responsible for the collective file. It's wise, for a number of reasons, to make at least one backup copy of all the material, whether on paper or on disk.

COLLECTING MATERIAL

When a collaborative project requires collecting material, whether in a laboratory, through library or electronic research, or from other people, most teams find that it's critical to use their resources—themselves—most effectively. Members don't want to duplicate each others' efforts by tracking down the same information. Equally important, though, they don't want to leave one member to struggle alone when others could help. And, most critically, they must keep in touch so that what one member is feverishly collecting does not become obsolete by what another member has discovered. Here are some suggestions for collecting material collaboratively:

Decide how to divide up the work. Again, consider the relative preferences of the group members. Some may love the challenge of tracking down an obscure print source through interlibrary loan, but hate the thought of conducting an informational interview. Different team members also may have background experience or contacts that make them especially qualified to work on a particular topic.

Clarify why you're collecting what you're collecting. Too often, team members can walk or read past something very valuable in their quest for "that stuff I'm supposed to get." But, if all participants have a clear sense of the purpose not only of the material *they* are collecting but also what others are after, they are better able to identify what and how much to bring back.

Set up a system for recording or arranging what's collected. It may even be worthwhile to develop a form or checklist that identifies what should come back with each collection. For example, team members should know what source information they will need to gather so that they don't have to go back later to ask an interviewee's job title or qualifications.

Keep everyone informed of progress—or lack of it. We worked with one three-member team that set up a sheet detailing who would do what by when, and then used various colored highlighters to identify each person's responsibility. Yellow blocks meant S. was working on it, purple meant D. was handling those details, and blue meant B. was responsible. As the members collected or generated what they were working on, they put an upward-pointing arrow beside that item. When they were having trouble with an item, they put a downward-pointing arrow. That way, all team members knew where to offer ideas or suggestions, or could work on those items when they had spare time.

REVISING

Most of the global revising suggestions we offer in Chapter 4 work equally well in collaborative situations. In fact, many of them are more effective if done by teams. Conversely, some of the suggestions for completing local revision really require an individual approach. No matter which strategies your team uses, these suggestions will make your efforts more productive.

Determine when to undertake each type of revision. In general, it's wise to complete *some* global revision before starting to edit a text. However, some documents—and some sections of some documents—can be edited before undertaking a global revision. In short, it depends. But it's probably most critical that team members know who's doing what with which part of the text so that they don't either duplicate or obliterate each others' efforts.

Decide in advance how disputes will be settled. There's seldom only one way to organize, illustrate, or state an idea; disputes are a natural part of team revision. But it's wise to have some plan in place for settling them before they come up. Teams sometimes agree to ask an outside trial reader to make a decision. Or they may decide to work toward a compromise that incorporates both—or all—of the suggestions that come from the group. Or they may choose to abide by a style handbook's recommendations, although those are sometimes open to multiple interpretations, too.

Use team members as trial readers. One of the best reasons to write collaboratively is to have "built-in" trial readers. So, use each other for this purpose. You might assume that everyone working on the same text would automatically be able to read and comment on different sections without the setup you would supply to an "outside" trial reader. But that's a mistake. Be just as careful—if not more so—to prepare your team members to read and comment; your setup may, in fact, help them re-see a part of the document they are working on. Use the coversheet suggested in Chapter 4, or modify it to fit your needs.

Be a conscientious trial reader. When asked to give a review, whether on a sentence, a paragraph, a section, or on a whole document, remember these guidelines:

- Be sure that you understand the background of the text—its audience, purpose, and level of completion. If the writer has not given you specific questions to respond to, ask for them.
- Look at the text as a whole. Flip its pages front to back, just "seeing" the text rather than reading it.
- If there's time for more than one reading, read the text through once to develop a general understanding of its content.
- As you read the text a second time, note your responses to the writer's questions.
- Ask yourself, "What are the two major strengths of this text?"
- Ask yourself, "What are the two major weaknesses? How might the writer go about remedying them?"
- Ask yourself, "What would be a one- or two-sentence summary of the text?"
- Be nice. Do unto others' work what you would have them do unto yours. The point is to end up with more effective text, not enemies. Criticism is much more effective when it is constructive.
- Be careful to point out what is already especially worthwhile and effective in any text you review. We all want to know what we're doing right so we can do it some more.

Check the final version for consistency. It's easy to overlook minor differences among pieces of a text that have been generated, revised, and edited by a team. For instance, one section may use the abbreviation "U.S." while another uses "US." To assure a fully integrated and consistent document, it's a good idea to spend one final editing pass checking for these details.

8

Understanding Reading

Overview

Reading is a cognitive activity central to our lives. Reading is so pervasive that we often read without ever being aware of it. Products of a literate society, we are surrounded by and respond to a text-laden environment. The invention and use of text has totally changed our lives and, as some argue, how we think. Aside from conventional texts such as newspapers, magazines, novels, and so forth, texts such as license plates, billboards, food packages, computer screens, and street signs all engage our abilities to read. And each different kind of text calls for a different kind of reading and need for that reading. A stop sign engages our reading attention only briefly, but most of us react, and react specifically, to the message in that text. We stop. A speed limit sign calls for a related yet distinctly different kind of response.

Our environment dictates that we read. But of more particular focus here is the kind of reading you do in your course work and in your development as an authority in a particular discipline. Our individual abilities, tastes, and specific needs usually determine what we read and how we respond to it. Unfortunately, much of what we are expected to read is not what we would choose if left to our own devices. Or, what we are expected to read is not as easy to read or to understand as we would like it to be. The purpose of this chapter is to acquaint you with some strategies and techniques to make the reading you do more effective, if not easier and more enjoyable.

HOW READING WORKS

Reading is one of the more complex kinds of critical thinking we commonly engage in. What we do with the information and how we extract that information are affected by our purpose for reading. The design of the text we read also affects our response, sometimes as much as our purpose for reading it. The substance of the text, its content, is another feature. Our capabilities are another; they are called into question continually every time we encounter a text. Our experience with a particular kind of text and its content also affects our response. A lot to manage, and yet, when was the last course you took on how to read? Beyond elementary school, most of us are expected not only to know how to read, but to be proficient readers, and to get even better at it.

As we move more and more toward becoming professionals in our respective fields of study, the texts we encounter become more and more specific in design, in purpose, and in importance. They usually become more difficult as well. For example, a junior in accounting who was encountering IRS tax codes for the first time remarked that she wasn't reading English any more. She has to extract specific information from text such as this:

> ***Figuring Estimated Tax on Nonconvertible Foreign Currency***
>
> *If the host country does not require you to pay an income tax on the amount of your grant, you figure the amount of your estimated tax that may be paid to IRS in the nonconvertible foreign currency by the following formula:*

$$\frac{\textit{Estimated adjusted gross income to be received in nonconvertible foreign currency}}{\textit{Estimated entire adjusted gross income}} \times \textit{Total estimated U. S. tax} = \textit{Part of estimated tax attributable to amounts received in nonconvertible foreign currency}$$

If you are required to pay your host country an income tax on your grant, you must subtract any estimated foreign tax credit attributable to your grant from the part of estimated tax attributable to amounts received in nonconvertible foreign currency. (6) (Publication 520, Rev. Nov. 87; Internal Revenue Service)

Our understanding of what we read and how to use that understanding is what makes us authorities in our respective fields. As this student found, it is not necessarily an easy or enjoyable task.

We recently asked a class of technical writing students, juniors and seniors from a variety of technical fields, to tell us what reading is. Most of their responses conveyed the picture of a student hunched over a textbook with a highlighter, busily painting pages. Their "activity," most conceded, was to passively absorb and memorize page after page of yellow and purple sentences extracted from the fountain of wisdom called a textbook. They viewed reading as it has been traditionally taught—a writer provides a text, which the reader reads. Visually, the process looks like this:

Writer → (Writing) → Text → (Reading) → Reader

FIGURE 8.1 Traditional View of the Reading Process

What few of these accomplished students who had survived into their junior and senior years of university studies recognized was that the nature of reading and writing is much more complex and a lot less linear than Figure 8.1 represents. Reading is an interactive process shared by three highly complex entities with different agendas, strategies, and contexts. Still too simplistic, the following illustration does provide more of a sense of the complexity called reading:

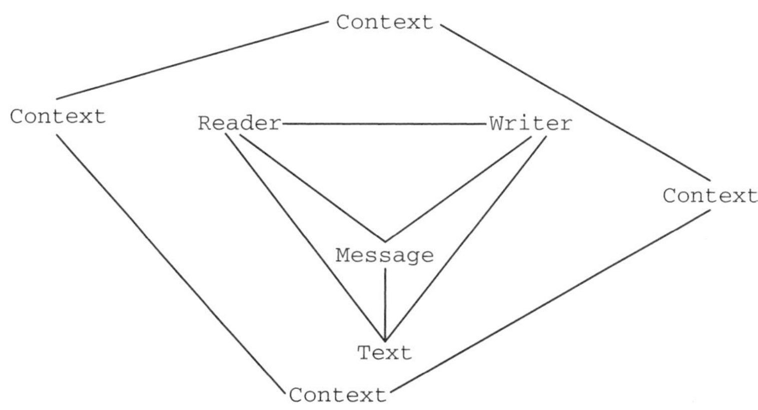

FIGURE 8.2 Illustration of the Reading Process

A thorough understanding of the natures and processes of your reading is not essential. However, some idea of what reading involves and what you do as a reader will make you a more effective one. The following pages provide a basic understanding of this model and its terms to help you apply them to your own context for your own purposes. Briefly, we discuss context, text, and the reader. Writing and the writer, which we discussed earlier, should already be familiar to you.

THE IMPORTANCE OF CONTEXT

Reading is a context-specific activity; that is, it occurs in a frame of reference. You read an anatomy and physiology text for an anatomy and physiology class, chemistry for chemistry, finance for finance. Taking a particular course with a particular instructor who assigns particular texts establishes a context. Context shifts from class to class; more specific context occurs within each one. Granted, contexts change, sometimes frequently, but examining the context can often ease your understanding of the material and what your instructor expects of you.

Usually categorized as temporal, spatial, causal, or some combination of all three, context is created by the environment around you and the myriad of purposes in and for such an environment. *Temporal context* is where you are at a given time. It can be as simply distinguished as beginning, middle, or end. *Spatial context* encompasses the social, the cultural, the historical. *Milieu* is a fancy word for it. It exists because, in the words of John Donne, no man (or woman, for that matter) is an island. No reader, writer, or text is independent of his, her, or its sources and origins. *Causal context* grows out of the interaction of time and space. Yet, it is distinct because it directly links to purposes. For instance, a poster in a vacuum cleaner store proclaims "Hoover sucks." Such a poster has a much different purpose to its message in a Hoover outlet than in an Electrolux or Kirby store because a particular context exists in each store. Discovering the contexts—temporal, spatial, causal—can take you a long way toward enhancing your understanding of text.

Certain questions help establish the context for your reading. Answer the following questions as they apply to this text and the course or context in which you are reading it:

- What is the context of the text?

  ____

  ____

  ____

- What is the immediate context for *my* reading the text?

___

___

___

- What is the larger context for this reading?

___

___

___

- How and where do I fit into these contexts?

___

___

___

- Why am I here?

___

___

___

Providing yourself such a frame of reference for your reading and for the texts you read enables you to *locate* a reading in relation to the course, other classes, professional relevance, and your life.

ELEMENTS OF TEXT

Whether media philosopher Marshall McLuhan's aphorism, "the medium is the message," holds true or not, the type of text we encounter affects how (and whether) we understand its contents. The kind of reading approach we use, as well as the habits and attitudes we bring to the text, are often determined by what kind of text it is. A poem has a much different appearance and set of communication strategies than a novel. We bring certain expectations, activate specific sets of background knowledge, and engage appropriate comprehension strategies when reading Coleridge's "Rime of the Ancient Mariner." Melville's *Moby Dick* requires other responses and actions from us. They are different kinds of text. Dickens's *Great Expectations* is much different from Landon Jones's demographic study of the baby boom, even though they have the same title. Obviously. Yet, how often do we stop to consider the different approaches we use when we encounter different texts and their different effects on us?

A book is "more than the cover." In many respects, it is a container holding a message, which evolves from your interaction with the contents, the text. Containers hold many different substances with different tastes and effects. A text, like any container, has a design to it, a design that is informed by the substance it contains. And most texts are fairly standard in design, even though they may cover widely different content areas. Becoming familiar with the "conventions" of books will enable you to gain access to their contents much more effectively.

Most books, especially textbooks, have the following components:

Title page
Copyright page
Preface
Table of contents
List of illustrations
Introduction
Chapters
Glossaries
Appendices
References
Indices

(Technical reports and articles usually have a standard format as well. We discuss those later in this chapter.)

Familiarity with these structures enables you to get to specific information quickly. Less obviously, however, these conventions fit in with your unconscious anticipation of them. Your background knowledge of types of texts allows you to organize and accommodate each of these units as you encounter them. Knowledge about texts in French, for example, lets you know that they have the table of contents in the back, an approach that throws American readers a bit until they get used to it.

Usually, unknowingly, we bring a map or diagram of text with us when we read. The key is to recognize that we need to bring different maps to different text types, and to consciously select the appropriate reading strategy at the appropriate time. A molecular biology textbook requires you to select among all of your maps for (a) textbook, (b) biology, and (c) molecular biology. Not having a specific map for molecular biology will slow you down at first, but if you have a map for biology textbooks, you will quickly adapt your reading to this more specific text.

When you encounter a new text, it is immediately important to determine what kind of text it is (and thus the appropriate map). Obvious, right? But how can you do this? A title is not enough by itself, but pay attention to it. A cost accounting text is organized and presented differently from a tax accounting text. The title usually tells you which is which. Then examine the title page and its reverse, the copyright page. The first may give an additional subtitle that further clarifies the purpose and scope of the text, and the latter will give you an idea of how current the text is. Thirty-year-old tax accounting texts may not have quite what you are looking for. And even if it is assigned reading and you have no choice, it's still important to be aware of the timeliness of the content.

Some readers, especially inexperienced readers, tend to overlook or ignore information about the author. They figure, "What does it matter?" It matters. Note how many writers were involved, where they are from, what their credentials are, whether you know their other work. Part of developing expertise in your profession is discovering that it is a community in its own right, often much smaller and more intimate than you imagine. Writers also have their own purposes for writing texts. Who they are and where they come from are important clues to what they have to say about a topic and how they present it. Try to learn what you can about the authors of the books you read. You invest your time, your energy, and your money in a text. Get some idea of whom you're investing with.

Students also often overlook a book's preface entirely. It is invaluable. Prefaces set up the book as a whole. Look at the Preface for this book. Note in particular that it is written primarily to teachers; the Introduction, however, is written primarily to students. A book's preface usually specifies the audience and purpose the book aims at, provides a general scheme of what it contains, and reveals some things about the author(s). Prefaces are usually more informally written than the text proper. "Listen" to the preface's author in a relaxed mode. Also note who else has been involved in the creation of the text. Textbooks, especially, are often written collaboratively—by committee, to some extent. Before a textbook is printed, it has been reviewed and examined at several stages of development by other professionals in the discipline. Their critiques and input are taken seriously by the writer, or the book doesn't get published. The preface or an accompanying acknowledgments page notes who these people are. As you develop a sense of your discipline's "community," you will begin to recognize its prominent figures, whose involvement often indicates the text's merits.

Tables of contents are vitally important. Treat these as you would a map to a destination you're eager to reach. A table of contents is the outline, the blueprint, the schematic to the book as a whole. It lets you know where you're going and often gives you an idea of how rough the terrain is and how long it will take to get there. Having a sense of the topography and its relative distances is something you do all the time; consciously bring this facility to your sense of text.

The more specific the table of contents, the more encouraging. Text is organized on at least three levels:

- *Superordinate,* or top level, where the main ideas and "big pictures" reside
- *Ordinate,* or midlevel, where supporting ideas help develop, substantiate, and explain the main ideas
- *Subordinate,* or lower level, where detail, support, and evidence act to clarify, extend, and make concrete the arguments, concepts, theories, and other generalizations. Fact, example, definition, description, analogies, and other devices are often found at this level.

The table of contents should give you a sense of the text's organizational levels. Turn back to our Contents and note the format or typography of the unit and chapter headings. Inventory other features that might come in handy: items such as glossaries, lists of tables and illustrations, appendices, and indices are there because they make life easier for the reader, not the writer. Find out early if they're available, and use them.

Essentially, your first few minutes with any text should be physical. Look hard and thoroughly at it. Move through a lot of pages. Thumb quickly from front to back. Keep an eye out for illustrations, diagrams, and text displayed in boxes or sidebars. Try to assess chapter lengths and organizational plans. Develop a sensitivity to subheadings. Ask yourself these general questions about the text:

- What is the main purpose this text tries to address?

  ____

  ____

  ____

- What devices or strategies does it use?

  ____

  ____

  ____

- Who is the apparent audience for this text? How does this fit me as a reader?

  ____

  ____

  ____

- What kinds of strategies and devices do I need to use here to be a successful reader of this text?

___

___

___

- Why am I reading it?

___

___

___

You may have to get through the rest of our book to answer some of these questions, but now is the time to become sensitive to these concerns and to start identifying what you can. Although the last question may be answered as easily as "Because I have to," try to probe a little deeper. Ask yourself why you need to read, ignoring the immediate response, "to pass the course." Even better, ask yourself, "What can I gain from this text?"

Texts often have handy devices in each chapter or unit designed to forecast what is covered in that section. Variously called "Preview," "Chapter Outline," or "Overview," they act much like a table of contents does for the book as a whole. Many effective readers turn these into questions as a prereading quiz to identify what they already know—and don't know—about the chapter's topics. Use them to create a mental frame or map of what's ahead. As you read, you flesh out the ideas and materials you have been "warned" about. You also will have a better idea of what to look for, what's important.

Other, more discrete signals can help you make use of a text. The internal structure of chapters and segments within the text usually suggest the nature of the material you're responsible for. Common textbook arrangements involve enumeration (listing), temporality (chronology), comparison/contrast, cause/effect, and problem/solution. These *modes* of development, or ways of thinking, are key to understanding an author's intention. You may be familiar with them from high school and freshman composition courses. They occur in mass media texts as well. For example, Carl Sagan's now famous 1983 *Parade* magazine article "Nuclear War and Climatic Catastrophe: A Nuclear Winter" is clearly an instance of cause and effect—nuclear war will cause dramatic climate changes. *Consumer Reports* magazine is noted for its comparison/contrast approach in testing consumer goods. Recognizing a text's organizational approach helps you organize your understanding, retention, and response.

An initial difficulty nonexperts have with a specific discipline is its vocabulary. Technical reading is technical because it's filled with the field's jargon, often a whole new vocabulary comprising long, foreign-looking, difficult-to-pronounce words. Even everyday terms are not used the way we use them every day, but have highly specific and specialized meanings. Some of the "reading" is not even in words but is presented as drawings, tables, charts, or formulas. The more expert you become in your field, the more proficient you will become as a specialized reader in that field. It is one of the ways you become an authority or expert. Your vocabulary will develop just like muscle—you use it, you get it; you don't, you won't.

Developing this new proficiency as an expert reader in your field is one reason you are in school. Course work and textbooks are designed (theoretically) to help you build this proficiency. Developing your sense of field-specific terminology, or vocabulary, constitutes one part of the process. Most of us, however, gave up vocabulary lessons in the seventh or eighth grade and are loath to begin them again. In some instances, we may be stuck with memorization: the tried and true flashcards can help. But now you also have purpose and context for your vocabulary building. You'll be able to identify the words you need to know by the frequency of their occurrence. Many texts have mini-dictionaries, or specialized glossaries, in the front or the back. And indices not only are handy tools for finding things fast, but they are also helpful in developing your command of terminology. An index will get you to a term, word, or name in a context, or better yet, a variety of contexts. These devices are in a text because they make a text more useful. Proficient readers are proficient not necessarily because they are smarter than everybody else, but because they take advantage of the tools writers and texts make available to them.

There are instances, of course, when even good readers get into trouble. Sometimes it's the writer's fault: poor organization, misperceived audience, a badly constructed purpose, and many other things can go wrong with the text itself. Sometimes you don't have the background, and you find yourself over your head in a particular content area. Don't give up. Researchers have identified a number of techniques that good readers use in dealing with text that makes little sense, regardless of the reason. In such circumstances, they:

1. Ignore the troublesome passage or word, and read on
2. Suspend their judgment until clarification occurs
3. Begin to form tentative hypotheses that reconcile the confusing or unclear material
4. Reread selected sentences to check for clues that they missed
5. Reread chunks of text to try to solve the difficulty from context
6. Go to an outside authority such as another text, an instructor, or other experts in the field

(adapted from Collins and Smith)

Note that each step becomes increasingly disruptive to the overall reading process as the reader increasingly moves out of and away from the text. Note also that each step requires increasingly complex behavior, which means more energy expended and more cognitive clutter. But also note that step 1 is the most frequently used. Many readers won't admit it, but skipping particularly difficult, obtuse, or badly written material often solves the problem. If the material is essential, later references will probably clear up your difficulty. The best approach is to get through the entire reading first, then come back and puzzle out what you didn't get.

Another way of dealing with any kind of reading, but especially helpful with troublesome or difficult material, is to seek out parallel or supplemental sources. We're not talking *Cliff's Notes*. Parallel texts are those that address the same topics, have the same purposes, and use similar arrangements. Supplemental texts provide more material, perhaps much more than you need or want. They are often listed under headings such as "Additional Readings," "References," "Works Cited," or "Bibliography." Specialized dictionaries and manuals are necessary accompaniments for most professionals. Start collecting and using them now.

Getting a double dose of the same topic may seem excessive, but often different texts present the same information more accessibly. Professionals interested in business and government, for instance, read the *Wall Street Journal*, *Fortune*, and other publications, usually as many as they have time for, rarely relying on one source or method of presenting information. As unique as we all are, what works for some may not work as well for others, so find a text on the material that works for you. Ask an instructor or colleague for additional material, consult with other instructors teaching the same course, investigate in the library, or browse in the bookstore. Most often you're responsible for understanding the material in a text, not the text itself. If the text is not working for you, get some help. To get you in the habit, list below several additional or alternate text materials that will help you in a course you're currently studying:

1. ____

____

2. ____

____

3. ____

____

4. ____

____

UNDERSTANDING THE READER

The individual, the context, and the type of text all affect reading and how it is accomplished, but certain features of a reader's process are common enough among most readers to discuss briefly. Reading specialists pretty much agree that readers share the cognitive features of background knowledge, comprehension, and habits and attitudes.

Background Knowledge

Learning and reading theorists increasingly point to the importance of background, or prior, knowledge as key to any type of reading. This background knowledge is what a reader knows before encountering a text. Every reader has it. Background knowledge involves the history, the training, the education, and the cultural experiences you bring to a text. It encompasses any previous experience you have had with a particular text type, its content, and the way the material is presented. Some cultures, for instance, view the constellation Sagittarius—a kind of visual text—as an outline of an archer, whereas others view it as a teapot. Our experiences and perceptions help determine the shape each of us sees in the text.

Background knowledge is especially critical in encounters with advanced texts in a particular discipline. A student in first-semester statistics will have trouble with hypergeometric distribution. But that's because that beginning student lacks the understanding of basic principles and vocabulary necessary to readily follow this more advanced concept.

Background knowledge is cumulative. It is an activity automatically brought to any task, and one that is continually engaged. Furthermore, it is continually expanding and recursive, as opposed to linear. As you encounter text, especially new text, you add to your background knowledge; or in many cases, you alter existing knowledge to accommodate this new material. How any of us does this is still greatly disputed by cognitive theorists who study such things. In essence, however, background knowledge reinforces Heraclitus's idea that you can't step in the same river twice. After you have read a text, you will be different. How different—and in what ways—depends on you, the text, and how you've read it.

Comprehension

Comprehension is, to be simplistic, what you understand about the text you have read or are reading, and what you do with this understanding. Comprehension is highly dependent on background knowledge and at its various stages determines what you turn new background knowledge into. Fairly common agreement among reading researchers suggests that three basic levels of comprehension exist during most reading activities:

- *Literal*: Our understanding at this level most closely approximates the actual text. It provides us with the *gist* or an overall sense of what the writer is attempting to convey.
- *Interpretive*: We integrate and infer at this stage. It is our understanding of what is between the lines.
- *Applied*: At this, the most complex level, we respond, react, and express. We go beyond the lines of the text, incorporating and accommodating it and its content into our background knowledge.

As readers, we move continually among these levels as we encounter text. Our emphasis in this book is on operating at the applied level, where experts operate when they encounter text in their discipline.

Obviously, this is a simplified and somewhat compressed presentation, but we think it gives you an idea of the cognitive activity underlying your reading. You are far from passive when you read. How active you are, however, is relative. Good readers are quite busy when they pick up a text and attempt to use it. Understanding some of the strategies and techniques of good readers will lead you to more fully explore your own reading process, and by doing so, make the time you devote to your reading more effective.

Habits and Attitudes

Of critical importance, and commonly overlooked by readers, are the attitudes they bring to a reading task. The very word *task*, often used euphemistically to describe something that needs to be done when we would rather be doing something else, connotes an attitude toward reading. Often you're reading because someone, likely an instructor, has told you to do so. People mostly resent being told what to do and would many times rather be doing other things than reading three chapters on agrarian land reform in Latin America. Think positively about the assignment if you can; if you can't, be aware that you resent this particular reading task—and that your resentment will cut your reading effectiveness.

Habits are a big part of attitude. We develop habits of reading, which help shape our attitudes toward what we read. An effective technique to improve your reading is to be aware of the habits you read with. Take a moment and describe below what your habits are when you read:

____

____

____

Now read on and see if your habits can stand some modification. We'll try not to get too prescriptive or dictatorial about what you should do. We understand that people require different environments and have different habits when they read. But it's important for you to become aware of yours. Then experiment with some alternate habits we suggest.

Note, first, that different kinds of reading may require different habits. Darwin's *Origin of Species* requires a different kind of attention than Kachigan's *Statistical Analysis*. Second, establish your most effective habits for the task at hand and replicate them as often as possible when you read. A favorite chair, a special lamp, a time of day—habituate yourself to reading. Once you've established a pattern, you can concentrate on what you are reading, not how or where. Think about the following suggestions, but do so in relation to what you already do. Some of our points may seem obvious, but we are continually amazed at the number of readers who are oblivious (or pretend to be) to the habits they bring to reading:

- Establish a comfortable air temperature: too warm can make you drowsy; too cool can make you numb. Bright, overhead lighting causes glare on the page, which can strain your eyes.
- Know what sustenance you need to ease the task, be it coffee, soft drinks, munchies, or whatever.
- Find a space where noise and movement are kept at a minimum. Some professionals arrive at their desks an hour early to get the quiet (and first cup of coffee) they need to get the essential reading of the day done.
- Try also to read in a nonreclining position. Sleep specialists suggest bed is for two things and reading is not one of them. Besides, active readers need to be in a position to write when they read.

Now, reconsider your description of surroundings. Using the questions below as guidelines, compare what you wrote with our pointers. Begin by looking closely at the environment you choose to read in. Inventory your conditions:

- What is the Climate?

____

____

____

- What is the Lighting?

____

____

____

• What are the Accompaniments?

____

____

____

• How is the Quiet?

____

____

____

Our little acronym, CLAQ, queries the obvious. Yet, we invariably find readers at the swimming pool frustrated at their efforts to get through a text. Harsh lighting, the heat, sweat dripping on the pages, splashes from the pool, and other easily imagined distractions create poor conditions for any kind of serious reading and digesting of material.

Also, read with a little foresight. Plan your approach to a text. Most instructors give adequate time for you to digest the material (whether you think so is another matter). Professionals, however, rarely have enough time. But both instructors and bosses rely on you to develop your own means of getting done what needs to be done. Most texts are broken into units that can help you manage your time. Allocate these units within your time constraints. Break the assignment into "chunks," easily digestible "meals." Simple arithmetic on your part and the natural divisions found in most texts can ease a lot of the anxiety and frustration of trying to get through two hundred pages of, say, Hegel's *Phenomenology of Mind* in one shot. Writers work in small chunks when producing what you read; as a reader you should allow yourself to consume in the same way. One of Edgar Allan Poe's rules for writing a short story was that it could be read in one sitting. Determine what you can *effectively* read in one sitting and then manage your time accordingly.

Once you have your physical approach to reading well in hand and are faced with a particular reading task, consider your attitudes toward the writer. The writer has an agenda. Whether it is to make an argument, convey information, train you in a methodology, or some other aspect of your professional study, the text has a purpose. That purpose and its means of achievement may be at odds with your experiences, ideas, and beliefs. You don't have to believe everything you read. Recognize that a text has an effect on you. It may be one you want, or it may not. The adage seen on bumper stickers, "Question Authority," applies to texts as well. A caution, however. Be prepared to defend and support your exceptions. "It was gross," as one student commented about Margaret Mead's *Coming of Age in Samoa*, is neither criticism nor very articulate opinion.

Finally, when you've done all that we've just suggested, stop for a minute and consider a little thing called "motivation." Learning theorists and researchers continually point to its value. Successful learning does not take place without motivation. You bring it with you to the task. Or develop it as you go. Or never have it. But it is helpful to acknowledge to yourself how motivated or unmotivated you are. All of this advice and all of this technique about reading won't help until you want it to.

The following questions will help you better understand yourself as a reader. Answer them in the context of the course you're currently enrolled in:

1. What background knowledge do I bring to this course?

   ____

   ____

   ____

2. What is my familiarity with the text I'm expected to read?

   ____

   ____

   ____

3. What comprehension levels are expected of me in this reading?

   ____

   ____

   ____

4. What kind of environment is most appropriate for me as a reader of this kind of material?

   ____

   ____

   ____

5. How is this material valid and appropriate for my needs? Invalid and inappropriate?

   ____

   ____

   ____

6. What are my attitudes and reactions?
   - Positives: ______________________________

   ____

- Negatives: ____

____

7. What are my motivations?

____

____

____

AN ADDENDUM: READING AND THE NEW TECHNOLOGIES

The current explosion of computer use dramatically changes how we encounter text. Rapid increase in the use of e-mail, electronic bulletin boards, the World Wide Web, and interactive CD-ROM texts all push information at us in startling ways. One thing in common among all these technologies, however, is that they involve a reader interacting with a text. Research is only now beginning to address what these new technologies are doing to how we read, but as we move "on-line" with texts, we must bring some of the same critical awareness of what we're doing and why to the reading tasks expected of us.

Although we are still a long way away from abandoning reliance on paper texts, evidence suggests that some traditional print texts are being replaced by electronic ones. And we'll be honest: at this point, we're not able to offer you a great deal of specific help. However, we believe that, although the texts themselves are changing in their appearance and delivery, readers are somewhat slower to adapt. We are reasonably sure, also, that the same principles and strategies that critical and attentive readers bring to paper texts will work for you in your encounters with electronic texts.

▶ 9

Writing and Drawing in the Margins

Overview

Annotating

Visual Writing: Shifting Words to Pictures

Model Building
Outlining
Flowcharting

So far we have discussed how reading works. This chapter presents writing strategies you can use to get a better understanding of the material you read. Later we focus on writing activities that are physically separate from your reading; summaries, abstracts, précis, and journal or notebook writing usually are done on separate sheets of paper. For now, we demonstrate writing strategies that take only a small space, often just the margin at the top or bottom or alongside the text you're reading. Because these strategies are used *as you read*, it's important that you pick up a pen or pencil whenever you pick up a text to read it. Now is a good time to get in the habit. Grab a pencil and read on.

Before we explore these writing strategies, one note of caution. We recommend these writing strategies because we believe they are valuable resources for understanding what you read. But we strongly recommend you only use them on materials *you own*. Nothing is more disconcerting and distracting to a library user than to find someone else's notes in the margins. For books you don't own, use the strategies we'll show you in the next two chapters. Or, use photocopies from a text. (Some enterprising students we know even photocopy standard size pages onto oversize sheets so they have even more margin to write in.) Once the copy is yours, don't hesitate to write your way to better understanding.

ANNOTATING

Many students rely on colored markers to highlight words or sentences as they read. Highlighting is a convenient way to set off a passage of text, and the makers of these pens are happy you use them. But have you ever gone back later to review your highlighting only to discover that you have no idea why you marked something? Worse yet is to look back later and realize you've painted half the text. At that point, who knows what's really important?

Here are some simple, immediate cures to this happy highlighting syndrome:

- Write the key term in the margin next to its highlighted definition.
- Identify a sentence that summarizes a paragraph or larger unit as "summary."
- Label essential ideas as "key."

We've modeled some of these types of notations later in this chapter to show you how some readers might do it.

Though they take very little time, adding these brief notes improves your reading and understanding in several ways. First, jotting a word or two in the margin is an effective memory tool; your notes help connect larger chunks—what you highlight—with smaller, more manageable chunks of information. Second, these little notes also provide excellent reference marks when you're scanning through the text later to find that certain word or idea. Like a thumb-index on the side of a dictionary, one- or two-word marginal notes get you where you want to go faster. Finally, and most important, if you train yourself to add these comments each time you highlight something, you're less likely to merrily paint your way through the book.

But annotation, as this process is called, has much more potential as a reading strategy than merely labeling a marked word or sentence. One of the more fascinating aspects of reading is that, no matter how many times we read a passage, each time we read, our reactions to it change a little bit. Additional knowledge, a new perspective, a seemingly unrelated conversation, even a good night's sleep—because they change our context, these factors change the way we react to a text and what we get out of it. Sometimes, too, reading brings us moments of insight. While reading a geometry book at age twelve, Albert Einstein penciled in the margin, "The proof makes no sense, because if we can assume that these prismatic spaces are capable of being flattened out, we could just as well say it of the cylinder" (Hoffman 23).

Active readers, like the young Einstein, keep track of their perceptions by writing comments about the passage in the margin. Like the dialectical notebook we describe in the next chapter, this type of annotation is an effective way for one piece of writing (your comments) to "talk" to another (the text). The key is to capture your responses immediately, before they get away. If a sentence or paragraph leaves you wondering about reasons, ask "why?" in the margin; if you disagree with an opinion in your reading, write a counterargument. When you come back later, you may find the writer has convinced you to agree, or you may be able to answer your original question. Conversely, you may still disagree or have additional questions. Experienced readers recognize these nagging marginal notes as a rich source for potential research and writing topics. The ongoing conversation between the text and your comments gives you the opportunity to respond to what you read and, later, to respond to your responses. It's a helpful way to work through a difficult piece of reading.

Such comment annotations also have other practical uses. Part of becoming expert in a field is discovering when, how, and why to ask questions. Yet many students are afraid to practice this skill, at least out loud. They may believe their peers understand everything and they'll look "stupid" by asking. Some may even believe that old adage, "It's better to be silent and thought a fool than to open one's mouth and remove all doubt." Clever, but untrue. Still others may not have *formulated* their questions yet when the opportunity to ask is offered.

Writing comment annotations as you read is a good way to identify areas you need or want to ask about. When you reread them later, you may be able to answer your own questions. That's a good way to get a better understanding on your own. But if you're still not sure what the writer means, or why, or how it all fits together, you'll be ready to ask. And chances are pretty good that other readers will have had similar questions.

In a later chapter, we discuss writing summaries, abstracts, and précis as methods for condensing a longer piece of text. Making annotations is also a particularly helpful tool for generating these. As you read, you can use one-word annotations to identify the major topics that need to be mentioned in your summary or précis. When you finish reading a section, say a chapter or article, collect your annotations into a list in the margin, if there's room, or on a page of your notebook. Your list will provide a topic outline of the passage and from there, you can begin to draft your abstract.

Just as you may want to use annotations to identify the content of a passage you're reading, you can also use marginal notes to clarify the structure. Besides the larger and more obvious clues about structure—title page, preface, table of contents, and chapter overviews—that provide a roadmap of a text, writers very often give readers a more detailed set of signposts to guide them through individual passages. For example, if you see a sentence like this one that begins "For example," you have certain expectations about the rest of that sentence. Although writers sometimes choose to set off lists of points by numbering them, at other times they may choose to embed the list in a passage. In that case, you'll likely find words such as *first, second, finally,* or *one reason* followed by *another reason.*

The complex texts you read often include complex chains of these cues to help guide you through the material. But these signposts won't do you any good if you don't see them. Make them stand out by noting them in the margin. At the beginning of a list, jot a word or two to let you know what's in the list: *reasons, examples,* or perhaps *arguments.* Then, add a number and a one-word note in the margin next to each item as it comes up. Like the other types of annotation we've discussed, these signposts work both as a memory aid and as a quick reference tool. You might use them to generate a summary, or just to find your way through a passage.

Every reader/writer uses annotations slightly differently. After you've done it for a while, you'll develop abbreviations and strategies of your own that make your notes unique. (That's one reason we don't want you to annotate materials you don't own; your notes wouldn't make sense to someone else anyway.) In each paragraph below, we've illustrated a different type of annotation: identification notes, comments and questions, and content outline. You'll recognize these paragraphs from earlier in this unit. Turn back to them, look at your own annotations, and compare them with ours. These are not the "right" ways or the only ways to write in the margins. But they should suggest techniques that will work for you.

Identification Notes

Reading is one of the more complex kinds of critical thinking we commonly engage in. What we do with the information and how we extract that information are affected by our purpose for reading. The design of the text we read also affects our response, sometimes as much as our purpose for reading it. The substance of the text, its content, is another feature. Our capabilities are another; they are called into question continually every time we encounter a text. Our experience with a particular kind of text and its content also affects our response. A lot to manage, and yet, when was the last course you took on how to read? Beyond

READING = complex things that affect rdng:

Good Point

elementary school, most of us are expected not only to know how to read, but to be proficient readers, and to get even better at it.

Content Outline

Types of context:

1) Temporal = where you are

2.) Spatial = social, cult., historical

3) Causal = time + space + purpose

EXAMPLE

Usually categorized as temporal, spatial, causal, or some combination of all three, context is created by the environment around you and the myriad of purposes in and for such an environment. *Temporal context* is where you are at a given time. It can be as simply distinguished as beginning, middle, or end. *Spatial context* encompasses the social, the cultural, the historical. *Milieu* is a fancy word for it. It exists because, in the words of John Donne, no man (or woman, for that matter) is an island. No reader, writer, or text is independent of his, her, or its sources and origins. *Causal context* grows out of the interaction of time and space. Yet, it is distinct because it directly links to purposes. For instance, a poster in a vacuum cleaner store proclaims "Hoover sucks." Such a poster has a much different purpose to its message in a Hoover outlet than in an Electrolux or Kirby store because a particular context exists in each store. Discovering the contexts--temporal, spatial, causal--can take you a long way toward enhancing your understanding of text.

Comments and Questions

BKGRND KNOWL: an activity?

Cumulative & altering

hmm.

Background knowledge is cumulative. It is an activity automatically brought to any task, and one that is continually engaged. Furthermore, it is continually expanding and recursive, as opposed to linear. As you encounter text, especially new text, you add to your background knowledge, or in many cases, you alter existing knowledge to accommodate this new material. How any of us does this is still greatly disputed by cognitive theorists who study such things. In essence, however, background knowledge reinforces

Can't see same movie again, either

```
Heraclitus's idea that you can't step in the same
river twice. After you have read a text, you will
be different. How different--and in what ways--
depends on you, the text, and how you've read it.
```

VISUAL WRITING: SHIFTING WORDS TO PICTURES

An architect's business card includes a drawing of a T–square and triangle. A wheelchair figure on a door means accessibility. Road signs indicate construction zones, S–curves, and crossing areas for trains, pedestrians, deer, cattle. We are surrounded by visual writing, pictures that represent words or ideas. We "read" these visual texts quickly, almost unconsciously.

You can use similar strategies as you read to shift words on a page into images that make the text more concise, easier to remember, more understandable. As with all of the strategies we discuss, some of these visual writing techniques will work more effectively for you than others; some will only work with certain types of texts. But becoming acquainted with them, trying them out, adapting them, is yet another way to become a more effective reader.

Model Building

In *The Double Helix: A Personal Account of the Discovery of the Structure of DNA*, James D. Watson describes the process that led to the discovery of the structure of DNA, deoxyribonucleic acid. Unless you've read *The Double Helix*, you might imagine Watson and his colleague, Francis Crick, shuffling about a lab in white smocks, beakers in hand, Bunsen burners flaring, searching for the structure of DNA. But that's not how Watson describes their discovery. Instead, he explains that their Nobel prize–winning breakthrough came, in part, from "drawing the fused rings of adenine [one element of the DNA molecule] on paper" (116). Later, these "doodles," as Watson calls them, became cardboard cutouts that could be shifted into different patterns. Finally, precisely measured metal models were built; these models ultimately confirmed the plausibility of Watson and Crick's mental image of DNA's double helical structure.

But you don't have to be a Nobel prize winner to doodle, or to understand the usefulness of model building. As you read, your mind often conjures up an image to represent the information in the text. Reading further, and still holding that image in your mind, you try to mentally add labels, move the pieces around, add or delete pieces, or flip the image over for another perspective. So you are effectively doing three things at once: reading, imagining your mental picture, and modifying that image according to the developing information in the text. We're all adept at this marvelous juggling act. We do it constantly. But it's not the most effective way to understand what you read.

Like a personal computer, your brain has only so much memory space to use at a given time. If you can just clear out the section occupied by the mental picture, you free it up for other important tasks such as reading and comprehending the text. Suppose that you pause briefly to make a quick sketch of your mental picture, right beside the text. Now you no longer have to hold quite as much information in your head. And because the drawing is down on paper, you can add labels to it and change its shape according to the text you're reading. You no longer have to devote valuable mental processing space to your internal image. More important, that image has become more permanent, something you can glance at months later and instantly remind yourself of all the information stored in the written text.

This technique—whether you call it "doodling" or "model building"—may not be what you usually think of as writing. But if you look around, you'll notice it everywhere: on students' notebooks, artists' sketchpads, even executives' cocktail napkins. Sometimes writers recognize their readers' need for a visual image to help them understand. We've included a couple of models in the previous chapter when discussing how reading works. But not all writers provide models, and not all models that writers provide will work for you. In fact, as with other writing strategies we describe throughout this book, creating your own model is more helpful than relying on someone else's.

Below is a model that two students in an education course developed together to help them understand a particularly important—but equally difficult—concept from the writings of Russian psychologist L. S. Vygotsky. This is the text they read, Vygotsky's definition of the "zone of proximal development":

> . . . the zone of proximal development . . . is the distance between the actual developmental level as determined by independent problem solving and the level of potential development as determined through problem solving under adult guidance or in collaboration with more capable peers. (86)

Although you may not fully comprehend their model, we think you'll agree that it's somewhat easier to understand than the text. And a lot easier to remember.

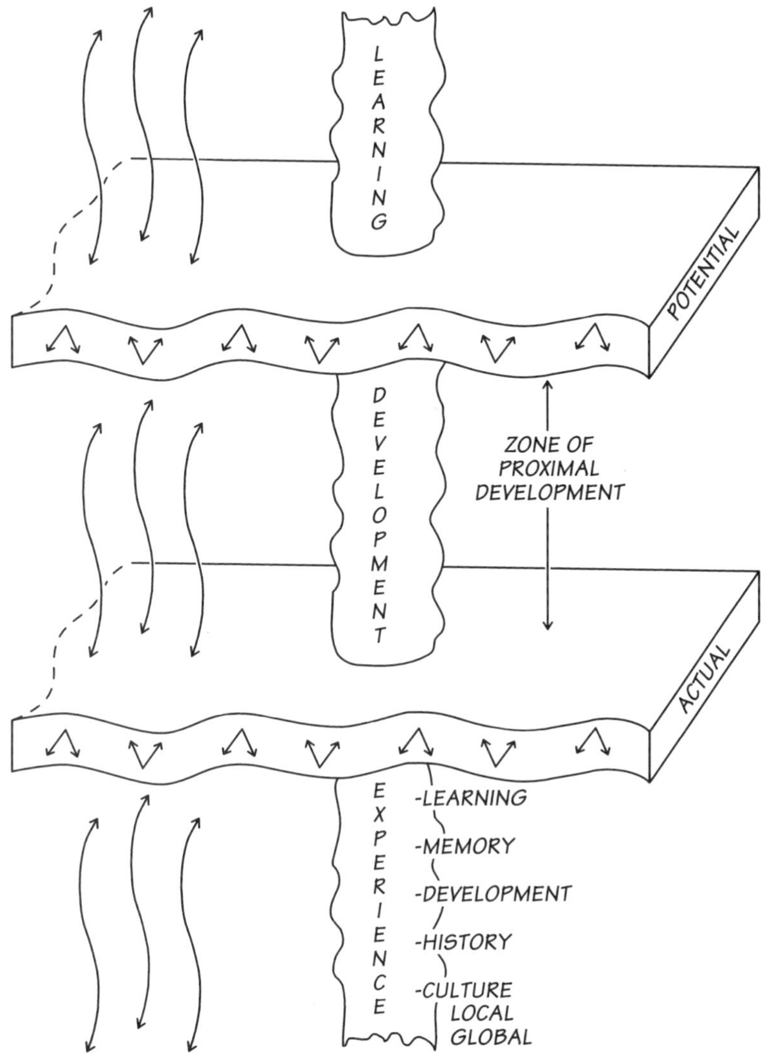

FIGURE 9.1 Model of Vygotsky's Zone of Proximal Development

Outlining

Almost everyone is familiar with outlining, especially the more traditional type. Many of us remember when making an outline was considered the first step in any writing task. (Many of us also remember "fudging." We did the outline last, after the writing was done, because it was a lot easier to outline something that existed instead of something we doubted would ever exist.) Outlining can be a very useful tool for writing. For the moment, though, we'll illustrate how you can use your outlining skills to become a more effective reader.

A formal outline of this section of our discussion might look something like this:

I. Visual Writing: Shifting Words to Pictures

A. Introduction
B. Model Building

1. What it is
2. Why to use it

C. Outlining

1. Traditional outlining

a. What it looks like
b. How to use it
c. What it's good for

2. Less formal outlining

a.
b.
c.

From this outline, you can quickly identify the elements and the structure of our discussion. And because it is so formal—that is, it follows a very set form—you can also predict with some assurance and accuracy what will fit in slots a., b., and c. of subpoint C. 2.:

2. Less formal outlining

a. What it looks like
b. How to use it
c. What it's good for

Formal outlines can be very helpful generating tools for writing a summary or abstract, which we discuss later. Once you've outlined the text to be summarized, you can choose which levels of the outline to include in your abstract. The lower you reach in the levels of your outline for information, the more detailed—and longer—your abstract will become.

This type of outline also works well for making a table of contents or reference guide to a passage you're reading. By adding paragraph numbers, or page numbers if you're outlining a long article or book, you can build yourself an "index" for later reference. Both of these uses work particularly well in conjunction with annotating.

The value of formal outlining is that it collapses a long text into a much shorter space. At the same time, though, an outline retains the shape and content of the original text. And because you decide how detailed to make your outline, you can expand and contract it according to the amount of understanding you have. For example, if you're outlining a particularly difficult passage of a long text, you might want to expand your outline of that section into sentences. Where your understanding is much clearer, you may only need words or short phrases to capture the essence of a passage.

Another outline of this section of our discussion, a less formal type, might look like this:

Visual Writing

Intro

Model Building

Outlining

1. Traditional	Appearance	Structured
	Uses	Generate summary
		Build road map
	Value	Shortens longer text
		Flexible
2. Less formal	Appearance	? (No rules)
	Uses	Reorganize ideas
		Highlight specific points
	Value	Completely flexible
		Personal

As you can see, this type of outlining is not governed by the "rules" usually associated with formal outlines.

If you were to outline this same section of text, your outline would likely be different because you would focus on different elements. For instance, you might rearrange the information to set off Value from Appearance and Uses, like this:

	Appearance	**Uses**	**Value**
Traditional	Structured	Generate summary Build road map	Shortens longer text Flexible (expand/contract)

Less Formal	? (no rules)	Reorganize ideas Highlight specific points	Completely flexible Personal

Because this type of outlining encourages the flexibility to create a *personal* image from the text, it also allows you to rearrange the information from that text in a way that suits your needs and understanding. As in the example just given, you might want to highlight a specific aspect by setting it

p. 33 – Phaedrus (p. 152)
p. 25 – Chautauqua
p. 24 – writer
p. 65 – description (p86)
p. 84 – reason
p. 93 – scientific method
p. 93 – writing to solve problems
p. 98 – Einstein
p. 121 – Pirsig comments on this Book
p. 123 – teachers/students
p. 126 – Zen
p. 129 – teaching college
p. 134 – dogma
p. 144 – welding; power over metal
p. 145 – instructors
p. 153 – essays
*p. 156 – freshman rhetoric
p. 161 – university rhetoric
p. 162 – correctness
p. 170 – 500 essay about U.S.
p. 172 – Evils of imitations
p. 176 – grades of knowledge
p. 185 – definitions
p. 189 – goals
p. 190 – esthetics
p. 191 – quality in writing
p. 224 – freshman composition
p. 229 – pioneers
p. 231 – religion, art, science
p. 232 – Poincaré
p. 247 – care: quality
p. 247 – Christ letter to mom
p. 249 – cognitive overload (process)
p. 260 – technology ↔ art
p. 261 – quality and tech.
p. 264 – quality and peace of mind.
p. 265 – value quietness
p. 272 – gumption

"The real cycle you're working on is a cycle called 'yourself.' "

The study of the art of motorcycle maintenance is really a miniature study of the art of rationality itself. Working on a motorcycle, working well, caring, is to become part of a process, to achieve an inner peace of mind. The motorcycle is primarily a mental phenomenon.

–Robert M. Pirsig

p. 288 – Mu
p. 293 – cycle called youself
p. 304 – composition was
p. 306 – style Phaedrus field
p. 315 – Logos vs myths
p. 324 – Aristotle dull generalization
p. 325 – chart this Duane
p. 326 – structuralism
p. 331 – Coleridge
p. 343 – horgeness
p. 344 – "Poor Rhetoric"
p. 346 – Phaedrus
p. 353 – generations **

p. 162 "itsy-bitsy rules"
p. 162 "table manners"

FIGURE 9.2 Personal Index for *Zen and the Art of Motorcycle Maintenance*

off to one side. Or you might mark with a star or a bullet different key features so that you can focus on them when you review your outline later.

The possibilities for using and adapting outlines are only as limited as your imagination. Try outlining an article or a section of a book you're reading for a class—perhaps even an entire book. Figure 9.2 shows how one reader outlined Robert Pirsig's *Zen and the Art of Motorcycle Maintenance*. This outline has really become the reader's index, written on the inside of the front cover. Each item refers to a page in the text where a marginal annotation, a label that corresponds to the word or phrase here, identifies a passage on the topic. A quick glance at his outline will tell you what topics this reader was most interested in.

Flowcharting

If you have studied computer programming or organizational structures, you probably are familiar with flowcharts, the diagrams programmers and managers use to plan and modify programs and work flow. If you have managed to avoid these areas, you are still familiar with the concept of flowcharting. Any time you follow a set of directions for any procedure—a recipe, assembly instructions for a child's toy—you are following a flowchart. We usually think of flowcharts as representing a series of actions that must, or at least should, be done in a particular order. But they can also represent other types of logic besides chronology. Cause and effect relationships, a standard element of much historical writing, can also be captured effectively in a flowchart.

Just as computer programmers use them to put together a text, you can use flowcharts as you read to take apart a text. Here are two example texts and flowcharts to illustrate what we mean. The first is a description of the Battle of Agincourt in 1415 between an English army, led by Henry V, and a much larger French force. We supply a chronological flowchart; try drawing a model of the battlefield to help you visualize the battle.

At dawn on 25 October both armies had been in position all night. . . . The French, whose 25,000 included 15,000 mounted knights, drew their riders up in five ranks, the first two ranks dismounted, with a few crossbowmen in among them. The English formed three groups, four ranks deep, of dismounted men-at-arms, with wedges of archers between them. On the wings, facing inward, were two more groups of archers. For four hours nobody moved. The French knights were arguing about whether or not to charge, and by 11 a.m. there was a lot of jostling and pushing. . . . No knight wanted to be in the second rank at the charge. . . .

DAWN
Fr. = 25,000
in 5 ranks

Eng. = 3 groups
4 ranks ea.
2 grps archers

4 HRS
No movement
11:00 A.M.
Fr. arguing

> Meanwhile Henry had moved his men forward to within bowshot of the French, about 300 yards away. . . . Still the French shoved and muttered, but did not move. Henry decided to make their minds up for them, and ordered his archers to fire into the air. Arrows from a thousand bows rained on the French, galling the horses and wounding the tightly packed mass. Suddenly, the French charged, apparently without any central order, straight across the mud at the English. This time Henry's archers fired for the horses, bringing down riders in their hundreds. Many suffocated in the mud . . . ; many others were dispatched by English archers running forward to slide a knife between the joints in their armour. In half an hour it was over. (Burke 59–61)

Eng. move forward.

Eng. fire arrows into Fr.

Fr. charge w/o order

Eng. archers kill horses & riders

11:30 A.M Battle over

This next example describes the series of events, and effects, that followed a single action, the building of the High Aswan dam on the Nile River in Egypt. The dam was intended to do two things: to collect and regulate water for irrigation and to produce electric power. In addition to our cause–effect flowchart on page 141, you might use the margin to annotate the structure of this text.

> First, the plain has been deprived of the annual fertilization by flooding that served it so well for five thousand years. . . . Now the Egyptians will have to add artificial fertilizer to the former floodplains of the Nile—which will cost money.
>
> Second, controlled irrigation without periodic flushing salinates the soil, bit by bit. There are methods for correcting this, but they too cost money. . . .
>
> Third, the sardine catch in the eastern Mediterranean has diminished from 18,000 tons a year to 400 tons, a 97 percent loss, because the sea is now deprived of floodborne nutrients. . . .
>
> Fourth, the rich delta of the Nile is being eroded away by storms on the Mediterranean. In the past, a nearly "steady state" existed between the deposition of silt by the river and the erosion of it by the sea, with a slight positive balance in favor of deposition, which gradually extended the farmlands of Egypt. With deposition brought to a virtual halt, the balance is now negative and Egypt is losing land.
>
> Fifth, schistosomiasis (a fearsomely debilitating disease) has greatly increased in the Nile valley. The disease organism depends on snails, which depend on a steady supply of water, which constant

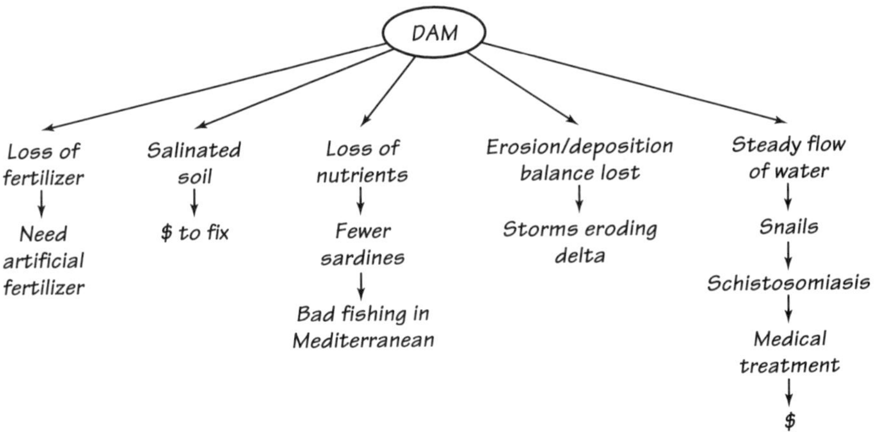

FIGURE 9.3 Flowchart

> irrigation furnishes but annual flooding does not. Of course, medical control of the disease is possible—but that too costs money. (Hardin 40–41)

We encourage you to write in this text a lot. Use all the white space available to write annotations, sketch models, and draw flowcharts. Doing so will help you understand and remember what you read. And it might even make your reading more enjoyable. So, please write in this book.

▶ 10

Creating Journals while Reading

Overview

Dialectical Entries

Résumé/Curriculum Vitae

Graphic Representations

Genealogies
Time Lines/Chronologies

Throughout this book we suggest ways to use writing as a tool for creating as well as conveying your understanding. In this chapter, you'll learn how to use writing to help you read materials—textbooks, scholarly journals, and the like—more effectively. The activities and strategies in this chapter usually require some space to develop and expand. Therefore, we recommend that you get in the habit of collecting them in some systematic way, which we call a reading journal. It really doesn't matter how you house your journal. (There are many names for such collections, from *learning log*, to *commonplace book*, to *reading diary*. We've simply chosen to use *journal*.) You may want to use a spiral notebook so it's easy to keep all of your reading activities in one convenient place. Or you may wish to use loose-leaf paper in a three-ring binder so that you can easily remove and reinsert pages. Or, if you love to do everything on computer, you may want to keep printouts in a pocket folder.

DIALECTICAL ENTRIES

The word *dialectical* is related to the word *dialectic*, but they have nothing to do with dialects. A dialectic is a method for getting at the truth by comparing/contrasting two sides of an issue. The philosopher Hegel proposed dialectic as a critical thinking tool by using the components thesis, antithesis, and synthesis to solve a problem or to analyze an idea.

Many people have found dialectical journal entries among the most effective strategies for reflecting on ideas—especially those found in reading materials. Ann Berthoff has developed this into a strategy that begins by first drawing a vertical line down the middle of a page—or a computer screen. At the top of the left half of the page, write the heading *Reading Notes*. At the top on the right side, write the heading *Comments and Questions* (see Figure 10.1). Above these two headings you may wish to note the date of the entry so you can keep track of the history of your thinking. You should also make some bibliographic note so you don't forget which piece of reading is the subject of your entry. This also helps you practice following a style sheet and can be used later to build a works cited/references list.

The blank dialectical entry below will give you a visual image to guide you as you create your own entries. You might use it to record responses to something in this book—or something you're reading in another textbook.

You may wish to record reading notes on the left side of the page while you read or after you have read the piece once. Or you may wish to do both.

Dialectical Entry

Reading ______________________________ Date ____________

Reading Notes	Comments/Questions

FIGURE 10.1 Blank Dialectical Entry

The advantage of recording notes *while* you're reading is that you are able to record ideas while they're fresh in your mind—before they escape you.

The guiding principle for writing comments and questions on the right side of the page is to jot them down as they occur to you. You'll find that your comments and questions will appear at all sorts of times. Some of them, of course, will occur as you read, before you even record a reading note on the left side of the page. Some will occur as you're writing a note. Others may come to you as you're listening to a class lecture or participating in a discussion. And still others may occur at odd moments: while walking to school, while eating dinner, while lying in bed. Whenever they occur, though, you need to catch them before they slip away—perhaps forever.

Here's the dialectical entry that a student, Mike, did as he was beginning to read Thomas Kuhn's *The Structure of Scientific Revolutions*:

Reading Notes	Comments/Questions
"Attempting to discover the source of that difference led me to recognize scientific achievements that for a time provide model problems and solutions to a community of practitioners" (p. viii).	Here Kuhn says that paradigms are used by their respective communities (fields, I suppose). I think it is important to note that Kuhn, when studying w/ behavioral scientists (social scientists) was struck by many disagreements between the social scientists that concerned the nature of legit. scientific problems. Kuhn admits that natural scientists probably *do not* have a better hold on the answers than do the social scientists, but there *aren't as many controversies*. Because of this, Kuhn has delved into the paradigm, in an attempt to discover why there existed such a great difference between the social scientists and natural scientists.
". . . there are circumstances, though I think them rare, under which two paradigms can coexist peacefully in the later period" (p. ix).	This might be important later.

FIGURE 10.2 Reading: *Structure of Scientific Revolutions*
Date: *04/12*

Mike's reactions to Kuhn's opening remarks may not accurately reflect Kuhn's thinking—indeed, Kuhn says so little about the social sciences that we must conclude that Mike is guessing at what must have gone through Kuhn's mind. What is important here, though, is that Mike is using the entry to explore his own "reading" of Kuhn's ideas. Mike records not only what the text says, but also what he thinks about it.

RÉSUMÉ/CURRICULUM VITAE

When we apply for jobs, our applications include résumés. In the academic world, the term *curriculum vitae* is used instead of *résumé. Curriculum vitae* is Latin for "the course of one's life." It's often abbreviated as *CV*. Just as creating your own résumé helps you identify your key experiences and abilities, writing a résumé or CV for a historical figure can help put that person's life and work into perspective. While reading a biography such as Banesh Hoffman's *Albert Einstein: Creator and Rebel*, for example, you might develop a CV for Einstein such as the one below as a chronological trace of his life and work.

Curriculum Vitae

Albert Einstein

```
Personal Information
Born: March 14, 1879; Ulm, Germany                  (p. 11)
Sister: Maja (1881-1951)                            (p. 242)
Married to Mileva Maric in 1903                     (p. 39)
   Divorced in 1919                                 (p. 134)
   Mileva died in 1948 in Zurich                    (p. 240)
Children: Hans Albert, born 1904                    (p. 39)
   Eduard, born 1910                                (p. 39)
Married to Elsa Einstein (distant cousin)
   in 1919                                          (p. 134)
   (Elsa died in 1936)                              (p.230)
Children: Ilse                                      (p. 250)
   Margot                                           (p. 250)
U.S. Citizenship (granted Oct. 1, 1935)             (p. 234)
Death: April 18, 1955; Princeton                    (p. 261)
Awards, Honors
1913, Elected to Royal Prussian Academy
   of Science                                       (p. 100)
1921, Nobel Prize for Physics (photoelectric
   effect)                                          (p. 54)
1921, Honorary Degree, Princeton University         (p. 145)
1925, Gold Medal, Royal Astronomical Society
      of London                                     (pp. 135, 253)
1929, Planck Medal                                  (p. 157)
```

FIGURE 10.3

Continued

FIGURE 10.3 *Continued*

Education

1885–1889: Catholic Elementary School, Munich	(p. 16)
1885–1893: Violin Lessons	(p. 20)
1889–1894: Luitpold Gymnasium (high school), Munich	(p. 19)
1896–1900: Federal Institute of Technology, Zurich	(p. 27)
1905: Ph.D., University of Zurich	(p. 55)

Positions

1902–1909: Swiss Patent Office	(p. 35)
1902–1906: Technical Expert, Third Class	(pp. 35, 82)
1906–1909: Technical Expert, Second Class	(pp. 82, 87)
1908: Bern University	(p. 87)
Privatdozent	(p. 87)
1909–1911: Zurich University	(p. 88)
Associate Professor of Theoretical Physics	(p. 88)
1911–1912: German University, Prague Full Professor	(p. 94)
1912–1914: Federal Institute of Technology, Zurich Professor	(p. 100)
1914–1933: Kaiser Wilhelm Institute, Berlin Director	(pp. 100, 167)
1930–1931: California Institute of Technology Visiting Professor	(p. 159)
1933– : Institute for Advanced Study, Princeton	(p. 170)

Selected Publications

1906, "A New Determination of the Sizes of Molecules," *Annalen der Physik*	(pp. 55, 56)
1907, E=mc^2 paper, Jahrbuch der Radioaktivitat	(p. 81)
1915, The Foundations of the General Theory of Relativity	(p. 130)
1921, *The Meaning of Relativity*, Princeton University Press	(p. 146)

Selected Adresses

1909, "The Development of Our View of the Nature and Constitution of Radiation," Eighty-First Congress of German Scientists and Physicians, Salzburg	(p. 93)
1930, Paper offering proposal for circumventing Heisenberg's indeterminacy principle, Sixth Solvay Congress, Brussels	(p. 190)
1933, "On The Method of Theoretical Physics," Oxford	(p. 170)

The extracted material serves as an outline in which you capture key elements of a life. The technique can also be used to sketch out a historical period, an intellectual movement, the discovery of a scientific principle, or the development of a technology. This strategy encourages you to use an alternative kind of text, the résumé, to think about large textual or intellectual constructions. Just as your own résumé is designed to represent essential attributes about you for the purpose of getting a job, this résumé is constructed to identify essential material for a course or research project.

GRAPHIC REPRESENTATIONS

Sometimes when we read, it's difficult to see relationships among people, events, and ideas. One way to make those relationships clearer is to graphically represent them. These representations can take many forms. The résumé described above is one form; here are some others.

Genealogies

There are some obvious uses of genealogies. In a history course you might, for example, chart the lineage of the kings and queens of a particular monarchy. But you might also extend this kind of visual representation to other kinds of course work or reading. In a literature course you might construct a genealogy like this of the characters in the Oedipus cycle:

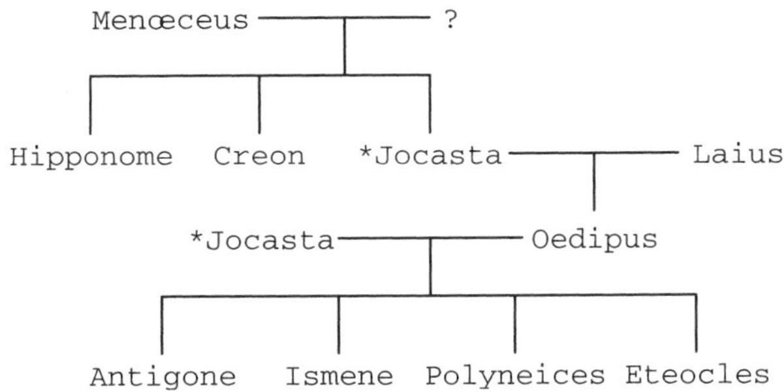

FIGURE 10.4 Character Genealogy

*Jocasta is both the mother and wife of Oedipus. She is both the grandmother and mother of Antigone, Ismene, Polyneices, and Eteocles.

Or you might examine the lineage of an idea. One student, having trouble keeping track of the concept *structuralism* and how it has influenced thinking in fields as various as linguistics, anthropology, art, psychology, and literature came up with the following:

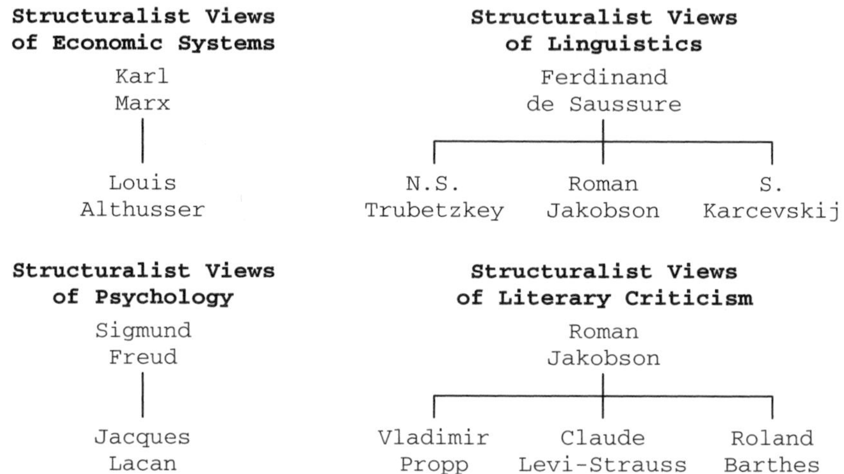

FIGURE 10.5 Idea Lineage

Time Lines/Chronologies

This is a highly simplified view of a very complex concept; it is certainly incomplete. What it does accomplish, though, is to raise questions about the ways in which certain structuralists in the fields of economics, psychology, linguistics, and literary criticism influenced others in those fields. What these four representations fail to do is give a sense of the chronology of the people included in them. By adding a chronology to these genealogies, we can more clearly see whose ideas preceded or followed those of others.

A partial time line/chronology for structuralism might look something like this:

Time Line/Chronology

1818—Birth of Karl Marx
1856—Birth of Sigmund Freud
1857—Birth of Ferdinand de Saussure
1867—Publication of *Capital* (Marx)
1883—Death of Karl Marx
1896—Birth of Roman Jakobson

1901—Birth of Jacques Lacan
1901—Publication of *The Interpretation of Dreams* (Freud)
1908—Birth of Claude Levi-Strauss
1913—Death of Ferdinand de Saussure
1914—Publication of *The Psychopathology of Everyday Life* (Freud)
1915—Birth of Roland Barthes
1916—Posthumous publication of *Course in General Linguistics* (de Saussure)
1918—Birth of Louis Althusser
1939—Death of Sigmund Freud
1955—Publication of "The Structural Study of Myth" (Levi-Strauss)
1962—Publication of *Phonological Studies* (Jakobson)
1963—Publication of *Structural Anthropology* (Levi-Strauss)
1966—Publication of "The Insistence of the Letter in the Unconscious" (Lacan)
1970—Publication of *Reading Capital* (Althusser)

It is important to remember in using these reading strategies that you are developing memory aids. You are trying to extract the gist of your reading experience and present it in an abbreviated form that both organizes and reminds you of what you've read. In his book *Connections*, James Burke traces the development of numerous ideas and inventions. In one chapter, "Distant Voices," he explains how the development of the stirrup encouraged the development of more and more sophisticated military equipment, eventually ending with the atomic bomb. Burke brings in all sorts of non-military developments (e.g., the plow, electricity) that influenced the development of military equipment. Essentially, his account illustrates how military technology has led to other military technology. A time line that helps to distill Burke's chapter might look something like this:

Concept Timeline

2nd Cent. BC—Illustrations from northern India include loop into which rider's big toe fits

523 AD—Full stirrups appear in Hunan Province, China

Late 7th Cent.—Stirrup has reached Turkestan

8th Cent.—Stirrup appears in kingdom of Franks

1040–1120—Cantle at the back of saddle raised to give rider extra support

1044—First known recipe for saltpeter, main ingredient of gunpowder

1066—Norman cavalrymen defeat Harold (Sat., Oct. 14)

Late 12th Cent.—Saddle girth straps strengthened; more protective armor developed

11th–14th Cent.—Breeding for larger horses (21 hands) (e.g., Percheron)

1346—Welch longbow used at Battle of Crecy

14th Cent.—Bombards (early cannons) used in battle

1415—Henry V uses longbow to defeat French at Battle of Agincourt (Oct. 25)

1749—Electricity used to explode gunpowder

What Burke, the historian, has accomplished is a rich and complicated story that has many characters and events occurring over a long period. No matter how good a job he has done as Burke, the writer, he still is handing the reader the daunting task of keeping track of it all. The techniques above are critical tools designed to assist you as you think your way through all of the reading you are expected to do. They will only work, however, if you use them.

11

Using Abstracts for Reading

Overview

Defining Abstracts

Writing Informative Abstracts

Writing Evaluative Abstracts

Both reading and writing abstracts are effective means of thinking carefully, critically, and becoming expert. Professionals are expected to know how to use abstracts and how to write them. Now is the time to start developing proficiency with them. They offer immediate benefits as well, benefits such as enhancing your understanding and memory of the texts you read and sharpening your writing abilities. We first give you some information about where abstracts come from, what they are, and then, briefly, discuss how to write them—arguing all the while their benefits to you as a reader and writer.

DEFINING ABSTRACTS

Simply put, an abstract is a summary or a concise statement of the main ideas of a text. It is designed to convey the gist or body of ideas of a text in as few words as possible. Most professional abstracts are no more than 200 words (and often fewer), even though they may describe lengthy articles, extensive technical reports, or entire books. The longer an abstract is, the less valuable it becomes. An abstract's purpose is to allow a reader to review the content of a text in abbreviated form to determine if the text is pertinent or useful for the reader to pursue.

Abstracts can be specifically broken into a number of more specialized terms and uses; précis, digest, summary, minutes, condensation, abridgment, and review are just some of the various classifications. For our purposes we're going to divide abstracts into two major categories:

- *Sequential or Informative*: The summary retains more or less the original order of the ideas presented; the formal abstract, précis, secretarial minutes, and abridging digest are of this type.
- *Synthesizing or Evaluative*: The original sequence of ideas is altered to accommodate the needs of certain users or to provide coherence, clarity, or dramatic effect; location digests and reviews belong here.

WRITING INFORMATIVE ABSTRACTS

Sequential abstracts are perhaps better kept in mind as descriptive or informative abstracts. They report as concisely as possible what is contained in the text. An especially effective means of developing expertise in your discipline, as well as accumulating material for literature reviews and research surveys, is to abstract the studies and research articles you read. If you have been annotating your reading, using strategies we've discussed elsewhere, this is a surprisingly easy task.

Your increasing familiarity with text structure will also help. For instance, technical reports and articles usually have a standard format. Organized in a specific way, the following format is a convention that experienced readers expect:

Technical Report/Article Format

- Title Page
- Abstract
- Text

—Introduction

—Problem Statement
—Background
—Purpose and Rationale

—Method

—Subject
—Apparatus
—Procedure

—Results

—Summary
—Statistical Analysis
—Tables and Figures

—Discussion

- References
- Appendices

(Adapted from *Publication Manual of the American Psychological Association*)

Informative abstracts mirror this structure by reporting the objective, methods, results, and conclusions of a study in their original sequence. So your task as an abstract writer is to compress and select. Structuring the material is relatively straightforward: follow the original.

The aim of an informative abstract is to provide a gist or summary statement of what the text is about. A reader can then elect to read the entire article or pass over it in search of something more appropriate to his or her needs. The writer of the abstract, however, benefits by having a snapshot that jogs the memory of reading the entire article. The writer also benefits by having actively searched out, selected, and recorded the pertinent information. These activities ask the writer to aggressively interact with and critically review the text.

A wildlife management student wrote the following abstract from his reading of Thompson and Peterson's, "Does Wolf Predation Alone Limit the Moose Population in Pukwaskwa Park?: A Comment." A sense of the original article, approximately 2,500 words long, is conveyed here in fewer than seventy words:

> The authors dispute conclusions by Bergerud et al. (1983) stating that moose populations in Pukwaskwa Park are limited by wolf predation. Criticism is based upon what they feel are inadequate data and methods and a failure to consider other mortality factors. They provide alternate hypotheses based on the effects of severe weather, food availability, cohort vulnerability, yearling dispersal, and other mortality factors.

The student notes the key article that provides the basis for the study and then suggests the scope and purpose—all in the first sentence. The second sentence conveys the body of the report with its methods, results, and discussion. The last sentence lists some of the conclusions. The student has captured the essence of this article: it is now on file in the student's head and also on a notecard, in the researcher's notebook, or in a research database ready to be used in other projects.

Remembering and retrieving what you read are critical components of professional research. Daily practice at this form of summary enables you to create a ready-made database for projects far into the future. It further provides you with study materials for exams. Rather than reviewing entire texts, you review your summaries of those texts and return specifically to the ones that seem especially relevant or that you have trouble remembering sufficiently. A word of caution: Be careful to document your abstracts fully. Leave an "audit" trail so you can retrace your sources. Get into the habit of noting full references. The student who wrote the abstract included this citation, written according to the style guide used in his field:

Peterson, R. O. and I. D. Thompson. 1988. Does wolf predation alone limit the moose population in Pukwaskwa Park?: A comment. *J. Wildl. Manage.* 52(3):556–559

Should the student need to use this article, he has at hand a complete citation both for his Literature Cited section and for his retrieval of the article from this particular journal.

Another caution: Many articles and reports already include abstracts. Their uses and values are the same ones we've been discussing. However, simply reading or copying them does little for your development as a critical, perceptive reader. Nor does it contribute to your capabilities as a writer. Don't ignore these abstracts, but don't rely solely on them either. They are no substitute for your own active engagements with the text.

Try writing an informative abstract yourself. Seek out either a professional article from your discipline or use a chapter from a textbook. Read attentively, marking important points and noting their function according to the guidelines below. Then fill in the blanks:

Informative Abstracting Guidelines

Citation or reference:

____

____

____

____

Scope and purpose of text:

____

____

____

____

Relevant supporting background or literature:

____

____

____

____

Elements of body (methods, discussion, results, principal supporting points):

____

____

____

____

Conclusions or recommendations:

____

____

____

____

Three or four sentences should do it if you have fully grasped the essence of the original. Keep in mind that this process requires practice if you're going to develop some facility at it. But also keep in mind the benefits: not only are you creating a record of what you're reading, but you're also developing precision in your own writing. You're also closely attending to what other writers do as they write, thereby benefiting both from their content and from the strategies they use to present that content. Finally, if the material you chose already has an abstract, compare it with your own to check on your reading and to check on the author's ability to abstract.

WRITING EVALUATIVE ABSTRACTS

Our second category, evaluative abstracts, has slightly different aims and uses. Less formally structured than the sequential or informative abstract, the synthesizing or evaluative abstract is also less descriptive of the original text. As readers and writers, we evaluate and judge the relative merits and demerits of a text as we synthesize its content. If you recall our earlier discussion of reading comprehension, informative abstracts draw more on literal and interpretive reading, whereas the evaluative abstract requires more interpretive and applied reading. You might remember the distinctions visually, as shown below.

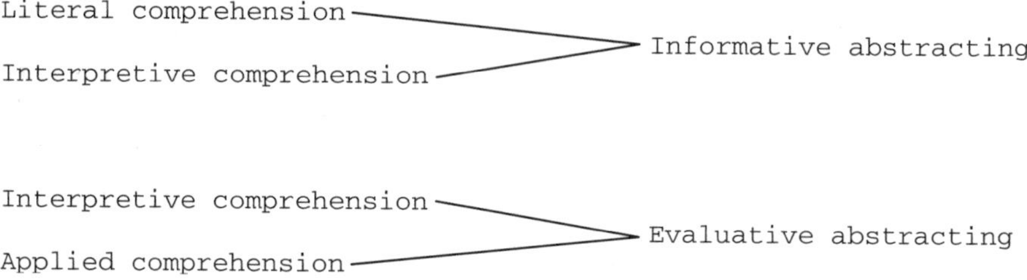

FIGURE 11.1 Comprehension Processes Involved in Abstracting

Evaluative abstracts enable you to more fully adapt a text to your own needs and objectives. They're usually as compressed as informative abstracts, but you're much more personally involved. You're called on to evaluate, judge, praise, condemn, suggest, or refute what you read.

The following is a systems engineering student's evaluative abstract of an article she read:

> Fink, P., J. Lusth, and J. Duran. "A General Expert System Design for Diagnostic Problem Solving." *IEEE 1984 Workshop on Principles of Knowledge Based Systems*. 45–52.
>
> The system discussed, Integrated Diagnostic Model (IDM), can possibly take expert systems one step closer to being more like a human expert. Most people first try to use their own experiences and intuition in solving a problem. If they are unable to solve the problem they then go to other sources. The idea behind IDM is the same. IDM will first model the reasoning process based on experience and basic knowledge in a particular domain to narrow the possible answers down, if not solve the problem. If that fails it will then use a deeper, physical knowledge base. Although IDM may not work well in certain domains such as voice recognition or chemical structure analysis, it is a very unique technique for the design of many diagnostic problem solving systems.

The author of this abstract evaluates the merits of this system and suggests its possible value. She compares the design to human problem-solving processes, describes the design's processes, and then notes its limitations. She concludes with an affirmative nod toward the system. All of this draws on the student's expertise in her field and requires her to critique what she's reading. She's determining the value of the information in the article, asking herself, "How and why is this valuable?"

Developing responses, reactions, and critiques of the material you read is central to becoming an expert, and writing evaluative abstracts develops this facility directly. Also, as you become more and more expert, others will rely on your comments and perceptions of various texts. Start preparing yourself for that role now. Select an article or text chapter and use the following guidelines to help direct your evaluative response:

Evaluative Abstracting Guidelines

Citation or reference:

____

____

____

Value of text (affirmative or negative):

____

____

____

Relevant supporting background or literature (material cited in this text or material not in text, but brought in by abstract writer to clarify or support):

____

____

____

Points of critique:

____

____

____

Conclusions or recommendations:

____

____

____

Abstracting is often called an art. In fact, there are professional abstractors, well paid and highly valued. Abstracts are recognized necessities, tools designed to provide wider access to the enormous wealth of information being generated daily. Becoming expert in their use and in their creation will increase your ability to think through ideas carefully and will greatly aid your success in whatever field or discipline you specialize in.

12

Understanding Active Listening

Overview

What Listening Is

Essential Types of Listening

Discriminative Listening
Evaluative Listening

Less Obvious Features of Listening

Bias and Other Emotional Filters
Physical Characteristics: Sight and Sound
The Listening Environment

The Roles and Characteristics of Listeners: Good and Bad

It's Monday morning and you've had a particularly grueling weekend. You've worked or partied or studied most of the time you weren't sleeping. You sit down in your first class of the week, settle in, look around, and take out a notebook. The bell rings, and the instructor walks in front of the class and begins talking, perhaps writing on the chalkboard or an overhead transparency.

Ostensibly, you're there to learn. But do you?

As students, we probably use our ears more than any other sense organ. Yes, we watch the instructor (who may or may not be visually interesting) and we take notes (which we may or may not be able to comprehend later). And, we believe, we listen closely to what's being said. But do we really?

Executives and other professionals regularly report that they spend more time listening to others than doing any other activity except sleeping. Some estimate that as much as 45 percent of their jobs directly involve a skill that few of us have ever been trained to do. Many of these executives report some training in reading and writing, and quite often in speaking, but little or none in listening. Yet, apparently it is the dominant communication "sense" used in professional life. It is also the first communication capability any of them, or us, use—something we seem to pick up, somewhere, way before speaking, reading, and writing.

How do we distinguish proficient listeners? Studies demonstrate the importance of this facility to our success at school and on the job. Research also points out the dollar cost of poor listening; incorrectly repeated telephone messages, poorly heard instructions, and badly followed directions are just the obvious results of poor listening that literally cost billions of dollars annually.

In the classroom or office, how do we know we're listening closely, effectively? What are we really doing during that time? What strategies and techniques do good listeners have for us to copy? What do you do as a listener? How do you respond? What actions do you perform? This chapter addresses some of these questions. It will help you examine what active listening is, how it happens, and how you can use writing as a tool to improve your listening facility.

WHAT LISTENING IS

Although we can close our eyes and not see, it is quite difficult *not* to hear. But hearing is not listening. Hearing is basically a physiological process dependent on the mechanisms of the ear responding to sound waves. Listening is the psychological or mental action on our part, just as reading is a psychological, mental, intellectual action that usually relies on sight for input. Derived from Old English and Teutonic roots, the word *listen* suggests the act of hearing attentively, the action "to give ear to." Effective listening requires an active, complex process involving several stages and a number of interrelated factors.

Our environment is full of sound, as you probably know if you have tried taping in a room full of people, such as a classroom. We are bombarded by the noise of moving, coughing, whispering. Yet, provided our interest is there, we can actively listen to one or more specific sound sources.

What we listen to depends on what we are listening *for*. Basically, four factors determine what we end up "hearing":

1. Readiness
2. Situation
3. Content
4. Signal

We are responsible entirely for our *readiness*, which includes such attributes as our experience with language, our vocabulary, our memory capabilities (or lack of), and our interests and attitudes toward what we hear. We discriminate among the various sounds in our environment, searching for what has an effect on us. The *situation* and the *content* of the message directly affect our listening capability as well. Furthermore, *readiness*, *situation*, and *content* are affected by and affect each of us individually, depending on the *signal* used to transmit the information. Getting off a railroad track when you hear a train whistle is a more or less immediate response to your *readiness* to respond to the nature and *content* of a *signal* received in a specific *situation*.

Simply put, we receive a sound (hear), perceive that sound and attach a meaning to it, and retain that sound, at least temporarily, while we decide how to respond. This is complicated by the facts that we rarely find an isolated, individual sound, and that most of our other senses are engaged while we listen.

To demonstrate this, stop reading for a minute, close your eyes, and just listen to what's going on around you. Isolate the various sounds and jot them down:

____

____

____

____

How many distinct sounds can you accumulate in just a minute or two? A car going by on the street outside, a police siren in the distance, the refrigerator, your breathing, a clock—these and other sounds are with us constantly, yet unless we listen for them, we filter them out of our attention. Of course, there is the inverse as well: hearing things that aren't there. Suspense stories have relied on this phenomenon at least since Edgar Allan Poe's story "The Tell-Tale Heart."

The active listening process is not unlike active reading in certain ways. We attend to some text features and not to others. Of course, crucial differences exist between reading and listening; some are obvious, some are not. Probably the most obvious, and surprisingly overlooked, distinction between reading and listening is that listening is almost completely instantaneous. You catch it or you don't. With reading, you usually have the opportunity to reread. Without recordings, you rarely can relisten. As a reader, you also have more control over both the rate of input and the environment of what you are "receiving." Listeners have much less control over how fast a speaker goes and where that speaking takes place. But listeners do often have the opportunity to interact "live" with the source, whereas readers do not. Finally, we're all more likely to be trained in how to read than in how to listen.

But there are similarities. Both reading and listening are integral to communication. Both are complex processes, often taken for granted and rarely examined by their users. Both involve actively attending to external stimuli. Neither is passive; they require active participation by you, the listener or reader. Context, purpose, and attitude are important considerations. Neither requires agreement on your part, only attentiveness and receptivity. Writer and speaker are only partially responsible for a reader's or listener's success. Both rely on background knowledge, symbol systems, and vocabulary.

Most important, mastering both active reading and active listening processes is critical to your professional as well as academic success. Recognizing their shared characteristics helps you to "borrow" techniques from one and apply them to the other. Recognizing their differences helps you compensate, apply, and accommodate the strengths and limitations of listening to a particular learning or work situation, and those of reading to others.

So far, we have not really distinguished one type of sound from another in relation to your listening. We're now going to shift our attention to the listening you do in your classes and in your professional life. Most of these listening tasks are language dependent. That is, the sounds you listen for are part of a symbol system that has evolved over a long time within a particular context, a culture. The sounds you listen for are just that, plural. We listen for sounds that are "chunked" into meaningful units. Language features such as phonemes, pauses, stresses, intonations, pitches, timbre, and amplitudes are all combined into whole discourse. We rarely are able to hear the distinct components, nor would they mean much to us anyway. Vocabulary is an essential feature of this chunking, but so are more global discourse features such as arrangement and other attributes involved in using language to communicate. We focus next on the essential types or categories of listening often expected of you as you become expert in your profession.

ESSENTIAL TYPES OF LISTENING

We've developed a checklist to help you analyze your listening tasks. These particular ones not only involve listening skill, but are at the same time related to the listener's purpose:

Purposes and Skills for Listening

- To get main ideas
- To hear facts
- To make valid inferences
- To get the central theme

- To retain pertinent content
- To hear details
- To take notes
- To develop curiosity
- To follow directions
- To judge relevancy
- To recognize what the speaker wants the listener to do
- To predict what will happen next
- To identify speaker attitudes
- To notice sequences of ideas and details
- To check for the accuracy of new information
- To evaluate and apply material presented
- To identify the main and supporting ideas
- To use contextual clues to determine "word meanings"

For classroom listening, this list can give you some clues to how your performance in the course will be evaluated. Are you expected to accumulate facts? Are you also expected to draw and apply inferences from these facts? How important is the sequence of the material? Identifying these elements can make your purposes for listening more obtainable.

Just as effective readers apply different strategies to different types of texts, active listeners shift their strategies depending on the texts they encounter. For the most part, the speakers you encounter in school and in the workplace are usually trying to persuade or to inform you. Often the two are combined. We will concentrate on these two areas because they have attributes that will make you a better listener.

Discriminative Listening

An informing speaker's key purpose is to inform, to explain. The discourse is *expository* as opposed to *persuasive*; its emphasis is reference-oriented, explanatory, scientific, technical. A discriminating listener's goal is to gather, understand, learn, and extend the information provided by the speaker—a common teacher–student situation, but one also found in every profession, at every level. Your task as a listener is to:

- Discover the speaker's main ideas.
- Detect and follow the speaker's pattern of organization.
- Gather and check the speaker's detail and support.
- Be aware of your own responses.
- Formulate questions.
- Attach the information to your own needs.
- Be prepared to act.

The first three of these tasks are made easier if you're aware of the principal types of text arrangement and a little bit about reason. Knowing these speaker and writer strategies will make your listening time more efficient. Remember, the speaker is not wholly responsible for the success of your listening. Listening is *not* passive.

You respond to what you hear, whether you're aware of it or not. Discriminative listening is aimed at tailoring your responses to fit the purpose of the listening. You attend a lecture to get information necessary for your professional development. You work with classmates to extend your knowledge and capabilities. You meet with colleagues to perform a job more effectively. The success of these endeavors is greatly determined by how well you listen, by the skills you bring as a listener, but it is also affected by your attitudes toward what you hear, your biases. Bias probably affects us much more than we are willing (or able) to recognize, and it's often very subtle. In a later section of this chapter, we'll show you some ways to note what turns your ears on, and what turns them off.

Evaluative Listening

Evaluative listening occurs when you encounter a speaker whose key purpose is to persuade you toward a specific action, whether it's to buy something, to adopt a certain attitude or opinion, or to act in a way commensurate with the speaker's goal. The speaker aims to influence your response. At the same time, that speaker tries to elicit a specific response from you. Often it's difficult to distinguish persuasive discourse from informative. Most communications involve both, distinct only in degree. Advertising, marketing, propaganda, politics, much of the legal system, and many religions rely on persuasive strategies and their effects on listeners. Expository strategies assume more discrete, and sometimes unrecognizable, persuasive aspects such as arrangement of information, methodology, technical terminology, cultural biases, and other highly embedded discourse features. For your own sake (and sometimes, protection), the more aware you are of how others influence you through your ears—whether their primary purpose is to inform or to persuade—the better off you'll be. Listening in no way means agreement. Active listening means paying attention to what's going on, and to what's being done to you.

Most persuaders use these four elements on listeners:

- Get the listener's attention and maintain it.
- Relate the listener's wants and needs to the speaker's purpose.
- Show how the speaker's recommendations fit the listener's purposes.
- Elicit a specific response or action from the listener.

Examine a thirty-second radio or television spot. Good ones get your attention, keep it, tap into your desires, convey how beneficial this item is to you, and get you to buy or subscribe to whatever is being pushed. Persuasion is not something a speaker does to a listener. Persuasion occurs when the listener goes along with the speaker.

We've come up with three points, called The Three Knows, that you should keep in mind as you listen to a speaker. They apply to informative as well as persuasive discourse. They apply to politicians, advertisers, the writers of this book—anyone who wants to influence you in any way, which probably applies to almost everyone you encounter.

The Three Knows of Listening

1. Know thy subject.

    - The more expert we are in a field or discipline of study, the better we can evaluate a speaker's contribution to it. This means developing not only a deep understanding, but also a wide understanding of the subject at hand.

2. Know thy tools.

    - A kind of Golden Rule applies in a persuasive speaker–listener relationship: Do unto others what they would do unto you. Learn persuasive techniques and strategies both for your own use in speaking situations and to avoid having them used on you without your knowing.

3. Know thy self.

    - Recognize the immediate effects a speaker is having on you. Recognize also that evaluation and appraisal of these effects, of a speaker's influence on you, is more effective (from your point of view, not necessarily the speaker's) if you can delay your response. Take some time to reflect on what you are being told. Note any changes in your attitudes and perceptions, and why those changes took place.

An effective way to develop your facility at listening and at incorporating your understanding of The Three Knows is to write down your observations, to keep a log or journal of your perceptions. Keeping your own Listening Inventory, like the one on page 166, for a couple of weeks is a good way to begin.

TABLE 12.1 Listening Inventory

Amount of Time	Type of Activity	Type of Listening	Purpose for Listening	Biases	Self-Evaluation

Type of Activity: Indicate what you were doing at this time (e.g., in class, at work, eating, sleeping) and why (e.g., to prepare for a test, relax, make points).

Type of Listening: Categorize your listening as Discriminative, Evaluative, or some mix.

Purpose for Listening: Identify what you were trying to do, as a listener (e.g., to get instructions, to identify key points, to stay awake).

Biases: Note any features, either physical (e.g., the speaker's appearance) or emotional (e.g., the topic's relationship to you) that may have affected your listening—either negatively or positively.

Self Evaluation: Rate your activeness as a listener on a scale of 1 to 10, with 1 being sound asleep and 10 indicating you were hanging on every word.

LESS OBVIOUS FEATURES OF LISTENING

Making the most of your active listening involves more than just an understanding of what listening is. So far, we've discussed the global aspects of listening, its general characteristics. The following section delves into some of the less obvious features of our listening. Our intention here is to enhance your listening as a protective device and to build a sense of consciousness into your listening. These features are to a great extent determined by the speaker or source of the message, but this only makes your attention to them more important. First, we discuss biases and emotional filters. Second, we note certain effects a speaker's physical characteristics can have on listeners. Third, we briefly discuss listening environments.

Bias and Other Emotional Filters

One feature of listening we all need to examine more closely, and usually don't, is the bias we bring with us to a listening situation. Bias is a feature in all of us. It helps make us unique, although sometimes unpleasantly. Sometimes it's culturally inculcated in us as well. For instance, the word *propaganda* often triggers a negative response from most of us. Probably one of the more disturbing consequences of high-tech communication is the development and power of propaganda, at least in its negative connotations. Propaganda devices rely on listener biases. Propaganda itself is neither good nor bad—it's simply a means of conveying a particular attitude or belief to others. Our negative reactions to the idea come from what has been done in the name of propaganda and from some of the techniques developed to accomplish those aims. Propaganda, however, cannot work very well if we are doing our job as active listeners. Nor can it work if we become more self-aware, more conscious of what our personal feelings and attitudes are and where those feelings and attitudes come from.

We've described here some of the more common propaganda devices to be on the watch for. These devices rely on your not critically evaluating what is being conveyed, on not listening closely and actively. They instead rely on eliciting emotional response, on arousing the biases of the listeners and using that response to turn off more objective analysis that might interfere with the speaker's aims.

Warning: Not All of What You Hear Is Good for You

- *Name Calling*: As its label implies, this device is used to evoke a negative response by labeling someone or something. It's a matter of identification. Children use it with obvious vengeance, but adults are just as susceptible, although often more covert about it. For example, as Jim Wright resigned under duress as House Speaker, he referred to activities in the House of Representatives as "cannibalism."
- *Glittering Generalities*: Similar to Name Calling, this labeling device categorizes an issue or person in a positive way that supports the speaker's cause. In political campaigns, the labels *liberal, conservative,* and even *moderate,* may be tossed around by all sides, but with no definitions offered by anyone.
- *Plain Folks*: This approach relies on listeners responding to the speaker's message by perceiving the speaker as being one of them. Ad campaigns, like those featuring Orville Redenbacher and his grandson, frequently use this strategy.
- *Transfer*: This attempts to associate what listeners already feel positive about (for instance, the Pledge of Allegiance) to the speaker (a patriotic American).

- *Testimonial*: A particular kind of transfer, in which listeners are expected to associate an admired person with a cause or product (a very visible advertising technique is to use sports or media celebrities to promote a product—Michael Jordan for Nike shoes is an example).
- *Card Stacking*: This device presents only one side of an issue particular to its purpose—only the positive or only the negative (a salesperson is unlikely to note shortcomings of a product).
- *Band Wagon*: An appeal based on the desire to be like someone admired, or to join the crowd (beer and soft drink commercials seem to rely on this approach a great deal).

None of these tactics should be unfamiliar to you. We've all been subjected to them at various times. We're all probably guilty of using some of them occasionally. They're powerful tools of persuasion, but only if heard uncritically. Some rely on the ethical appeal of the speaker, some on slips of reason, some on the emotional response of the listener—all rely on your unconsciousness of them to be effective in getting a speaker's message across.

Physical Characteristics: Sight and Sound

Other characteristics found in a listening situation bias our responses as well. Working with a group of teacher-trainers recently, we ended up discussing the physical characteristics of some of the new teachers. One trainer talked about the advantages a particular teacher had—he was young, good-looking, and articulate. Capturing the class's attention was easy: members of the opposite sex were immediately attentive based on this teacher's appearance, and members of the same sex were more attentive because of his articulateness. But another teacher-trainer had to caution one of her new teachers about the way she wore her hair—this young teacher had long, blond hair that was drawing as much attention as what she was saying.

The dress-for-success phenomenon is another indication of our growing attentiveness to personal presentation, to being noticed. Much has been made about "power ties" in politics. The physical appearance of the speaker affects how we respond to that speaker, at least immediately. Gender, physical attractiveness, manner of dress, body movement, and other visually apparent features influence how we listen to the information being conveyed.

Less visual triggers are everywhere, too. As humans, we rarely are able to separate totally our emotional responses from our intellectual ones. We need to be attuned to what kinds of "buttons" we have and then accommodate them to the situation and our needs as listeners. What is actually being said and our perceptions of what is being said are often not the same. Without getting involved in a discussion of *What is reality*? and *Is objectivity possible*?, we do want to point out that the more aware you are of what *you* bring with you to a listening situation and how that affects what you take away with you, the better off you'll be.

One way to do this is to think about your emotional responses as a sieve or screen through which you sift information. Mentally hold this sieve up to a light. What comes through? Your awareness of your responses determines how many holes there are, their shape, and their size. If you have only a few, small, rigidly defined holes, you might think about putting in a few more.

The following items trigger both positive and negative responses in listeners. Fill in some specifics about what really sets your teeth on edge when you're in a listening situation. You do need to keep in mind that certain characteristics that can't be helped (big ears, for example) have little to do with what a speaker says and shouldn't influence your critical listening.

- Speaker's voice:
- Speaker's physical appearance:
- Topic:
- Speaker's strategies:
- Language:
- Listening environment:

The last three items often affect us as much as the first two. For instance, some people absolutely refuse to discuss religion or politics—you probably have your own experiences that might justify this. But, we all have issues or topics that we cannot be objective about or are overly sensitive about. *Why* is a matter for a psychologist. For the purpose of becoming a more effective listener, though, learn to recognize those topics you have trouble discussing with emotional distance. Jot down a few of them below. Think of issues, concerns, or topics that you are uncomfortable listening to, much less discussing:

____

____

____

____

Write next to each item anyone you think you could talk to about these topics. Then consider why. What attributes do these people have that you might be able to develop for yourself?

Just as what's being said affects us, how it's being said influences our emotional responses. Voice quality and tone, regional and social dialects, certain words, and grammatical structures are language features that we respond to whether we are aware of our responses or not. Much of traditional grammar (what we thought we learned in grammar or grade school) was developed to make us sound like everybody else. Research suggests that the more a speaker sounds like us, or like what we think we should sound like, the more likely we are to give credence to that speaker.

The Listening Environment

We also respond better (or worse) to a listener depending on the environment of the listening situation. Aside from features such as distraction levels, acoustics, and sound quality, the visual space we find a speaker in helps determine our response. News media have refined this almost to art. One demolished building looks much like another, yet consider how often we find a television news reporter standing before a pile of rubble relating the latest bomb blast, earthquake, fire, or like disaster.

The particular environment of most listening situations is beyond our control. The speaker may or may not have much say about this either. But our response, or at least recognition of our response, is up to us. And we usually have some say about where we locate ourselves physically in relation to the speaker. Some educational researchers suggest that where we choose to sit in a classroom directly relates to our success in that class: those who sit front and center do better than those sitting in the back and off to the sides. The evidence is not entirely convincing, but it's something to consider.

Earlier, you analyzed things that trigger negative responses, that hinder effective listening. Now try to determine ways of overcoming these responses. Suggest to yourself new approaches to the situation to overcome the barriers you've identified:

- Speaker's voice:
- Speaker's physical appearance:
- Topic:
- Speaker's strategies:
- Language:
- Listening environment:

We're not going to help you here by suggesting our own ways of dealing with these. There simply is no one right way. Rather, the effectiveness of this approach is in your attempt and in the recognition that you bring to the attempt. Explore and experiment.

THE ROLES AND CHARACTERISTICS OF LISTENERS: GOOD AND BAD

We bring many habits with us when we listen. These habits are established early in life and are reinforced continually. Many of them are triggered automatically. These habits distinguish good listeners from poor ones. Try the Listening Habits Quiz to see if you can distinguish the good from the bad. Put a *G* or + beside those features you see as good listening habits and a *B* or – beside the bad.

Listening Habits Quiz

_______ Writes everything down
_______ Is impatient
_______ Can repeat what speaker says
_______ Jumps to conclusions
_______ Doesn't rush the speaker
_______ Fidgets
_______ Responds with nods
_______ Follows speaker with eyes
_______ Raises questions
_______ Understands speaker's attitude
_______ Remains poised
_______ Changes subject
_______ Watches the clock
_______ Doesn't respond
_______ Loses temper
_______ Anticipates next point
_______ Daydreams
_______ Dislikes the speaker
_______ Listens for more than facts
_______ Responds emotionally
_______ Reviews and summarizes
_______ Evaluates speaker's points
_______ Resists distractions
_______ Takes a lot of notes

You should have identified an equal number of good and bad habits. Pretty easy? Do a little self-analysis just after you get out of a class. Underline the items that describe your behavior. Next, spend a few minutes listing other habits you have as a listener. Be sure to include *both* good and not-so-good habits, underlining the more positive ones. Now do a simple tally: count the items marked *G* or + and underlined and assign five points for each. Subtract five points for each *B* or – that's underlined:

Good Habits	***Not-So-Good Habits***

How good a listener are you? What areas do you need to focus on to be a better one? Awareness of your listening habits and attitudes is critical before you can alter them. However, good listeners benefit by having better relations with others; they "find" more opportunities; they are more productive; and they are remembered for it.

▶13

Writing and Listening

Overview

Research suggests that we learn more visually than we do aurally—a lot more. Yet, we spend more time in speaking and listening situations than we do dealing with visual information. We have certain advantages with visual discourse, but we also have opportunities with spoken communication—if we are willing to work a little. You can hear much faster than most people talk. Although the actual figures vary, researchers have determined that people normally talk at between 125 and 150 words per minute. We can quite easily listen and comprehend between 600 and 800 words per minute. This gives us a lot of time, time to listen actively to what's said, time we often use attending to almost anything else. After all, who's to know what we are actually listening to? Unfortunately, what usually shows somehow, somewhere, is that we are not or were not listening.

Awareness of how listening works and of your own listening habits are important but a bit remote from immediate application. The material we've covered in the previous chapter is designed to affect how you think about listening as much as how you do it. This chapter presents some ways to enhance and change how you listen. We discuss some of the reasons for taking notes while listening and suggest some things to consider before taking notes. Then, we present some specific techniques to enhance the way you use writing while listening.

WHY TAKE NOTES?

Why *do* we all take notes while we listen? If listening and taking notes seem so inseparably related, there must be some reason, right? Before we list some reasons we've thought of, take a few minutes to jot down some of your own.

____

____

____

By filling in those blanks, you've just discovered two of the most important reasons for taking notes while listening. And they're the same reasons to use writing while reading:

- Writing makes us think.
- Writing helps us remember what we've thought of.

These are the very reasons we make lists before going to the grocery store. In fact, we would even argue that writing a store list is merely taking notes on the internal (sometimes external!) conversations we have with ourselves as we plan our trip. Because "thinking of" and "remembering" are often competing activities in our brains, we separate them by doing them on paper.

Another reason for taking notes while listening is to assure *that* we are listening. In short:

- Writing makes us concentrate on what we're doing.

As we listen, we are constantly bombarded by a multitude of distractions: the movements of the speaker, the view out the window, the fashion statement being made by another listener. By focusing on writing notes, we can effectively shut out many of those distractions and, we hope, be more active listeners.

Another obvious reason for taking notes:

- Writing records what we've heard.

The notes we take "capture" talk and give us a permanent record of it. But, unlike a tape recording, it's an abbreviated, edited record. We rarely need or want a complete, verbatim record. (On those occasions, we do record on tape.) Instead, we want just enough to reconstruct the essential part of the message. In making a grocery list, we don't write, "Go down the bread aisle and pick out one loaf of whole wheat—don't get distracted by the expensive seven-grain loaves." No; the word *bread* is enough.

Finally, one of the most important—and often most underused—reasons for writing notes:

- Written notes can later be expanded and extended in new and different directions.

Because they are almost never "complete," notes can become the building blocks of new ideas. A page of notes may become one side of an ongoing conversation between the past—when the notes were made—and the future—when they are reread. In this sense, notes become the repository not of already-thought thoughts, but of potential ideas that haven't been considered yet. To give a very practical example, as a student you've no doubt had difficulty coming up with an idea for term projects or major papers in your classes. It's a frustrating situation, trying to "think up" a topic. But those topics are often right there before you, in your notes.

PREPARING FOR NOTETAKING

Imagine for a moment that you've just walked into a room for a class or a committee meeting. You know you're going to need to make some notes about what happens. How do you get ready? Write down, in order, all the steps you go through in preparing:

____

____

____

Probably the first thing you wrote is something like: "Take out pen and paper." What about sitting down? Most people don't consciously consider where they sit; they just find a seat and sit down. Communications specialists and sociologists have recently begun studying how and where people choose to sit when they meet in groups. These studies have focused mostly on the way seating arrangements reflect the roles of the participants. But our own informal observations of students in classrooms—as well as faculty members, and others, in committee meetings—over the past several years suggest to us that these choices also affect the way people take notes and what they write in them.

For example, in a classroom, some students prefer to sit all the way in the back of the room, and others tend to sit right in front. What's the difference? First of all, it might be a specific physical need: those in back may be farsighted and those up front may have difficulty hearing clearly. Although these are extremely important considerations for effective listening and notetaking, there are some other effects of seating location that we believe you should think about. For example, if the class activity depends a great deal on the instructor's (and, perhaps, the students') use of a chalkboard in the front of the room, those who sit in the back may have an advantage seeing a larger view, an "overview" of the thinking in the room. Those up front, however, may see the details easily, but have trouble seeing broader, general connections. And those sitting by the doors or windows will likely be subject to distractions and interruptions.

Small meetings often take place around a long table. If there is a chairperson who presides over the meeting, some people find it very difficult to take notes if they sit immediately next to that person. Two reasons for this come to mind. First, because the chairperson is the center of attention for the whole group, it's easy to become very self-conscious about all of the other members watching you take notes (and, perhaps, wondering what you're writing down) when they're actually looking at the chairperson. Second, your close physical proximity can make it very difficult to look at the notes you're taking and also to make eye contact with the chairperson. A little more distance can make it easier to glance back and forth between the two.

We can't suggest that any particular location in a room is necessarily better than others for taking notes. But we do suggest that, unless your seat is assigned, you should consider how various locations will affect your ability to take effective notes. In other words, think before you sit.

Choosing the right materials to use is also an important factor in preparing to take notes. The proliferation of writing instruments of every shape and type, from the simplest number two lead pencil to those ingenious combination highlighter/ballpoint pens, suggests that manufacturers recognize the needs of individual writers. So, too, with paper. Spiral bound notebooks, top-bound legal pads, loose-leaf paper, artists' sketch pads, even that favorite of elementary school, the Big Chief Tablet—all of these and many more to choose from. Most of us have a favorite set of implements we use to take notes.

But favorites are not always best. Taking notes on a discussion of inferential statistics, for example, may require drawing graphs and plotting points. That's a lot easier to do in pencil on graph-lined paper than with a pen on unlined computer paper. By the same token, the sketch pad that might be fine for notes in a history of architecture or art history course may be a frustration for taking notes in another type of history course. Even the spacing of the lines, whether narrow or wide ruled, can determine how effectively you take notes. In general, consider carefully how the materials you choose will work for what you're doing. A good mechanic *could* use a hammer to adjust the carburetor on your car; but you'd probably prefer he use a tool more specifically designed for the job. The results would no doubt be better.

Your list of preparatory activities for notetaking may also have overlooked another important strategy: prelistening planning. If you have formulated expectations of the probable topics to be covered, you can anticipate shifts from one topic to another. In short, knowing *what* to listen for will make noting it much easier.

There are many different ways to preplan notetaking. For instance, annotations you've made while reading often suggest topics or questions to anticipate in a discussion of that reading material. If you've outlined the reading material, copying each of the top-level headings onto a separate sheet is a good preparation for notetaking. In lecture situations, either in classrooms or in professional conference meetings, speakers often preview their presentations with a list of topics to be covered. Sometimes these appear on a handout; sometimes the speaker announces them as part of the introduction to the talk. In either case, part of your preplanning should be to recognize and jot down these cues for your notetaking.

Even if you believe you don't have any clues about what you'll be taking notes on, you probably do. As creatures of habit, we are prone to follow patterns, often unconsciously. Your years of sitting in a variety of classrooms have exposed you to many of these patterns. Stop and think for a moment about how the "average" class session runs. What are the usual elements? The content differs slightly from one situation to the next, but the pattern is pretty constant:

- Introduction (establishing the purpose, handling old business, getting started)
- Middle (diving in and doing, often separating into smaller units)
- Finishing (wrapping up and tying off, clarifying, sometimes projecting ahead)

If you stop to consider these patterns for a moment *before* they begin, you'll be able to anticipate the shifts you need to make while taking notes.

And you'll also find that you *can* predict, with pretty fair accuracy, what you'll want and need to write down. Not thinking about these patterns may leave you trying to make a map of where you've been without knowing where you were going.

Finally, many notetakers don't consider what they're eventually planning to do with their notes before they begin making them. In fact, we suspect that many student notetakers never figure out what to do with their notes. We'll address that problem a little later. However, if you intend to go back over your notes and extend or add to them, you need to leave room to do so when you take the notes.

One common strategy is to draw a vertical line separating each blank page into a two-thirds and a one-third slice. The notes are written in the bigger section; the follow-up goes in the smaller one. Another strategy, the dialectical notebook that we demonstrate in Part 1, involves putting notes on one page and the writer's responses to them on the facing page. It works well if you take the notes on the *back* or left side of each page and save the fronts—the right-hand, facing page—for the responses. Of course, if you're taking notes on loose sheets of paper, it's a good idea to number and date the sheets as you go along: once mixed up, pages of notes can be incredibly difficult to reorder.

All of these seemingly obvious considerations, from where you sit to what you use and how you preplan, are important to the quality and effectiveness of your notetaking. Good preparation doesn't guarantee that you'll find notetaking easier or better; but it goes a long way toward those ends.

STRATEGIES FOR TAKING NOTES WHILE LISTENING

As with all kinds of writing, there are as many ways to take notes as there are notetakers. And each individual must develop a whole set of notetaking strategies for different occasions. In the following discussion, we describe a number of notetaking techniques in detail and point out some of the advantages of each. It is up to you to try out and adapt these and other techniques to your needs and the listening situations you find yourself in.

Outlining

Probably the most familiar type of notetaking is outlining. There are at least two general types of outlines: formal (complete with Roman numerals and subpoints) and informal (arranged visually with indents to indicate levels). Each type works well for different listening situations.

Formal outline notes work well for formal presentations, when the speaker also follows a formal outline. In fact, experienced speakers will give their audience a copy of the outline—either as a handout or projected on a screen—to help them follow the presentation. If you *do* get a copy of the outline on paper, don't spend your valuable time recopying it. Instead, fill in details as you listen, either on the handout itself or, if there isn't room, on separate sheets. Use the heading numbers as shorthand labels to cross-reference your notes to the handout. Or, use the first few minutes of the presentation to copy the outline from the screen. But don't copy the whole outline at the top of the first page; instead, put each of the major headings on a separate page and leave plenty of white space between the subpoints. Then, keep extra blank pages handy for overflow notes. If the outline is numbered, use the numbers to cross-reference your notes and the handout. This preplanning will help you anticipate what to listen for.

At other times, speakers don't share their outlines *overtly* with their audience. Still, you may be able to construct one by listening closely for key words—called "signposts"—that indicate what level the speaker is on. (Some of the most common signposts are highlighted in CAPITAL LETTERS in the following discussion.)

During the early part of a presentation, speakers usually mention the MAIN POINTS they will cover. When you hear these, that's your cue to write each one at the top of a separate page. Then, listen for a word like FIRST or a phrase such as "MY FIRST POINT" or "LET ME BEGIN WITH." These are often followed by a reiteration or restatement of one of the points you've already written down, and it lets you check to see that you heard and noted the topic correctly.

As the speaker develops a point, you might hear cues such as "SEVERAL REASONS" or "A NUMBER OF CASES," which indicate a list of subpoints, the first level of indent in your outline. If the speaker quickly runs down the list, be sure to leave space after each of these items: the speaker will probably go back to develop each one further, and you'll need that space. At other times, you won't hear a preview of the list. Instead, the speaker will pause and develop each point along the way. In such cases, listen for a "LAST" or a "FINALLY" to indicate where the list ends.

Sub-subpoints (those signified by Arabic numerals and lower case letters on formal outlines) are often signaled by "FOR EXAMPLE." Another way to recognize these lowest-level ideas is by listening for specificity: numbers, dates, names, and facts are usually used to fill out a discussion.

Informal outlines are also a valuable system for taking notes. After all, not all presentations we listen to are formal. More important, not all formal presentations actually follow such formally structured outlines. Sometimes, for effect or simply for variation, a speaker may present a long list of examples—each one complete with statistics, dates, and names—before ending with the point they support. At other times, we may listen to "stream of consciousness" presentations: the speaker begins with one idea and is reminded of an example that brings up another point, which leads toward a completely new idea. On such occasions, formal outlining is a more frustrating than helpful strategy for taking notes.

An informal outline might work, though. Keep in mind that most texts (and spoken presentations are texts, too) can be analyzed according to hierarchies of two, three, or four levels: main points, subpoints, sub-subpoints, etc. In formal outlines, each of these is indented a bit further from the left margin and given a different kind of number or letter designation. Using the same spatial layout, but discarding the numbering, you can divide your page into "regions" for an informal outline that arranges the text both vertically and horizontally. (Some notetakers who use this method turn their pages sideways to give each region more horizontal space.) The far-left region is for very general points; the middle contains more specific ideas that support the general points; the far right is for highly specific facts. Listening for the signposts mentioned above, the notetaker can identify which region the information belongs in, and jot it down in that area of the page. As always, it's important to leave plenty of space throughout because you may need it later if the speaker returns to a particular point. Here's an example of this type of informal outline:

formal outline	linear		
		signposts	First Last
informal outline	nonlinear		get the pieces
	discussion		sort by region

There are several advantages to this informal "region of the page" system. First, regardless of the organization—or lack of it—in the presentation, your notes will identify the relationships among the pieces. If the facts come first, there's still room for the general points farther to the left on the page. Second, dividing the page into regions helps remind the notetaker what to expect and what to listen closely for. If you only have general points, you know there may be subpoints yet to come. Finally, if the speaker never fills in those gaps, but does pause to ask for questions, you can help yourself and your fellow notetakers by following up on those blank spaces: you have a ready set of questions to ask. And even if there isn't an opportunity to follow up with the speaker, you at least know where you need to fill in information on your own. Using this system, listeners can often salvage much useful material from those "stream of consciousness" listening situations that can be frustrating to capture in a more linear, point-by-point outline.

Re-Annotating While Listening

Spending years in and around classrooms, you've no doubt heard—or even said—"So-and-so's class is *so* boring. All he ever does is just say what's in the book. Why do I even need to go to class?" We might argue that this is seldom truly the case: most speakers, no matter how closely they seem to follow a printed text, add insights and experiences as they go along. But more important, and very often overlooked by those listening, is what the speaker *doesn't* talk about or mentions only in passing. The amount and kind of attention he or she pays to different points, as well as the content of the discussion, suggest how listeners can determine what is and is not important in the printed text.

In such situations, effective listeners use their time not to take a new set of notes but rather to re-annotate the text they've already read. The worst mistake that *in*effective listeners make is to decide, "I'll just listen and read the book later; after all, it's got everything in it anyway." When you *know* the speaker is going to follow a predetermined text—the agenda for a meeting, a preprinted speech, a textbook—read and annotate it in advance. Jot down your questions, note key terms to listen for, identify the organizing structure of the text. Then, as you listen, keep the text in front of you so you can make additional annotations, perhaps in a different color so you can distinguish them.

Because we think learning to re-annotate a text while listening to a speaker is one of the most important skills that distinguish experts from nonexperts, we'll also give you an example that illustrates the other side. In a third-year architecture course we've observed, we noticed that most of the students had a lot of trouble taking and using notes effectively. The instructor, who uses many slides to illustrate his lectures—often projecting them side-by-side on two screens—doesn't require a specific textbook for the course. Instead, he makes his lecture notes, which include sample exam questions and references for further reading, available for students to buy at a local photocopy shop. But most of the students don't buy the notes in advance of his lectures, despite his constant reminders about their availability. Some try to jot down important points (and thus miss looking at the slides); others just sit back, watch, and listen, hoping to soak up as much as possible. Then, just before each exam, students rush out and buy the notes, gather in small groups to try to answer the sample questions, and to "figure out" the instructor's notes. Most are frustrated.

We can't argue that all their frustrations would be solved by simply buying the notes in advance. After all, learning is often a frustrating experience. But we will argue that these students, like all students who strive to become experts in their chosen fields, need to discover the advantages of prereading and annotating, as well as re-annotating as they listen.

Annotating Notes "On the Go"

In our discussion of writing strategies for effective reading, we point out several strategies for annotating a written text: responding with comments and questions; highlighting key terms and ideas; enumerating lists; drawing pictures, diagrams, and flowcharts. We think each of these strategies is equally useful for annotating a set of notes as you take them.

But one of the problems notetakers must face is time. Unlike a written text, which stops "moving" when you stop reading, the spoken text—and thus, the notes on it—just keeps spewing out like paper from a computer printer gone wild. There usually isn't a "pause" button. Effective notetakers recognize this problem and find ways to annotate their notes "on the go." Here are some techniques, along with some suggestions on how to use them.

Because you can seldom "stop" taking notes long enough to annotate the text as it spews out, the obvious strategy is to *leave space to add annotations later*. But those blank spaces may remain blank, even later, if you can't remember what you intended to put in there. Immediacy is all-important. So, some notetakers *keep a separate jot list of key words* that come up so they know what to go back to later and develop further in their notes. Another technique is to *highlight terms or concepts in your notes* as you make them: it takes only a second to underline—or double underline—a word or two so it will stand out later when you scan your notes.

Responses and questions may be instantaneous in the mind of the notetaker, but they can take more time to formulate and write down. Many notetakers *develop systems of shorthand to identify reactions* to what they hear and write down. Some we've seen, along with various "translations," include those below:

Some Notetaking Shorthand

!!	Good point; I agree; I need to think about this more
NO	I disagree; This is a negative example
+	I agree; This is an advantage
*	Note this: it's important!
??	This is doubtful; I didn't understand this
Y?	Why? What are the reasons for this?
ck	Check on this; Find out more information

These symbols can be further specified by adding a word that identifies the essence of the reaction or question: "?? sources" could stand for "What are the sources of this problem?"

Take a few minutes now to list some of the shorthand symbols you use, as well as your translations. Then, because there's seldom time to create them when you need them, add a few more symbols that you could use to annotate your notetaking. Most important, *practice* using these the next time you find yourself taking notes.

____

____

____

Capturing Visuals in Notes

The adage "A picture is worth a thousand words" was never more true than when applied to notetaking. One clear picture can help recall an hour's discussion. Effective speakers also recognize this advantage; they often use visuals to help get across complex concepts. But they explain their visuals, too, in effect giving listeners *both* the picture and the thousand words that go with it. The problem for the notetaker, then: "Which one do I try to capture? If I spend time noting the explanation, I might miss the diagram that makes sense of it. If I draw the visual, I'll miss the explanation." Drawing pictures, sketching models, making flowcharts, *and* taking notes—doing each of these separately is time consuming; trying to do them all simultaneously is next to impossible. Quickly copied visuals can become incomprehensible chicken scratches on a page of notes. But if you don't get *something* down on paper, you may not be able to reconstruct the visual image later, when you do have time.

One solution is to ask the speaker for a copy of the visual, if he or she hasn't already provided you with one. Photocopiers are everywhere, and they can save your valuable notetaking time. If the visual comes from or is based on one in a book or other easily available source, jot it down so you can retrieve a copy later. And don't be afraid to ask for the source if it isn't given. Professionals, whether writing or speaking, are always ready to cite the sources of their material.

At other times, the image may be more transitory, drawn on a chalkboard and erased to make room for more, for instance. In such cases, effective listeners must make the choice: which is most important to get down on the page, the picture or the words that go with it? Whichever you opt for, be sure to leave plenty of space to reconstruct the other one later. Also, if you decide to sketch the visual, be sure to put as many words as possible on and around it: label its parts, identify what it's supposed to represent, give it a name. This works the other way as well: a list of labels for the parts may help jog the memory enough to reconstruct a picture later. Whenever possible, though, get *something* down that reflects your perception of the visual. A few squiggled lines or a descriptive phrase on an extra piece of paper can often help hold a visual image in mind long enough to reconstruct it later.

USING OTHER TOOLS FOR TAKING NOTES

As a District Conservationist, Allen administers a two-county office of the Natural Resources Conservation Service (NRCS), a branch of the U.S. Department of Agriculture, in central Nebraska. Allen and the other conservationists in his office consult with farmers and ranchers, advising and educating them on the wise use of natural resources, primarily soil and water. Because their goal is to promote conservation both through education and through designing specific conservation methods, Allen and his staff are constantly looking for opportunities to offer their services. And because much of their work occurs in the field—literally, in farmers' fields and ranchers' pastures—they can't always reach for a pencil and notebook to jot down ideas.

Much of the work of a conservationist takes place in a vehicle, driving to and from meetings with farmers and ranchers, or, in Allen's case, driving the forty miles each day to his office from his home in a nearby small town. No matter where he's going, Allen is surrounded by his work. Out one window, he sees drought-parched pastures grazed down almost to the dirt—an erosion nightmare just waiting for a heavy rain or a week of wind to bring it to life. Out another window, his trained eye spots a few plants of leafy spurge, a noxious weed that can take over a piece of land and render it untenable. In both cases, the farmer or rancher may not even be aware of the problem, or may not know that the local NRCS office can help solve it. Part of Allen's job, then, is to identify these situations and to offer the expertise of his office for solving them.

If it's convenient, Allen may pull off the road when he sees a potential problem and mark its location on a map he carries in his truck. A one- or two-word note on the map usually suffices to remind him of what he saw there. But it's not always convenient to pull off the road and make even these few notes. Or the problem may be so severe that he feels it needs immediate attention. So, besides a map and notebook, Allen carries two other tools that help him make notes: a small portable tape recorder and a camera. When he doesn't have time to stop—if, for example, he's on his way to a meeting—Allen reaches for the tape recorder and records a few comments about the location and the problem. Back in his office, Allen can replay the tape, identify the location, and write a letter to the landowner offering to help solve the problem.

If he has time to stop, he often takes photographs; these are very valuable and powerful records for a number of reasons. First, photos can provide very convincing evidence that a problem exists, if that's needed. Second, pictures are powerful reminders: seeing them lying on his desk, Allen is constantly urged to do something about the problems they show. Third, photos are excellent references. If, for example, the rancher comes to his office in response to Allen's offer of help, the photos become the focus of their talk. But Allen doesn't just photograph problems; he also keeps a set of "solution" photos that he can use to show the positive results of conservation techniques. These, then, can further help his discussion with the farmer by illustrating what he's recommending and how it will be an improvement. Finally, Allen can eventually pair his "before" photos with those taken after the solutions have been applied and use these to convince someone else that conservation can work, and show how it's done.

The tape recorder is also a handy way for Allen to take notes on his meetings with a farmer or rancher. Very often their discussion takes place outside, as they walk around a piece of land, where it's inconvenient to pause and jot notes on a pad. But these are extremely important discussions: based on what he sees and what they talk about, Allen will write a set of written recommendations developed specifically for that farmer and that location. Because they may discuss a wide range of options, and because Allen wants to suggest the greatest number of possibilities for the farmer to choose from, he often records their walking discussions so he can recall all of the options they've talked about. And listening to these recordings back in his office, sometimes days later, also helps him remember and picture in his mind topographic details of the location that he might otherwise forget.

Finally, an important part of his job consists essentially of promoting his services and educating the public about conservation. So Allen gathers "success stories" using the tape recorder and camera. He keeps a stack of photos showing good and poor conservation practices—sometimes a single "fence-line contrast" photo that shows adjoining fields—to illustrate the occasional news articles he writes. The photos help make his article or presentation communicate even more powerfully.

With his tape recorder handy, Allen can capture comments from satisfied farmers, which he may later quote in a written article, or use in the occasional short radio programs about conservation that he does. For radio shows, he finds it much easier to tape "candid" interviews with speakers who would be too busy, or too nervous, to do a more formal interview in a studio. Equally important, because these discussions sound much more realistic to his listeners—complete with familiar farm sounds in the background—Allen believes they are more likely to convince other farmers to give conservation a try.

Tape recorders and cameras can provide useful, and very powerful, means for notetaking. But there are some rules of etiquette you should keep in mind when using these tools.

Rules of Etiquette for Using Cameras and Recorders

1. Never record conversations without *first* asking permission from everyone involved and clearly stating your purpose for making the recording. If anyone objects, don't tape. Besides being common courtesy, it's the speakers' right to know that they're speaking "on the record."

2. Get permission before taking a photograph if the photo includes a person.
3. Never use a tape recording or photo for any purpose other than the one you stated when you got permission to make it. That *includes* sharing the tape or photo with your colleagues.
4. If you discover that your tape or photo might be useful for another purpose—for example, if you'd like to include the photo as part of a written document—get a separate permission for that purpose. (That's why professional photographers ask for names, addresses, and phone numbers of their subjects.)
5. Take care to keep tapes and photos together with other materials, such as written notes, that will guarantee your remembering exactly what they meant when they were made. Both tapes and photos have enormous potential for "interpretation," especially when they get separated by time and distance from the context in which they were made. For this reason, if you have any doubts or your memory seems at all fuzzy, don't use the material in the tape or photo.

▶ 14

Preparing Oral Presentations

Overview

In numerous polls of human fears, many people report being more afraid of speaking in public than of dying. If you really want to scare people, ask them to stand up and make a speech. Most of us are comfortable with the attention we're paid in everyday, face-to-face conversation. We believe our ideas are listened to—most of the time, anyway. But we don't feel as though they're under constant scrutiny. If we address a group of people, everything we say automatically becomes Public.

In this chapter, we ask you to look closely at what you already know how to *do*. Becoming conscious of and building on your knowledge of the similarities—as well as the differences—between writing and speaking situations is a first step toward becoming a more expert and confident public speaker. More important, awareness of these connections between writing and speaking will help you use writing to prepare and present your ideas effectively, both in writing and in oral presentations.

ANALYZING SPEAKING SITUATIONS

There are some obvious differences between formal and informal speech, just as there are between formal and informal writing. Informal speech, like most diary and letter writing, is spontaneous, unplanned. It just seems to bubble out. Although you may plan to meet and talk with your friends, you seldom plot out the topic(s) and the course of the conversation in advance. In fact, if you do, your friends are likely to notice right off and ask you what you're doing. Informal speech develops on its own; it's self-generating, dynamic, recursive, redundant. How many times have you noticed, after several minutes of talk, that a conversation seems to be back where it started? Talking in circles is a fairly common feature of informal speech.

Formal speech, however, is planned. Even those brave souls willing to risk life, limb, and reputation in that most dangerous speaking event, the extemporaneous speech, prepare something in advance, "just in case." And the more spontaneous, dynamic, and self-generating a presentation seems, usually the more preparation and practice it has behind it. There are relatively few formal speaking situations in which the contents will generate themselves the way informal speech grows. Instead, speakers must determine, at the very least, what topics arise and, implicitly, which ones do not. That is, they maintain control over the situation.

Just as writers carefully organize formal documents, speakers also make decisions about the arrangement of formal speech. In general, oral presentations tend to follow linear patterns, usually the beginning-middle-end structure also common to formal writing. Indeed, try for a moment to imagine an oral presentation that follows any other pattern. It has achieved such status that it's often reduced to this simple formula for success:

- Tell 'em what you're going to tell 'em (Introduction)
- Tell 'em (Body)
- Tell 'em what you told 'em (Conclusion)

This is overly simplistic; and it's no guarantee either for effective writing or effective speaking. But it does point out an important similarity between formal writing and formal speech: both rely on a certain amount of recursion and redundancy.

In formal situations, recursion is planned. The speaker or writer *chooses* to return to an earlier point to reiterate it; or, the entire presentation is tied together by returning to an opening scenario during the conclusion. Particularly in speaking situations, repetition and redundancy aid memory—both the speaker's and the listener's. All of us know a little bit about the connection between repetition and memory from singing the alphabet song. Some of us still sing that song, although perhaps not out loud, when we're trying to file things alphabetically. By contrast, when informal speech or writing turns back on itself, it's often because a speaker/writer has decided the topic isn't finished yet. Or, it's a way of stalling for time while the next idea is formulated.

One important aspect of informal and formal speech concerns who talks when. On the surface, it seems that a clear and obvious difference exists here between the two ends of the speaking continuum: in informal speech, everyone gets to talk; in formal speech, only one person does. But that distinction is as false as the notion that, in writing—regardless of whether it's more or less formal—only the writer "talks."

It's true that, as informal speech progresses, regardless of the number of participants, it generally shifts from one participant to another in a system of "turns." Sometimes, in very animated or hostile situations, the turns overlap so much that conversation becomes chaos. Most of the time, though, it's pretty orderly. The rules that determine whose turn it is to speak, as well as those regarding how to initiate and how to relinquish a turn, are among the first elements of communication we learn as children. Language acquisition experts studying the interaction between infants and their parents have noted how adults create whole conversations by "playing both parts," alternately asking and answering questions. As their speech develops, children begin to take part and become more adept at this conversation game. Sometimes they even conjure up imaginary friends and practice playing both parts, just as they have seen adults do.

An easily identifiable feature of informal speaking, then, is that it's fairly democratic. Every participant has essentially equal power to add to or to direct it in new—or old—directions. The pejorative phrase "one-sided conversation" accurately describes what happens when this no longer holds true: one speaker gets the upper hand, usually to the annoyance of everyone else. Most of the time, we might say, everyone shares the work. But what is most often overlooked is that the "work" includes both speaking *and* listening: just as there is no conversation when only one person speaks, there can be no true conversation if everyone speaks. Just as there can be no written communication without a reader.

In formal speech situations, however, the atmosphere seems just the opposite—essentially autocratic. The speaker does have both more power and more responsibility in the communication. He or she controls, either implicitly or explicitly, the content, the direction, and the pace of the speech. But here, too, there is a common misconception that the speaker does all the work. Hardly. The speaker's power lasts only as long as the audience listens. Because listening, like reading, is less easily observed, it's often overlooked as an important element of communication. Both reading and listening are activities that audiences must be encouraged to participate in.

In informal speech, and writing, the other participants are generally familiar to us. When we write memos or talk to our colleagues, we know them by name, often quite well. Furthermore, we also know—without having to think about it—what they know and don't know, their level of expertise on a variety of topics. They, in turn, know the same about us. This is, in fact, precisely why most of us find it difficult to strike up a conversation (informal speech) with a complete stranger: we don't yet know anything about our audience, nor they about us. And that's precisely why the best way to strike up conversations with strangers is to ask them to talk about themselves, their interests, their work—and to do the same in return. The key to informal communication is familiarity.

In formal speaking situations, at least some members of the audience are usually unfamiliar to the speaker. Thus, effective speakers consciously consider, in advance, who the audience will be, what they know—and don't know—about the subject of the presentation, and what attitudes they may have about it. Reciprocally, effective speakers also establish for the audience who they are and what they know. This is often called establishing source credibility. Because it's automatically there in informal situations, based on our familiarity with the other participants, we naturally expect it to be instantaneous in formal situations as well. Thus, the most important period in a formal speech is the first several seconds. During that short time, an audience forms its impressions of a speaker based on what the speaker says, does, and how the speaker looks. Think of how fast this is. But think also of how television commercials—quite expensive ones—rely on 15 to 30 seconds of air time to capture your attention and sell you a product. It's essential, then, that the speaker consider, in advance, what the audience will see and hear during those all-important first seconds.

The purpose of a formal speech, too, must be carefully considered in advance. Unless a speaker knows precisely what he or she is trying to accomplish, it's unlikely that the audience will figure it out, or that it will be accomplished. In informal speaking situations, the purpose of the talk is often implicit, or developed on the go—or, at times, nonexistent. "Just shooting the breeze" is reason enough for lots of informal talk. But speakers in formal situations determine their purpose and state it explicitly, even when it seems obvious to everyone present. This is yet another way in which formal speaking compares with formal writing: to accomplish its intentions, those intentions have to be clearly communicated to all of the participants.

In summary, you can use the following to help you analyze a speaking situation:

- What is the level of formality of this situation? Compare it with a writing situation at the same level of formality.
- Who are the members of the audience? What is their relationship to the speaker? What role are they expected to play in the communication?

- What is the speaker's role? What impression does the speaker create? When? How?
- What is the purpose of the presentation? Where and how is it made clear?

WRITING THE PRESENTATION

No matter how confident you feel about *writing* a clear and effective text, presenting information orally can be a very discomforting experience. But keeping in mind two key principles can help alleviate some of this discomfort:

1. Know your material very well.
2. Encourage your audience to become active participants.

In discussing preparation as a key to effective oral presentations, we can't overstress the importance of time. Even a brief, informal talk requires extensive work over a long time to prepare. In fact, we would argue that short presentations require *more* work and *more* time to prepare because they must be very "tight" to fit the time constraints. To a point, the more time you can spend preparing, the more confident you'll feel about your presentation. But putting together a presentation involves a number of different activities and can't be accomplished, effectively, overnight.

Knowing your material well is also obviously important; after all, the point of any oral presentation is to communicate something you know to someone else who doesn't know it—or at least someone who doesn't know it as you do, or from your perspective. More important, though, is the confidence you'll gain from thorough preparation on your topic.

The best way we know for you to become well acquainted with what you know is to write it down. As we've explained elsewhere in this book, writing forces us to think, to explore, to clarify, to connect, and to remember. So, begin preparing your presentation by writing down what you know about your subject. You could make lists of ideas, write out a quick first draft of your presentation, try making an outline—any of the many writing strategies that you know can work equally well for this purpose.

In many cases, oral presentations are based on written documents. For example:

- A biochemist researcher reports on her most recent project at a conference.
- As part of a senior design project, an architecture student presents his design to a jury of faculty and practicing architects.

- A marketing consultant addresses the board of directors of XYZ Corporation on the feasibility of expanding their product line to include wunkles as well as widgets.

In each of these cases, the oral presentation is simply impossible to prepare until the written document—research report, design drawings and program, feasibility study—is complete, or nearly so.

Presenting this work orally, each of these speakers will rely on the knowledge gained from writing the document. But on those rare occasions when an oral report is not based on a written document that serves some other purpose, effective speakers *create* such a document anyway, both explicitly and implicitly. Explicitly, they jot notes, create headings and subheadings, draft and revise large chunks of discussion, arrange and rearrange their ideas *on paper*. Implicitly—internally—the same processes occur: noting ideas, sorting them hierarchically, creating and recreating a developing text. The more they work on the external document, the more the internal one, the one they will present orally, gets polished. And besides its value in preparing the oral presentation, a written draft can later become a finished document, one that would not have existed except for the oral presentation. For example, after a successful presentation on her company's first-quarter earnings, the speaker's boss asks for a draft of her report. Imagine the impression she makes—as well as the time she saves—if she hands him the draft as they leave the conference room rather than a day or more later.

So, a useful first step in preparing an oral presentation is to *work through a written draft on the topic*. It doesn't have to be fancy. In fact, it may be a mess, just a list of (seemingly) random ideas. Or, it might be one long paragraph that wanders all over the place. Then again, it could be a 25-page document, complete with appendices and illustrations. We don't want to stipulate exactly what you should have written; but we can't overstress the value of having something written before you start. The weakest oral presentations are often those that have no writing behind them.

Now, once you have some kind of written draft, dismantle it; but do so in a particular way. *Pull out the headings and subheadings of your text and make an outline of your material.* If it's not a fully completed text, write what *would* be its headings and subheadings. These are really the key to developing an outline, anyway. This step works especially well on a word processor, where you can cut and move large blocks of text quickly. Many word processors and presentation software packages have a built-in outline view that will collapse and expand a long document at the click of a mouse button. But pen and paper do just as well—and they have the added advantage of reinforcing your ideas as you recopy them.

The outline you generate acts as a shorthand overview of your material. It's much smaller and easier to work with than the entire document. It's also much easier to see "holes" in an outline than in a full text. Set aside the full text for a while: save it in a separate file in your word processor or put it away in a drawer until later. For the moment, you don't want to be distracted by its detail.

When you have a working version of the content of your presentation, you need to consider two other important elements of the communication situation: your audience and your purpose. So, pause for a few minutes to *write full responses to these questions*:

- Who, exactly, are the members of my audience?
- What do they already know about this topic?
- What *don't* they know about this topic?
- What do they *want* or *need* to know about this topic?
- Why is this audience listening to me; that is, what special qualifications or knowledge have they recognized in me?
- What do I want to accomplish from my presentation?
- What temporary or lasting effects do I have in mind?

With responses to these questions before you, look back over your working outline. Reconsider your material in terms of the audience and purpose you've just written. For instance, does your outline include lots of material your audience already knows? Or, does it lack important background they must have before you can achieve your purpose? Are you discussing only general information without getting to your special knowledge?

PLANNING THE PRESENTATION

At this stage you also need to reconsider all three elements—audience, purpose, and content—in terms of time. So, *make a time budget*. If, for example, you have a total of 15 minutes for your oral presentation, plan to talk for 10 minutes and allow 5 minutes for questions/comments from the audience. Try to divide your available time according to the material you have so far and your best estimate of the time needed to cover it.

By the way, *never* talk so long that you don't have time for questions and comments, no matter how important you think your material is. If it's really important, your listeners will ask questions that allow you to fill it in. And audiences generally presume that speakers who don't leave time for questions either have planned poorly or are in love with the sound of their own voices.

Trying to create such a time budget usually points out the need for the next step in the process: *Limit your material*. First, remember that no one ever wants to hear everything, no matter how interested *you* may be in your material—or how interesting you think you can make it for your audience. Use these questions to help you decide what to include:

- What material *must* I present? (For example, necessary background knowledge, history, consequences)
- What material *must* I leave out? (For example, complicated procedures, technical explanations, data)
- What material *could* I present, if there's time? (For example, problems encountered, unusual but tangential findings)

Second, given the way we generally perceive ourselves and the things we're interested in, it's usually the case that you can cover only half of what you think is "absolutely essential." So, go back through your "must include" and "could include" responses and number them according to their priority. Now you're ready to trim your material again, by about half. In our experience, this still includes too much, but it's closer to reality.

Next, *arrange your material and recalculate your time budget*. Although you'll probably want to stick with the arrangement you developed in your original outline, also consider how you can organize your material to shape the communicative force of your presentation. For instance, you'll want to put the most important points in the middle, where you're most likely to have your listeners' undivided attention and when you'll feel most confident and at ease. It's also a good idea to place one or two of your "could include" points near the end, just before your concluding remarks. This is your "padding," just in case you talk faster than you expected. You can easily cut these extra points without adversely affecting your overall purpose.

ILLUSTRATING THE PRESENTATION

Once you're satisfied that you have adjusted the material in your working outline to fit the communication situation and the time budget, you're ready to *prepare visual displays and handouts appropriate to the length and content of your presentation*. You've no doubt seen presentations in which no handouts were used; instead you and your fellow listeners may have been dazzled by visual displays created with one of the new multimedia or presentation software packages.

Such visually powerful presentations can be very successful. But before you invest lots of money—and time—in either handouts or multimedia presentations, we strongly recommend you consider the pros and cons of each. (For brevity's sake, we'll use the general term "multimedia" to include presentations involving—individually or together—computer software, projection systems, audio and video, both tape and digital—and other nonpaper media.)

Creating and using a handout as part of your presentation does have several advantages. First, writing the handout is yet another way to become familiar with your material. Second, it provides your listeners with an excellent listening tool, one that helps them follow your presentation. This, in turn, helps you: your listeners can focus more on your message and less on trying to outguess where you're going and how you're going to get there. Finally, distributing a handout, and *going over it quickly at the beginning of your presentation,* is an excellent way to establish your rapport and authority with an audience, and to settle your anxiety before you get to the important material you want to present.

Of course, handouts have their disadvantages, too. If you haven't planned for a handout as you prepare your presentation, you may find yourself "throwing it together at the last minute," which can hardly make for a good impression. There's also the cost of copying (not to mention the environmental impact of all those pages), plus worrying about having enough copies. Finally, when you use handouts with an oral presentation, you must carefully consider when—and *how*—to distribute them, as well as when and how to refer to them. Integrating a handout with your talk is a bit like dancing: it takes some coordination, some timing, and a fair amount of practice.

One clear advantage of preparing a multimedia presentation is that it encourages you to think more about the visual impact that your ideas will have on your audience. Sometimes—yes, *sometimes*—a visual presentation *is* worth a thousand words. Second, many presentation software packages include or can connect with word processing software. That way, you can quickly pull in headings or text directly from a document you've been writing. These packages also often include many files containing pictures, images, or diagrams (commonly called "clip art") that you can use or modify, saving you some time and frustration developing your own. Finally, such effects as dissolves (in which one image melts away as another appears), pop-ups (in which additional information "pops up" on screen when a button is clicked), and video with sound simply cannot be done on paper. And, yes, multimedia presentations are *fun*, both to create and to watch.

Keep in mind, however, that multimedia presentations can be very distracting for listeners. They generally must shift their eyes and ears away from the speaker—and the point he or she is making!—to shift into another mode of "listening." It's pretty easy to have too much of a good thing; in the multimedia context, it's called "visual noise."

Next, there's the problem of the *equipment* you need, both to prepare and to project such presentations. (In fact, we've attended sessions at which the speaker spent more time explaining the multimedia equipment—how it works, what it costs, where to get it—than on the presentation topic!) Finally, multimedia packages require some time to learn and some creativity to use well. Many packages are extremely user-friendly: they have "standard" backgrounds, effects, and clip art that the software will overlay on your text at the click of a mouse button. The result is that your presentation, regardless of its topic, may look like everyone else's when your viewers are expecting something quite a bit more spectacular.

Once you've decided whether you want to use handouts, multimedia, or both, give plenty of time to developing and polishing them. The following guidelines, developed through our own trial and error and lots of observation of both successful and unsuccessful presentations, will help you create effective materials of all types to support your presentation.

An outline of your presentation is perhaps the most common and most useful aid for both you and your audience. If you're working from a fully developed written text, use some of its headings as major points on your outline. Also, the lead sentences or concluding summaries from each section of your text may indicate the subpoints. In presenting your outline, be sure to leave some blank space between the points. On handouts, it's a good idea to double-space the entire outline. You'll fill in the details during the presentation and your listeners need room to take notes if they wish. Equally important, the extra white space on the page or screen affects the psychological impact of your message on your audience: lots of words crammed together may make them think, "Oh, no; he's going to drone on for hours!" Finally, avoid using more than three levels in your outline; two levels is usually enough.

Other useful types of materials include drawings, diagrams, charts, statistical data, and other visual texts that often appear as appendices of written documents. Whether you choose to include these on handouts, show them using electronic media, or both, carefully consider whether you need or want to use such visual texts. Ask yourself: Will they help or hinder my presentation? Will they be more effective if each member of my audience has a copy or if I show them to the whole group at once? Will the audience need much time to "read" each one?

All visual text should be extremely concise, clearly labeled, uncluttered, and easy to read. A good rule of thumb is to allow fifteen to twenty seconds: if a visual can't be taken in and deciphered by the average reader in that short time span, it's not going to work. One way to test visuals on paper is to drop them on the floor. If you can read them easily while standing up—with your eyes approximately five to six feet away from them—they should be simple enough to work well for your audience. Test multimedia materials the same way, but from across the room. You also must keep in mind that, as you speak, you'll have to give up those fifteen to twenty seconds of your time to let your audience take in each visual text.

Supplying individual paper copies of visual texts can expedite their use: everyone can look over them at leisure. However, you will have more control if you display them using a projection system, even something as simple as an overhead projector or a flip chart. When you control the images, you can choose exactly when to show them—for greatest effect—and when to put them away. One common mistake we see presenters make is to leave a visual on display for many minutes after the talk has moved on to another topic. Invariably, many members of the audience are still staring at the picture and not listening to the speaker. A third possibility may be the most advantageous: you could choose to include copies of your visual texts as handouts—for later reference—but to control the projected image during your presentation.

All of these considerations should not discourage you from using visual texts—either on handouts or in multimedia—with your oral presentation, however. A good, clear picture *can* make the difference between understanding and confusion, especially in an oral presentation. We've also noted that many of the follow-up questions that audiences ask refer back to a visual text, suggesting, at least, that they are very important memory devices.

It also may be advantageous for you to print different sections of your handout on different colored paper, especially if it's several pages long. For instance, if you have a single outline page and three visual texts, put the outline on top, on white paper, and each of the visuals on a distinctive color. Then, during your talk, you can direct listeners to "Figure 1, on the blue page." But don't get too carried away; some colors make reading very difficult.

The same is true with multimedia: subtle changes in background—such as color—can help you alert viewers to shifts in your topic. But be sure it's readable. Despite the many, many possibilities that multimedia may provide, most experienced presenters return to a very simple philosophy: less is more.

Some of the more effective visual aids for oral presentations are three-dimensional objects—photos, samples, models, prototypes, etc.—that can't be reproduced for the entire audience. These, too, present both advantages and disadvantages that you must weigh carefully. Many times these visual aids are too small to show to the entire group; the alternative is to circulate the object throughout the audience. At other times, the object may be too large, too fragile, or too valuable to circulate. (We remember one speaker who circulated a Troy ounce of gold and then nervously watched it pass around the group, his presentation completely forgotten.) You may also need to use the visual aid as you give your presentation, demonstrating how your new widget works, for example. In all cases, the value of such materials can be lost because the audience doesn't know exactly what to focus on. So, a less detailed visual representation of the object (a line drawing or sketch, perhaps) with specific labels will help you draw attention where you want it. And it provides your audience a handy reference later.

Regardless of how (or if) you choose to illustrate your presentation, we suggest that you indicate on your outline where you will refer to diagrams, objects, or demonstrations. This lets your audience anticipate them and also provides another important set of signposts to guide you and your listeners through your presentation. The same is true for question-and-answer pauses. In a short presentation (20 minutes or less), it's usually better to take questions at the end. But if you're explaining very detailed procedures or describing a complex idea, it may be useful to stop and clarify before you move on. Either way, do indicate on your outline—and state this clearly, at the beginning of your talk—when you will take questions from the audience.

PRACTICING THE PRESENTATION

The last step in preparing any oral presentation is the one that almost everyone knows is needed. Still, it's the one that usually receives the least attention. *Practice giving the oral presentation* at least once before a live audience. More than once is even better. There's a good reason so many television shows are filmed before a live audience: there's no way to get realistic reactions without real people. Try out your presentation on an individual or a small group who accurately represent the actual audience. If you'll be talking to a lay audience, then a spouse or roommate can give you feedback. If your audience will be knowledgeable on your subject, your trial audience needs to be knowledgeable as well. The primary purposes of such a practice session are to check your time budget and to find out, based on feedback from your test audience, what material needs to be added or deleted. They also may suggest ways for you to reorganize or streamline your presentation for better effect. If you're prone to high anxiety, practicing before a small audience will help reduce your fears: it's easier to speak before a small number of listeners than a full room. Finally, a practice run further establishes the material in your mind. Ironically, the best way to achieve a spontaneous-sounding oral presentation is to practice it.

It's also useful, if possible, to practice where you'll be giving the presentation, or at least in a similar environment. You might sound really good in a small study room at the library, but you'll need a lot more volume to fill a classroom with thirty people in it. Equipment, too, takes some getting used to. Try out the overhead, slide projector, or presentation software. Practice putting transparencies on, focusing the image, changing slides. Know what button to press to advance to the next slide or screen. Get used to the microphone, if one is to be used. As listeners, we've all cringed at the screech of feedback or strained to hear the speaker who's just a tad too far away from the mike. Finally, during the practice session it's also a good idea to develop backup plans, just in case the bulb burns out, the mike stand breaks, or the software crashes.

PREPARING THE PRESENTATION: A REVIEW

Here's a quick reminder of the suggestions we've discussed in this chapter.

1. Allow *at least* one week to prepare, more if possible.
2. Work through a written draft on the topic.
3. Pull out the headings and subheadings of your draft and make an outline of your material.
4. Analyze your audience by writing full responses to these questions:
    - Who, exactly, are the members of my audience?
    - What do they already know about this topic?
    - What *don't* they know about this topic?
    - What do they *want* or *need* to know about this topic?
    - Why is this audience listening to me; that is, what special qualifications or knowledge have they recognized in me?
    - What do I want to accomplish from my presentation?
    - What temporary or lasting effects do I have in mind?
5. Make a time budget.
6. Limit your material by responding to these questions:
    - What material *must* I present? (For example, necessary background knowledge, history, consequences)
    - What material *must* I leave out? (For example, complicated procedures, technical explanations, data)
    - What material *could* I present, if there's time? (For example, problems encountered, unusual but tangential findings)
7. Arrange your material and recalculate your time budget.
8. Prepare handouts and visual aids appropriate to the length and content of your presentation.
9. Practice giving the oral presentation at least once before a live audience.

These suggestions focus primarily on the first of our key points for effective oral presentations: Know your material very well. By the time you've worked through all of these strategies, you should feel very confident about your knowledge of the material. Now—and not a minute before now—you're ready to consider some strategies to employ during the presentation itself that will help you convey that material with the greatest confidence and effectiveness.

▶ 15

Strategies for Giving Effective Oral Presentations

Overview

Setting Up

Previewing

Introducing Yourself and Your Purpose

Moving through the Script

Showing Your Expertise

Most public speakers would probably agree that preparing is 75 percent of the effort involved in any oral presentation. But they would likely also agree that the remaining 25 percent—giving it—is far more difficult. Knowing your material well, creating wonderful handouts and visual aids, and practicing take time and hard work. But they do not necessarily guarantee *giving* an effective presentation.

We believe one reason many speakers, both expert and novice, feel so much pressure during oral presentations is their perception that they are doing all the work. They see speaking as active, listening as passive. Given this view of the situation, is it any wonder speakers get nervous? After all, don't we all get nervous when someone watches us work? But for both speaking and listening—and the communication as a whole—to be effective, they must *both* be active endeavors.

The strategies we suggest in this chapter focus on achieving the second key principle of effective oral presentations: Encourage your audience to become active participants. That doesn't necessarily mean that they, too, will speak during your presentation, although we think that's nearly always desirable. But there are many ways, both explicit and implicit, to draw an audience into a public speaking situation. We think the value of doing so is obvious: it's both easier and more effective to work *with* an audience than *for* one.

SETTING UP

Perhaps the most common problem speakers have is not getting started, but rather getting started *too soon*. Before their audience is settled and prepared to listen, before they have distributed their handouts or set up their equipment, sometimes even before they've taken an adequate breath of air, many speakers launch into their first point. With nerves fluttering, and perhaps worried that time is quickly dwindling, they take off like Pony Express riders with one foot in the stirrup.

If you hope to engage your audience and to invite them to become participants in your presentation:

- *Get set up before you begin.*

Give them time to settle in their chairs, to prepare to take notes if they wish, and to focus their energy on listening. Getting set up is also just common sense. Even the most relaxed and experienced speaker can't do two or three things at once; and there are some general "housekeeping" activities to take care of before the talk begins.

So, before you start to talk, distribute all your handouts, making sure that each person gets one. We wish we could recommend a quick, quiet, and efficient system for this; but years of experience in classrooms only reinforce our belief that no such system has yet been devised. If there are extra copies (and there should be; always *over*estimate), ask someone seated near the door to give a handout to any late arrivals. While handouts are circulating, you can arrange your script, organize your visual aids in order of their use, check your equipment to see that it works, and find a comfortable place to stand before your audience. Finally, don't be afraid to rearrange the furniture if necessary. It's better to get rid of or bring in a lectern before you start than to try to jostle one around in midpresentation.

During your practice session, you should determine exactly what equipment you need and where it will be best placed *for you*. We suggest you try out as many different combinations as possible during practice sessions. Lecterns or podiums can provide taller speakers a useful prop to hold their papers at the appropriate distance; for shorter speakers, they often become a tree behind which to hide from the audience. Conversely, short to average-height speakers may find that a flat surface (the top of a table or desk, for example) allows them to see their material and the audience to see them. But tall speakers who try this same arrangement usually treat the audience to a fine view of their scalp as they stoop to see their papers.

It's also important to try out visual aids in advance to make sure that they will work as planned. Nothing is more frustrating than discovering, during a presentation, that the posters you worked so hard to produce are too limp to stand up on the easel. Knowing this in advance allows you either to add reinforcements to the cards or to bring along a large clip to hold them in place. And getting things set up before you begin further assures that everything will work as planned. Or, as fixed.

PREVIEWING

Once you're set up, it's time to start talking. But you're still not quite ready to dive into the content of your presentation. And neither is your audience. Instead, use a few seconds to:

- *Go through your handout*, explaining what's on each page and pointing out when you'd like to answer questions from the audience.

Humans are curious creatures. Give them a three-page handout and, before you know it, they'll be peeking at the last two pages to see what's on them. And, as active listeners, they *need* to know what's on those pages so they can anticipate shifts and follow your talk. So, rather than ignoring their curiosity, or discouraging it, it's better to capitalize on it; then, your listeners will be better prepared to focus their curiosity on what you're saying.

If yours is a multimedia presentation:

- *Create an overview screen* to use as you preview the key points you'll cover and explain when you'd like to answer questions from the audience.

This opening screen is critical because it not only identifies your key topics but it also helps establish the "look" of your presentation. Use it to check visibility ("Can you see this clearly in the back of the room?") and adjust colors, if possible. This is also a good opportunity to let the audience know whether you can "back up" or review a previously shown segment of your presentation. Finally, if you're using both handouts and multimedia, explain how you expect the audience to use both: for instance, "You can just watch the screen and then use the handouts later for reference."

INTRODUCING YOURSELF AND YOUR PURPOSE

At times, you may be introduced by someone else who may or may not also mention the subject of your talk. Other times, you're on your own. But in either case, it's a good idea to:

- *Introduce yourself and clearly establish the purpose of your presentation.*

First of all, you should always identify who you are, why you're interested in the subject, and what your background or credentials are. Because it's usually pretty easy to talk about oneself, the subject we each usually know the best, it often helps reduce those immediate jitters. (Remember, though, that you can't tell them everything.) Stating your interest in the topic builds a rapport with the audience. Audiences will listen with interest to someone they know is speaking from interest.

Although it may sound pushy or downright egotistical, it's essential that you establish your credentials. Listeners, like readers, are less likely to grant authority and credibility to someone who does not assert them. Of course, you must be careful not to overstate, or overemphasize, your expertise on the subject.

Finally, stating the purpose of your presentation is an important cue to your listeners that they should be settled in. It's a clear signal that you're now ready to move through your material.

So far you're probably wondering how much of your valuable speaking time all of this getting ready has taken up. Actually, not very much. Definitely less than a minute; more likely between thirty and forty-five seconds. Is it worth it to you, as speaker, to "lose" that much time? Absolutely. The investment invariably pays off in a better-prepared and attentive audience. In turn, that means better understanding of what you're communicating. Not a bad return for thirty to forty-five seconds of time.

MOVING THROUGH THE SCRIPT

At this point, you're ready to:

- *Move through your script.*

As you do so, remember to use headings and keywords to signpost for your audience. For example, "The BACKGROUND for my research . . . " or "I CONCLUDE from my study that . . . " One way to judge how effectively you're using signposts—one way you can rely on your audience's active participation—is to watch for listeners poring over the pages of your outline or flipping back and forth among the pages of your handout.

This often indicates that they're lost; probably there are others who are equally lost but are just not showing it. To assure their continued participation, you need to get them back on track. Either pause and explicitly point out where you are in your handout or, more subtly, mention a keyword that will help listeners get their bearings.

What if *you* get lost? Those of us who learned to play a musical instrument as children still hear echoes of "No matter what happens, just keep going" ringing in our ears. But that's not such good advice in public speaking situations; it usually leads to babbling and floundering. It also makes audiences extremely nervous because they usually sense rather quickly when the speaker gets lost. Instead, do what expert speakers do: pause and find your place. It rarely takes more than five or ten seconds. Don't worry; your audience will wait for you. (They really have little choice.) And if you're *really* lost, admit it. Ask your listeners to tell you what you were just talking about, an excellent way to encourage their active participation. These unplanned pauses are also excellent opportunities to answer questions or go back and clarify a point.

Visual texts and visual aids are common causes of interruptions in the flow of otherwise smooth presentations. If you use them, be sure you've clearly indicated on your script where you want to refer to each visual aid. Stack them in order of their use and put them close at hand so you don't have to pause and search through a pile of papers for the one you want. It's also a good idea to mark on your script if you need to allow time for your listeners to digest a visual text. Finally, note on your script where you'll be finished with each visual aid as a reminder to put it away.

SHOWING YOUR EXPERTISE

A few obvious strategies for giving effective presentations are worth discussing simply because they are so often overlooked. These added touches will help you truly demonstrate your expertise. First:

- *Maintain eye contact with your listeners.*

Use their expressions to judge the loudness and speed of your delivery. You may even want to pause and ask if those in back can hear. Watch, also, for listeners squinting to see your visual aids: are your slides in focus? If you see lots of people staring at a flip chart, it might be a reminder to put it away if you're finished with it.

You also may be able to read misunderstanding or confusion on the faces of your audience, but be cautious: sometimes a blank stare is actually intense attention.

Also, remember to:

- *Watch the time.*

As if you didn't have enough to worry about, right? Hypothetically, this problem should have been resolved during your preparation and practice sessions. But presentations seldom move at the same rate on different occasions.

Having given the same presentation several times to different audiences, we've noticed that we sometimes expand or contract it by as much as a third. You may want to establish some time markers on your script: for example, write "8:00" next to "Conclusion" to indicate that you want to be on the Conclusion with eight minutes left, to allow five minutes for questions. If you get behind, *omit* less important points. Don't try to catch up; it's impossible. Don't try to summarize; it's impossible, too. And don't try to talk faster to cover more material; it makes you and the audience very nervous.

Finally, because we know that public speaking situations are one of the most terrifying, and most important, activities that professionals engage in, we offer these last suggestions, which we call "confidence builders":

- *Don't worry about minor errors as you speak.*

Everyone makes minor errors—in pronunciation, usage, and syntax—when they speak. In fact, one of the more interesting aspects of oral communication is that it works at all, considering the amount of "noise" and "error" that has to be filtered out. The most effective speakers ignore such small and infrequent glitches in their talk. They know that, as active participants, their listeners are focusing on *what* they are saying, not necessarily *how perfectly* they have said it. They also realize that their audience will let them know if they make significant errors that impede understanding.

And, never forget that:

- *You are the expert.*

Even if you don't feel it, by virtue of your physical position, front and center, you automatically have a certain status. And you are in control of the situation. Furthermore, your listeners have a very high regard for you and your knowledge; after all, they're listening to you, aren't they? They want to learn from you. You have something that they want or need.

Works Cited

American Heritage Dictionary of the English Language. New College Edition. Ed. William Morris. Boston: Houghton, 1981.

Baker, Mark. *Cops: Their Lives in Their Own Words*. New York: Pocket, 1986.

Berthoff, Ann. *Forming, Thinking, Writing: The Composing Imagination*. Montclair, NJ: Boynton/Cook, 1982.

Burke, James. *Connections*. Boston: Little, 1978.

Cantrell, Susan. "They Like It Late." *Tucson Citizen* 19 May 1989; B1.

Carson, Rachel. *Silent Spring*. New York: Houghton, 1962.

Collins, A., and E. Smith. *Teaching the Process of Reading Comprehension* (Tech. Rep. No. 182). Urbana: U of Illinois, Center for the Study of Reading, September 1980.

Cross, Geoffrey A. *Collaboration and Conflict: A Contextual Exploration of Group Writing and Positive Emphasis*. Cresskill, NJ: Hampton P, 1994.

Eiseley, Loren. *The Invisible Pyramid: A Naturalist Analyzes the Rocket Century*. New York: Scribner's, 1970.

Elbow, Peter. *Writing Without Teachers*. New York: Oxford, 1973.

Fink, P., J. Lusth, and J. Duran. "A General Expert System Design for Diagnostic Problem Solving." *IEEE 1984 Workshop on Principles of Knowledge Based Systems*. 45–52.

Gardner, Howard. *Frames of Mind: The Theory of Multiple Intelligences*. New York: Basic, 1983.

Gleick, James. *Chaos: Making a New Science*. New York: Penguin, 1988.

Hardin, Garrett. *Exploring New Ethics for Survival*. New York: Viking, 1972.

Hoffman, Banesh, with Helen Dukas. *Albert Einstein: Creator and Rebel*. New York: New American Library, 1972.

Huff, Darrell. *How to Lie with Statistics*. New York: Norton, 1954.

Krutch, Joseph Wood. *The Great Chain of Life*. 1956. Boston: Houghton, 1977.

Kuhn, Thomas. *The Structure of Scientific Revolutions*. 2nd, enlarged ed. Chicago: U of Chicago P, 1970.

Luria, A. R. *The Mind of a Mnemonist: A Little Book about a Vast Memory*. 1968. Trans. Lynn Solotaroff. Chicago: Henry Regnery, 1976.

Malinowski, Bronislaw. *Argonauts of the Western Pacific: An Account of Native Enterprise and Adventure in the Archipelagoes of Melanesian New Guinea.* 1922. New York: Dutton, 1961.

Pirsig, Robert. *Zen and the Art of Motorcycle Maintenance.* New York: Bantam, 1974.

Publication Manual of the American Psychological Association. 4th ed. Washington, DC: American Psychological Association, 1995.

Rhinelander, Philip. "Stereotypes—Their Use and Misuse." *Writing in the Social Sciences.* Ed. Joyce S. Steward and Marjorie Smelstor. Glenview, IL: Scott, 1984. 139–50.

Sadoul, Jacques. *Alchemists and Gold: The Story of Alchemy Through the Ages.* Trans. Olga Sieveking. New York: Putnam's, 1972.

Sacks, Oliver. *The Man Who Mistook His Wife for a Hat and Other Clinical Tales.* New York: Harper, 1987.

Thomas, Lewis. *The Medusa and the Snail: More Notes of a Biology Watcher.* New York: Viking, 1979.

Thompson, I. D., and R. O. Peterson, "Does Wolf Predation Alone Limit the Moose Population in Pukwaskwa Park?: A Comment." *Journal of Wildlife Management* 52 (1988): 556–59.

Toulmin, Stephen, and June Goodfield. *The Architecture of Matter: The Physics, Chemistry, and Physiology of Matter, Both Animate and Inanimate, As It Has Evolved Since the Beginnings of Science.* 1962. New York: Harper, 1966.

Vygotsky, L. S. *Mind in Society: The Development of Higher Psychological Processes.* Ed. and Trans. Michael Cole, Vera John-Steiner, Sylvia Scribner, and Ellen Souberman. Cambridge, MA: Harvard UP, 1978.

Watson, James. *The Double Helix: A Personal Account of the Discovery of the Structure of DNA.* New York: Atheneum, 1968.

Wurster, C., S. Wurster, and W. Stricklan. "Bird Mortality After Spraying for Dutch Elm Disease with DDT." *Science* 2 Apr. 1965: 90–91.

Index